RECONSTRUCTING CITIZENSHIP

SUNY series in National Identities
Thomas M.Wilson, editor

RECONSTRUCTING CITIZENSHIP

*The Politics of Nationality Reform
and Immigration in Contemporary France*

Miriam Feldblum

STATE UNIVERSITY OF NEW YORK PRESS

Published by
State University of New York Press, Albany

© 1999 State University of New York

For information, address State University of New York Press,
State University Plaza, Albany, NY, 12246

Production by Cathleen Collins
Marketing by Patrick Durocher

Library of Congress Cataloging in Publication Data

Feldblum, Miriam.
    Reconstructing citizenship : the politics of nationality reform
and immigration in contemporary France / Miriam Feldblum.
        p.   cm. — (SUNY series in national identities)
    Includes bibliographical references and index.
    ISBN 0–7914–4269–1 (alk. paper). — ISBN 0–7914–4270–5 (pb : alk.
paper)
        1. Citizenship—France.   2. National characteristics, French.
    3. France—Race relations.   4. France—Emigration and immigration.
    I. Title.   II. Series.
    JN2919.F43   1999
    323.6′0944′09049—dc21   98–45362
                                                                              CIP

10 9 8 7 6 5 4 3 2 1

For my mother, Esther Yolles Feldblum, Ph.D. (1933–1974)

Contents

Acknowledgments

"Walk with the wise and attain wisdom (Proverbs 13:20)," so began my mother's acknowledgments to her own study in American Jewish history, completed only a few short years before her untimely death at age forty-one. Today, my acknowledgments are for those who have provided wisdom and guidance, sustenance and support during this project. But, of course, these words cannot even begin to repay my debt to my mother and father who first enabled and encouraged me to embark on this path.

An early mentor, Byron Shafer, who first taught me about the study of political process, has continued to remind me throughout the years to always ask the next question. For his support and guidance, I shall always be grateful. At Yale University, three professors, David Cameron, David Apter, and Rogers Smith, encouraged and supported my initial studies of French citizenship and immigration politics. During the course of the project, I benefited greatly from conversations with Yasemin Soysal, Marty Schain, Daniele Lochak, Patrick Weil, Riva Kastoryano, Jacqueline Costa-Lascoux, Catherine Wihtol de Wenden, Remy Leveau, Ari Zolberg, Albano Cordeiro, and Abdelmalek Sayad. At Stanford, conversations with Philippe Schmitter, Douglas Klusmeyer, and Marta Seoane were very helpful. Yasemin Soysal, Gary Freeman, Martin Schain, Robert Deveigne, Meyer Feldblum, Chai Feldblum, Sholom Feldblum, Barbara Koziak, and William Deverell read different drafts and chapters of the book, and offered invaluable comments and advice. Of course, the responsibility for errors, omissions, and viewpoints is solely mine.

This book could not have been written without the generosity and financial support of several persons and institutions. In Paris, during the late eighties, Jacqueline Costa-Lascoux kindly provided me with a working space. Remy Leveau and Catherine Wihtol de Wenden allowed me to participate in their working group on Muslim immigrants at the Centre des études des relations internationales. A Centre national de la recherche scientifique grant to study dual nationality helped fund my research. I am also indebted to the members of the National Commission on Nationality, the immigrant activists, officials, and scholars, who generously took the time to talk with me. At Stanford University, the Center for European Studies and its Director, Philippe Schmitter, provided me with an office and visiting fellowship, which enabled me to complete the early drafts of this study. Like all recipients of the Center's generosity, I have to give a special thanks to Henrietta Grant-Peterkin.

The University of San Francisco graciously supported my continuing research in France with faculty grants and my writing needs with research assistance. I benefited from the wisdom and support of my colleagues in the Politics Department. My research assistants always worked beyond the call of duty; I thank them all, and especially Claire Van Zevern, who also read drafts and provided comments. In the Division of Humanities and Social Sciences at Caltech, I thank my wise colleagues, Bill Deverell and Jennifer Tucker, for their constructive commentary, and even more so, their continuous support. Rosy Meiron, secretaire extraordinaire, Sheryl Cobbs, and Susan Davis, the HSS Division administrator, provided invaluable and needed support, keeping this book and me on track. I am very grateful that a long-time friend and busy artist, Russell Rainbolt, took the time to create the cover design for the book. I owe special thanks to Tom Wilson, the *National Identities* series editor, and at SUNY Press, to Zina Lawrence and Cathleen Collins who actually placed this book on the road to publication.

As you may now realize, this project, like myself, has moved many times. I want to express my thanks to Chai Feldblum, Barbara Koziak, Yasemin Soysal, and Michelle Katz, who have stayed consistently with me (in spirit if not the same city) and the project. To Emlyn Hughes, who actually did move from New York, New Haven, Paris, Stanford, and Pasadena, I thank for those late night breaks.

This is the place where acknowledgments usually wind down. And if I had completed the book when only one son was born, there would be fewer baby-sitters to acknowledge. As it is, after Ariel came Isaac, and after Isaac came Noah. My warmest appreciation goes to Daniele Hadjedj, Dorothée Andermann, Anne Rossignol, Samia Messadia, and Sabrina Boullier. I also am grateful to all my friends in California and France, who came to the rescue when baby-sitting was needed. Last but never least, I thank my boys for their cheerful endurance, natural wisdom, and unpredictable lives.

CHAPTER 1

Studying Citizenship

A Political-Process Approach

Introduction

Broad

National citizenship has been a central and contested status in the modern polity. In formal terms, citizenship and nationality policies delineate legal membership in a state. Policies governing citizenship and naturalization determine who is a citizen, who has the right to citizenship, and what the criteria for citizenship entails. National citizenship also invokes — if not formally delineates — political, cultural, and social membership in the polity. In Europe, debates about citizenship and membership historically have accompanied political struggles over participation and voice in the community, cultural struggles over the parameters of the nation and national identity, and social struggles over the expansion of effective membership. Conflicts surrounding citizenship are once again resurgent across Europe. In contrast to past conflicts over citizenship, however, many of the current struggles are centered around foreigners and immigrants.

Fr |

This book is about the specific politics of citizenship reforms and immigration in contemporary France. Yet questions regarding changes in citizenship are *Europe.* relevant to European polities as a whole. Across Western Europe, the proliferation of citizenship and nationality reforms is striking. From the 1980s onward, numerous Western European states, including France, the United Kingdom, Belgium, the Netherlands, Germany, Switzerland, Spain, and Portugal, revised their citizenship, nationality, and naturalization policies. Citizenship reform brings up policy questions of formal criteria and entitlements. Many of the reforms were also part of broader conflicts over immigration and immigrant incorporation. These national citizenship and immigration struggles provoked debates about the meaning of national membership, national community, national identity, and the integration of foreigners and immigrants. In fact, policies concerning immigrant

1

incorporation have become visible and consequential features in both national and wider European politics. Taken together, the increasing saliency of citizenship and membership reforms, along with related issues of immigrant incorporation, have comprised a "new citizenship politics" in contemporary Europe.

This new citizenship politics, however, is puzzling on several levels. It has encompassed a variegated set of policy changes, social movements, and contentious politics. On the one hand, there has been a demonstrable trend of extending rights traditionally associated with state citizenship status and loosening the criteria for citizenship. Over the past decade, several European states that traditionally featured very limited opportunities for citizenship acquisition by foreigners have passed expansive reforms. They have granted local voting rights to noncitizens, introduced territorial bases for citizenship to supplement traditional lineage-based criteria, allowed the acquisition of dual nationalities, and eased naturalization procedures (Bauböck and Cinar, 1994; Hansen and Weil 1999).

Germany's citizenship law, for example, limits birthright citizenship to those of German lineage. But the state has begun to grant greater access to citizenship for long-term foreign residents and foreigners born and raised in Germany. A 1991 act gave these populations a claim to naturalization while a 1993 administrative revision clarified that both groups have an "absolute entitlement to naturalization." Most Western European states also have extended services and rights to legal residents that previously were limited to nationals.[1] On other levels, numerous popular movements have introduced into public discourse alternative conceptions of membership disassociated from formal state citizenship. International organizations and discourse have stressed the primary basis of "personhood" rather than "nationhood," to use Yasemin Soysal's terms, as a determinant factor in deciding individual rights (1994:163–164).

On the other hand, efforts to restrict access to citizenship and define exclusivist, nation-, or national-based conceptions of membership have also proliferated. Even as many European countries with traditionally closed citizenship policies have eased access to citizenship (like Germany), other countries with historically more open citizenship policies—specifically the United Kingdom and France—have tightened access. Legislative revisions of citizenship and nationality in Britain in 1981 and in France in 1993 constricted the traditional territorial criteria for citizenship existing in those two states. A new round of French nationality reform begun in 1997 rescinded some but not all of the earlier restrictions.

Nationalist and anti-immigrant movements are also resurgent across Europe. "France for the French" or "Germany for Germans" are typical slogans among nativist, anti-immigrant movements that have had different degrees of electoral and political success in European polities. And the attention to nation, national identity, and culture-based conceptions of citizenship has not been limited to conservatives. Calls for a revalued national citizenship and national identity have emanated from segments of the Left in France, Germany, Britain, Austria, and elsewhere.[2] It is important to note that these cross-cutting tendencies cannot be divided neatly along national or ideological lines. Rather, expansionist and constrictionist politics appear to cut across and within the European polities.

The current conflicts over citizenship are no longer solely or simply shaped by national parameters.[3] As the import of international and transnational factors has become more visible, it is evident that the new citizenship politics in Europe have been informed by a variety of international changes: transformations in the nature of citizenship in the modern world, the increased flows of labor migration to Europe in the postwar period, and European changes in the matters of national sovereignty and identity, particularly within the European Union. Along the same lines, the process of European integration also increased the saliency of domestic citizenship and immigration reform.[4] Since the early 1990s, the extension of European Union competency into numerous policy areas has led to more concerted efforts to harmonize national immigration and citizenship regulations.

Certainly, the multiple patterns of transnational convergence and divergence complicate any explanation. But the premise of this book is that to understand the transformations in citizenship, we must begin with the domestic changes in citizenship. How do we explain the puzzle of divergence and convergence in citizenship changes within European polities? The domestic changes contributing to transformations of citizenship are not only those that led to actual legislative reform. Failed reform efforts, nationalized political debates and rhetoric, moments of intense politics, ongoing activist movements, different kinds of state responses, divisive party conflict, and emergent ethnic and multicultural politics, including the formation and experiences of immigrant associations and communities, all constitute sites of changes in citizenship.

My approach calls for a reconsideration of the *domestic political processes of citizenship*. A focus on political process is not novel. After several decades of neglect and disfavor in political science, political-process-oriented approaches are once again returning (McAdam, McCarthy, and Zald 1996; Marks 1996, 1997; McAdam, Tarrow, and Tilly 1996). The approach has undergone considerable revision. In traditional political-process approaches, the core component was an examination of political agency.[5] Newer versions of the political process approach have gradually incorporated the interaction of institutions and agents, the role of structural constraints, and the influence of ideas and interpretations.[6] While most political process studies have confined themselves to studying social movements or related kinds of contentious politics, I believe the approach is useful in analyzing other types of policy and political change.[7] In my use of the approach to study citizenship, I identify three constitutive components of the political process: political agency, the interaction of institutions and agents, and the construction of ideas and interpretations.

Citizenship Reform as a Process, Not a Product

By taking a political-process approach, the point of departure for my analysis can be contestations over citizenship rather than immigration politics. Such a focus reverses the usual manner in which citizenship reform has often been examined, namely, as a product of broader immigration politics and national membership models.[8] In fact, much of the voluminous reflections on French citizenship and the reform struggles have been heavily informed by the literature on immigration politics.[9] A political-process approach to the contentious politics of citizenship and citizenship reform, however, leads us to directly address the influence of citizenship processes, including those that produced dualistic trends of divergence and convergence. To what extent did the specific emergence, type, and scope of French citizenship reform processes subsequently determine changes in citizenship practices and understandings? What was the impact of these processes on the specific character of the new citizenship politics?

In this book, I contend that the political processes through which the conflicts over citizenship were constructed need be examined as formative phases in the development of French citizenship. The political processes of French citizenship reform, including the processes of interactions among the state, parties, far right, and immigrant associations, and the construction of citizenship as a politicized issue, were formative not simply in terms of their outcome. In fact, the period examined most intensely here, from 1983–1988, produced no legislative reform. The lack of a legislative change did not disable the reform processes, which still contributed to the character and direction of French citizenship politics. I argue that crucial groundwork for the restrictive reform of French nationality finally passed in 1993 was laid down by the nature of the reform efforts in 1986–1988, including the debates over citizenship before the National Commission on Nationality in 1987–1988. Despite its popular association as a rightist measure, the 1993 restrictive revision of the French Nationality Code was not simply a product of rightist immigration policy but part of a new nationalist politics of citizenship that emerged in France during the 1980s. Likewise, a newly elected Socialist government spearheaded the 1997 nationalist reform whose expressed aim was the "reestablishment of the territorial right" to citizenship (*Le Monde* 11/29/97). In actuality, the reform and its proponents retained key components of the logic that emerged in the earlier membership debates. The politicization of citizenship in French national politics; the debates of citizenship, national identity, and pluralism; the Right's failed attempted at a restrictive revision in 1986; and finally, the National Commission's televised hearings of the proposed reform all combined to generate a "new nationalist politics of citizenship."

The term *new nationalist politics* requires some caveats. I do not use the term to identify exclusively the far Right in France and I do not use it interchangeably with "racial politics." The term is meant to distinguish the contemporary events from previous French nationalist politics. The historical origins of French notions of nationhood, the legacies of French nationalism, and their translations into conceptions of national identity are the subjects of a voluminous literature (e.g., Noirel 1992; Citron 1987; Tilly 1996; Greenfeld 1992). Rather than invoke the weighty burden of such history, I seek instead to evoke the enactment and orientation of the new citizenship politics.

While there is much scholarly disagreement about the theoretical understandings and historical phenomena of nations, nationalism, and national identity, the processes of constructing the foundations, contours, and parameters of the nation and national community are a visible part and product of nationalist politics (cf. Smith 1979, 1991; Gellner 1983; Hobsbawm, 1983, 1990; Greenfeld 1992; Brubaker 1996).[10] Nationalist politics frame and reframe national identities; they engender specific political and cultural orientations.[11] As Paul Gilroy has shown in his work on contemporary British nationalist politics, using the term *new nationalist* can stress the constructed nature of "complex cultural differences," where the conflicts operate at once on the terrains of culture and politics (Gilroy 1993:10). By using the term *new nationalist*, I aim to highlight the contemporary dynamic political processes by which national identity conceptions are at once reified and reconsidered, made essentialist and constructed.

In France, the new nationalist politics of citizenship extended beyond the far right across the political spectrum. I suggest in my analysis that an attenuated focus on the "rise of racial politics" or far-Right nationalism too often conflates racism, nativism, and nationalism. Le Pen's extreme Right, anti-immigrant movement may be accurately described as a nativist movement. But the new nationalist citizenship politics were variously characterized by voluntarist, republican-communitarian, and nativist arguments.[12] Moreover, the logic of the new politics was informed by both national and transnational developments. In other words, nationalist processes have assumed new features as both agent strategies and discourse are no longer limited to the terrain of the nation-state. A new array of actors and kinds of action are involved in the contemporary reframing of national identity and reconstruction of membership. French political rhetoric, for example, stressed national boundaries while relying on transnational discourses about the right to difference. From this perspective, the construction of the new nationalist citizenship was neither a replay of older French nationalism nor simply an extension of French national citizenship.

In a sense, this book endeavors to tell a large narrative about changing citizenship in Europe through a smaller (though no less dramatic) story about a decade of citizenship conflicts in France. I provide a detailed case study of the domestic politics of citizenship reform with three primary objectives. The first is to clarify the roles of the state, the political parties, and the immigrant groups in formulating the issues, institutionalizing the ways of reasoning and thinking about citizenship, and constructing the conflicts. The second is to provide an understanding of how political processes, and the constraints and imperatives of these processes, helped shape the emergent new politics of citizenship in France. The final one is to trace the contemporary reconstruction of citizenship in France up to its impact on other kinds of membership politics. In pursuing these aims, I intend to demonstrate why we need to "bring back in" the political process as a distinctive part of our analytical frameworks when we study citizenship.

The actual processes of citizenship reform have not been the usual focus of scholarly work on citizenship and immigration. For the most part, the current literature on changing citizenship and immigration in Europe has understood citizenship reform—or the lack of it—simply as evidence of existing patterns or as products of wider change.[13] While such analyses may incorporate the contingencies and episodic nature of the political process as part of an overall aim to explain a specific story of citizenship politics, their frameworks are anchored elsewhere. As part of my effort to bring serious analytical attention back to the notion of political process, this book stands in response to the political-culture, structuralist, and institutionalist studies of European citizenship and immigration in Europe, studies that have neglected the political process. My point here is not to dismiss the usefulness of such analyses but to show their limitations. These kinds of analyses raise questions about the contemporary changes in citizenship that their own frameworks cannot address.

Culturalist, Structuralist, Institutionalist, and Political-Process Analyses of Citizenship

What explains the puzzling changes in citizenship and membership in Europe? One approach to answering this question has been to examine contemporary changes from a political-culture perspective. From this perspective, the variegated citizenship politics reflect the different nationhood and membership traditions that characterize European politics. In his analysis of French and German nationhood traditions, Rogers Brubaker (1992) traced nationally specific, historical models of nationhood and membership in the two nations. According to Brubaker, the enduring and influential national models of ethnocultural membership in Germany and political-cultural membership in France shaped the path of contemporary citizenship politics. Beyond Brubaker, numerous American and European scholars also have subscribed to similar kinds of political cultural arguments, whereby entrenched "national models" of citizenship serve as explanatory variables in their attempts to understand citizenship and immigration conflicts (Weil 1991; Hollifield 1994; Schnapper 1991).[14] In other words, national models explain variation across states by situating the different citizenship policies and politics as reflections of the distinctive national membership models.

In the specific case of French citizenship, such "national model" frameworks explain the changes in citizenship and the increased salience of new citizenship politics in terms of a distinctive model of membership, immigration, and immigrant incorporation. The French model consists in part of Republicanist, political-cultural bases for national membership and in part of a statist or state-driven assimilation of immigrants as prospective French citizens. Both French policy-makers and scholars have in recent times caricatured an American and Anglo-Saxon model of ghettoized ethnic and racial conflict in contrast to their model of national integration and republicanist membership (cf. Schnapper 1991; Weil 1991; Lorcerie 1994).

Within such a framework, French popular and scholarly commentary highlighted the specific religious, cultural and historical features of Muslim, mainly North African, and especially Algerian immigrants in France. Conflicts over citizenship become an inevitable by-product of the tensions wrought by the presence of certain immigrants. Though its articulation changed across the political spectrum, different commentary argued that these kinds of challenges propelled the new citizenship politics, or at the very least explain why citizenship became so problematic in the contemporary period.[15]

The limitations of a political culture framework is underscored when we realize the extent to which it underestimates the dynamics of political processes. Such a framework tends to reify various historical and ideological strands into more or less static national models to be juxtaposed against other national models. It counterposes "challenges" brought by contemporary immigrants to the national membership understandings of the national model. Because the analyses take as a given the primacy of a national membership model, they are inevitably led to identify a problematic relationship between immigration and citizenship. They cannot take into account how the relationship became problematized. They downplay the manipulation and malleability of both national traditions and immigrant challenges by those engaged in reform struggles, for example, from the far-Right National Front to immigrant activist associations. In other words, the analyses situate citizenship reform as the product of political response shaped by tradition, without taking into account that reform processes also shape the outcome of political responses.

Not surprisingly, political-culture explanations become less convincing when the current proliferation of citizenship reforms is examined more closely. As noted above, Germany has begun to move away from its strict lineage criteria for citizenship and toward facilitating the naturalization of non-German immigrants. Moreover, several political leaders and parties in Germany have called for more fundamental membership reforms, including a modified territorial basis for German citizenship and the allowance of dual nationality. France, in contrast, moved away from its traditional territorial criteria for citizenship for second-generation immigrants and toward tightening immigrants' access to membership. From a political culture perspective, contemporary citizenship reforms at times appear to reaffirm national traditions of membership, but at other points they appear to flout the national model. To look primarily at national traditions and models to explain current reform outcomes either lays the groundwork for a series of national exceptions—as in French exceptionalism, German exceptionalism, and American exceptionalism—or leaves many questions unanswered about the dynamic character and direction of the reforms.[16]

Structural analyses are another important part of the literature seeking to explain changing immigration and associated citizenship politics in Western Europe. These analyses (e.g., Freeman 1995; Castles 1989; Cohen 1994) identify structural features and biases in West European polities, which operate as constraints or pressures on policy formation and implementation. From this perspective, intensifying citizenship politics reflect broader structural forces. Specifically, citizenship conflicts are considered product of regime constraints, immigration pressures, and immigration policy responses. Structural analyses often highlight different kinds of convergence in the new citizenship politics.

Some structural analyses have provided insight into the expansionist directions of citizenship reform. In his work on immigration regimes, Gary Freeman (1995) argued that structural biases of liberal democratic polities have shaped immigration and membership policy formation in expansionist directions. Notwithstanding hostile public reception, the direction of actual state policies and practices is expansive and not restrictive. In his work on the political economy of immigration policy, James Hollifield (1992) identified the influence of an individual "rights" regime in the domestic policymaking of liberal democratic polities. Other structural analyses have focused on the discriminatory and exclusionary push of the new citizenship politics. Robin Cohen has argued that the convergence in citizenship practices are part of a "new European pattern of exclusion" (1994:162). Cohen's analysis, while focused on Britain, extends to a discussion of the rise of racial politics in Europe.

The political rise of Le Pen and the National Front may suggest that a "racial politics" analysis would provide insight into the French case. Some scholars have contended that French immigration and citizenship reform conflicts are best understood when placed "in the context of the emergence of the politics of race" (Schain 1990; cf. Silvermann 1992).[17] In French scholarship, there are a large number of studies that stress the "effect" that the emergence of the extreme right politician and the diffusion of xenophobic, anti-immigrant rhetoric have had on shaping immigration and citizenship politics during the eighties. These studies use the terms *racial* and *nationalist* politics interchangeably to describe—almost exclusively—the politics of the far Right, and, at times, the majoritarian right.[18] They bifurcate citizenship politics between racist and antiracist movements.

From this perspective, the new citizenship politics in France should be foremost a product of far-Right success in politicizing immigration. In fact, the rise of Le Pen and the National Front coincided with the emergence of the new citizenship politics. In 1985, when Le Pen called for the revision of the French Nationality Code to increase the obstacles for foreigners and children of foreigners, his demands to lessen access to French citizenship were taken up by all the major parties of the Right as part of their electoral platforms during the 1986 national and local elections. When in office, the victorious conservative Chirac government led a strong though unsuccessful effort to revise the code.

But the Right was not alone in demanding reform. The limitations of a racial politics framework are evident by recalling the dimensions of the new citizenship politics it cannot easily address. This approach does not explain the processes by which the Socialist government, the Left parties, and immigrant associations in France moved from an endorsement of pluralist politics in the early eighties to a rejection of the "right to difference" for immigrants and their own emphasis on "national integration" by the late eighties. Such an approach obscures important commonalities in the language and logic between the Left and Right in France, which increasingly characterized the conflicts over citizenship. Its more nuanced versions situate citizenship reform as the product of a racialized immigration politics and policy responses (cf. Silvermann 1992). But even here, the approach does not explore the political processes of citizenship politics that contributed to such racialization.

Structural explanations, while insightful in sketching broad strokes across European citizenship politics, are less useful in explaining the specific characteristics of and the dissimilarities between the varied national politics. Both the United Kingdom and France passed restrictive citizenship measures: Britain's Nationality Act of 1981 and France's revision of its Nationality Code, after a decade of debate, in 1993. Both experienced increasingly politicized conflicts. But structural analyses are unable to account for some of the key differences in the character of the two conflicts. While citizenship debate in France centered on questions of nation and national community, the earlier British debates largely bypassed questions of national identity. While, the proponents and opponents of Britain's restrictive Nationality Act defined the conflict in terms of racial conflict, such a trend was vigorously resisted in France.[19] Inclusionary and exclusionary biases are neither the only dynamics at play in setting policies and shaping political or popular response nor are they similar across institutional settings.

The brief contrasts of Germany, France, and Britain outlined here point to the need for differentiated but dynamic analyses of citizenship reform. Some of the most promising studies of contemporary citizenship in Europe have been "new institutionalist" analyses. Earlier institutionalist studies were marked by their focus on studying how political institutions, and in particular the state, both constrained and propelled agents (Skocpol 1979; Nordlinger 1981; Evans, Rueschemeyer, and Skocpol 1985). New institutionalist frameworks focus on the determinative influence of institutional configurations. They also focus on specific institutional processes or pathways and the interaction between agents and political institutions. Yasemiñ Soysal's (1994) cross-national analysis of membership and immigrant incorporation in Europe identified different institutional configurations of national membership to explain variation in immigrant incorporation policy. For example, she showed the different incorporation patterns produced by French centralized, statist organizational arrangements, British and Swiss decentralized, liberal configurations, and German centralized semicorporatist model (36–39). At the same time, Soysal contended that a more general, pervasive transformation of the state institutional framework explains certain kinds of commonalities or convergence emergent in membership practices in Europe.

In his comparative study of immigrant political participation in France and Switzerland, Patrick Ireland (1994) argued that host-society institutions structured the participation of immigrant groups in distinctive ways. According to Ireland, different types of institutions, along with the different kinds of processes linking immigrants to such institutions, explained variation in immigrant participation. Adrian Favell (1997) contrasted the influence of French and British philosophies regarding integration and diversity through their institutional responses to immigrant incorporation. In his analysis, Favell argued that the power of such philosophies and ideas is mediated by the determinative role of institutional processes and pathways in policymaking.

These institutionalist explanations that focus on citizenship and immigration policy regimes do enable differentiated readings of the new reforms. Moreover, like other "new institutionalist" literature, these authors recognize not only the influence of institutions on agents, but also the interactive processes between institutions and agents.[20] But new institutionalist frameworks are actually very limited in their incorporation or examination of the political process.[21] While Ireland and Favell incorporated different aspects of the political process as part of their explanatory frameworks, their approaches emphasized state institutional processes to the detriment of political processes distinct from the state. Such frameworks relegate specific political responses as secondary to the institutional patterns and responses. However, the intensity of political responses in the new European citizenship politics has varied considerably. Some Western European states passed substantive expansive citizenship reforms without extended conflict, while others are enmeshed in lengthy battles. Indeed, the contrasting types and intensities of political response appear to be an important site to examine in order to fully understand the new citizenship politics.

A political-process approach does enable a focus on how the new politics of citizenship emerged. By using a political process framework, I can examine the extent to which national models and the related challenges of contemporary immigration are constructed as part of the conflict, identify the dynamic processes of the citizenship conflicts and reform efforts and assess the extent to which they contributed to the direction of citizenship changes, and address the impact of differentiated political responses. My conceptualization of political agency, interactions between agents and institutions, and the construction of interpretations is drawn in part from scholarly studies of the political process, and in part, from other analytical frameworks.

Our understandings of political agency and its relation to the political process have become more complex. As opposed to traditional political process frameworks, the political process is no longer defined as simply the activities of people striving for power. Rather, political agency is integrally related to the importance of contingency, structures of opportunity, and processes of interaction (McAdam 1982:37; Tilly 1978:135). More recent models have striven to underscore the influential determinants of the broader environmental context in shaping political agency and strategic action (McAdam, McCarthy, and Zald, 1996:7–17). In this book, I analyze the struggles over citizenship partly in terms of state and political party initiatives and responses as they confront both a rising far-Right movement and an emergent immigrant association movement.

If political agency is no longer solely determinative, the political process is also no longer defined as simply a neutral forum in which activities take place. The dynamics of the process can shape outcomes. Attention to the complexities of the political process, therefore, is critical.[22] Central to my political process framework is the assumption that change is multicausal, where the specific configuration of factors can shift from one phase to another, but a basic dynamic remains, one that includes a multiplicity of factors (e.g., agency, contingency, structures, and institutions). In my analysis, I seek to identify the different phases of French citizenship politics, and examine in each phase the interaction of political agency, contingency, institutions, and other structures shaping opportunity, strategy, and change.

While attention to the interaction of institutions and agents has always been part of political-process frameworks, institutionalist studies contain important insights. Institutionalist perspectives, in the words of March and Olsen, illuminate how political institutions "define the framework within which politics takes place . . . (defined by their structures of) routines, roles, forms, and rules . . . (institutions) organize a potentially disorderly political process. By shaping meaning, political institutions create an interpretative order from within which political behavior can be understood and provided continuity (1989:18, 52)." Citizenship practices traditionally have been an indicator and reflection of state sovereignty, regime type, and institutional orders. Throughout the analysis, I seek to uncover the extent to which French statist traditions and institutional practices shaped the debates over citizenship, and the ways in which different agents strove to reshape the political institutions governing citizenship. Both the historically embedded norms and institutional rules expressed through citizenship practices and ways in which political agency or political processes enacted transformations of those rules are central to the analysis.

The interpretations of institutional norms, ideas, and agency constitute another component of the political process. How were the conflicts over membership and immigration in France framed as challenges to a French model of citizenship? How was that model constructed as the common-sensical explanation for membership conflict? The anthropologist, Clifford Geertz defined the political process in part as a process by which the "maps of problematic social reality and matrices for the creation of collective conscience" are formulated (1973:220). The interplay of ideologies and interpretations, myths and symbols, which takes place within processes also shape political action.[23] In his study of race and nation in Britain, Paul Gilroy, the cultural studies scholar, contended that ideologies such as nationalism and racism are "structuring relations in society . . . shaping political action and giving it powerful common sense meanings" (1987:16). Drawing on such conceptual frameworks, I examine both the construction of ideas and ideologies, and as important, the influential role that processes of interpretation (and the processes that create what is common sense) play.[24]

Throughout my analysis of the different phases of the French citizenship politics, I seek to identify how different interpretations and ideologies of national membership, national identity, and nation were constructed and articulated through the political process. When looking at the notions of immigrant "challenges," the "national integration" of immigrants, or the French "model," I aim to uncover exactly how certain interpretations became commonsensical while other relationships were problematized. This perspective enables an analysis of how the relationship between immigration and citizenship has been mediated and shaped by the political process. It offers nuanced understandings of how specific episodes in the new politics of citizenship, including the conflict that developed around reforming the Nationality Code and the hearings of a National Commission on Nationality established in 1987, became formative moments in reconstructing contemporary French citizenship. Overall, the political process approach in examining citizenship reform (and arguably, policy reform more generally) concerns its capacity to illuminate such determinative dimensions of political, institutional, ideological, and strategic processes.

Thus far, I have focused on different kinds of approaches for studying transformations in citizenship. Almost all Western European countries have witnessed changes in their citizenship policies and membership practices. But among these countries, France has been the site of some of the earliest, most visible, and highly persistent conflicts over citizenship. My analysis concentrates on the French politics of citizenship reform and immigration during the years 1981 through 1989, and concludes with an examination of the nationality reforms of 1993 and 1997. The choice of France and this particular period of French citizenship politics is compelling for historical and theoretical reasons. France is characterized by a long history of immigration. French institutional rules and political history provide a state setting that features a mixture of territorial and lineage criteria for citizenship acquisition. The 1980s were marked by the rise of a strong and influential far-Right movement, the National Front, and of visible and strategic immigrant activist associations. Finally, during this period, France experienced a series of politicized and protracted policy conflicts.

French Citizenship Reform as a Case Study

France's long experience of immigration enables historical comparison. Unlike most other European countries, France has a substantive history of immigration and immigrant incorporation. Past conflicts and reforms covering citizenship and nationality in France often did involve foreigners and immigrants. Generally in the Western European politics of citizenship, a central and divisive issue has been the integration of the new immigrants, consisting mainly of the postwar flows of non-Europeans into Western Europe. Of the close to 20 million foreigners now estimated in Western Europe, approximately 11 million are of non-European origin, of whom over half are of Muslim origin.[25] Likewise, a key stake in French citizenship politics has been the integration of the Maghrebi or North African, Muslim populations into the French political and cultural polity. In the French case, unlike other European polities, useful comparisons and connections can be made with past debates about the integration of mostly European foreigners into the French polity. A historically informed focus on the new immigrants will directly address theoretical debates about the kinds of "challenges" posed by the new immigrants to the membership models and traditions of European polities.

French institutional and political history of citizenship enables a multidimensional study of citizenship. Unlike other countries in continental Europe whose nationality laws relied solely on lineage (*jus sanguinis*), France has long maintained nationality practices based on a mixture of territorial (*jus soli*) and lineage (*jus sanguinis*) ties. Like Britain, France fashioned a specialized kind of incorporation for its colonialist populations that was later extended to former colonialist populations coming to territorial France. Consequently, France has a larger population of immigrants who are nationals than many other European countries where immigrants have remained foreigners. It was only with the reforms of the 1980s that most other European countries incorporated territorial criteria in their nationality rules. At the same time, in contrast to Britain, where the proportion of (technically) foreign immigrants has remained small, France has consistently featured a large proportion of foreigners in its resident population (see Table 1.1).

TABLE 1.1.
Evolution of Foreign Population in France, 1921–1990

Year	Total resident population	French by acquisition	Foreign Population		
			Total foreign population	European* nationalities	North African† nationalities
1921					
Num × 1,000	38,798	NA	1,532	1,436	36
percentage	100%		3.90%	93.70%	2.30%
1931					
Num × 1,000	41,228	361	2,715	2,458	83
percentage	100%	0.90%	6.60%	90.50%	3.1%
1954					
Num × 1,000	42,781	1,068	1,765	1,431	227
percentage	100%	2.50%	4.10%	81.10%	12.90%
1968					
Num × 1,000	49,253	1,320	2,621	1,800	619
percentage	100%	2.70%	5.30%	68.70%	23.60%
1975					
Num × 1,000	52,599	1,392	3,442	2,103	1,122
percentage	100%	2.60%	6.50%	61.10%	32.60%
1982					
Num × 1,000	54,273	1,425	3,680	1,760	1,436
percentage	100%	2.60%	6.80%	47.80%	39.00%
1990					
Num × 1,000	56,635	1,778	3,608	1,309	1,412
percentage	1,000%	3.10%	6.40%	36.30%	39.10%

This table is based on census data, which I generally consider to be an underestimation of the total foreign population (George 1986).

NA = Not Available

*Includes Eastern Europe and Russia

†Algeria, Morocco, and Tunisia

Sources: Costa-Lascoux (1989a:19); George (1986); *Hommes et Libertés* (1985:7); INSEE (1992).

The French institutional structure of citizenship, therefore, has generated a combination of foreign immigrants and French nationals of immigrant origin, among whom are immigrants from former French colonies and territories. French political and social history of citizenship laid the stress on territorial criteria and assimilating the foreigner as a French citizen. In general terms, French citizenship laws were greatly shaped by the French Revolution and its aftermath, including the formation of the Jacobin state and French republicanist discourse, its colonialist experiences, as well as by specific demographic pressures, economic needs, and military exigencies (cf. Noiriel 1992; Brubaker 1992). The French tradition of citizenship invoked a direct linkage to the national state, varied political-cultural understandings of membership, and priorities of national integration.

On a substantive level, the usage of citizenship and nationality in contemporary French discourse has been marked by a blurring of their historical distinctions.[26] Nationality policies are often subsumed under the category of citizenship politics, and discussions of citizenship often extend to the domains of social, economic, and cultural membership and practices. To the extent that French citizenship is articulated as membership in the national community, the French historian, René Gallisot has contended that French membership traditions are consistently characterized by an ideological "confusion of nationality and citizenship" (1989:35). Key phases of the French politics of citizenship are marked by conflicts that invoked as much competing arguments about political and cultural membership as they did competing definitions of legal nationality status.

More than in any other European polity, therefore, citizenship struggles in France have been starkly defined in terms of the meaning of national identity, national community, and subsequently, national integration. The conflicts in France have been consistently nationally oriented and quickly politicized. Not surprisingly, the French struggles over citizenship clearly extended beyond formal policies and technical definitions of nationality as laid out in the French Nationality Code, which is the body of legislation governing the acquisition, attribution, and loss of French nationality.[27]

Studying the citizenship politics of France allows us to trace the historical and contemporary linkage between citizenship and immigrants. It enables us to reconstruct how the linkage was drawn before the current conflicts, and then to construct how it became redrawn, or to put it more critically, how it became problematized in the context of a divisive immigration politics. For example, from the immediate postwar period through the seventies, questions of citizenship were not considered in terms of immigration or immigrants. The linkage between citizenship and immigration was neither salient nor politicized. In the nineteen eighties, however, competing conceptions of national identity and national community, new kinds of rights, and changing integration priorities regarding immigrants all emerged as highly controversial, contested, and connected stakes in French national politics. A focus on changing linkages between citizenship and immigration, especially visible in the French case, will address ongoing theoretical debates about the determinative influence of historical, cultural membership traditions, and institutionalized state membership configurations on citizenship in Europe.

The rise in France of Jean-Marie Le Pen and the National Front enables examination of the role of the far Right in citizenship politics. Across Western

Europe, far Right, anti-immigrant parties are considered to be catalysts for restrictive politics, nationalist sentiments, and anti-immigrant measures. Within the context of its immigration politics, France witnessed the dramatic rise of both a national far-Right movement, the National Front, and partly in response, a variegated immigrant association movement. Both movements played strong roles in articulating the new citizenship politics. Beginning in the early 1980s, far-Right politicians and immigrant activists, conservatives and socialists, nativists and antiracists, all debated the meanings and criteria of French citizenship. Le Pen's National Front remains one of the most visible far-Right parties in Europe. A focus on the impact of the National Front on French citizenship conflicts will address ongoing debates about the influence of far-Right movements and racial politics on citizenship politics in Europe.

The protracted nature of French citizenship politics clearly enables a detailed examination of the processes and consequences of citizenship reform in Europe. For over a decade, and especially from 1983 through 1989, France experienced an intensifying series of electoral debates and policy disputes over citizenship. An exclusionary reform of the Nationality Code proposed in 1986 failed after two years of struggle. Despite seeming policy failure, substantive changes in citizenship and immigrant incorporation practices became evident, as manifest in the national crisis that developed around three schoolgirls who wanted to wear the Islamic *Chador*, or veil, in their school in 1989. Actual policy change, however, only comes about in 1993, when a restrictive revision of the code was finally passed by a newly elected and empowered conservative government. Finally, the rounds of nationality revision and debate have continued. In 1997, a newly reinstalled Socialist government proposed its own nationality reform, rescinding some but not all of the 1993 revision. A focus on the series of attempted reforms and the politics around the reform process will address theoretical arguments about the character and direction of change in citizenship in Europe.

The debates over pluralism, national identity, and citizenship during the eighties enabled not only the Right but also the Left and immigrant groups to elaborate versions of the "imagined political community" (Anderson 1983:15). Conservatives and socialists, nativist and multiculturalists elaborated ideologies of a "nation . . . simultaneously open and closed" (Ibid.:133), gave priority to defending the national identity, and finally, insisted on integration into the "national community." The slippage from defending varied conceptions of the national identity to justifying exclusionary stances spared neither the Right nor Left (Lochak 1987; Gallisot 1985). The arguments concerning citizenship and the challenges of immigration operated as a means to frame political programs and give meaning to political actions. Richard Handler has written that in the "interpenetration of nationalist and social scientific discourse," both nationalists and social scientists presuppose "boundedness, continuity and homogeneity . . . in their understanding of nations as entities" (1988:8). Certainly, the debates over citizenship and the definition of the French nation included not only politicians and political activists, but as important, French intellectuals and social scientists who engaged and contributed to discussions about the reality of the French nation or the need to defend a national identity.

Research Strategy and Plan of the Book

This book is qualitative in nature and employs analytical and interpretive methods. As part of a political-process approach, I examined the series of political debates and conflicts over pluralism, national identity, and citizenship in France during the eighties. The data for this project were collected mainly through on-site interviews, and archival and documentary research completed in France in 1988, as well as follow-up research completed in 1992 and 1994. Extensive interviews were conducted with officials in the Ministries of Justice, Interior, Social Affairs, Foreign Relations, and at the Council of State; with immigrant representatives from a wide range of associations, a majority being associated with the Maghrebi populations; with representatives from human rights and antiracist organizations; with officials of political parties; and with many of the social scientists who studied and contributed commentary about the debates, and changing politics.

In addition, in-depth interviews were conducted with thirteen of the sixteen members of the "Nationality Commission" or commission of experts that was formed in 1987 to discuss and issue recommendations on a revision of the Nationality Code (see Appendix A for a list of the agencies, parties, and organizations at which the interviews were conducted). The centralized features of French political and scholarly networks, nearly all of which were based in Paris, facilitated the interviewing process. These interviews were intended to gather information about organization, perspectives, strategies, and particular events, as well as to capture the prevalent discourses.

In terms of archival work, this research has drawn on internal documentation of the Ministry of Foreign Relations, the Bureau of Nationality in the Ministry of Justice, and all the internal memoranda, reports, and documentation of the archives of the Nationality Commission located in the Council of State. In terms of documentary research, the research has drawn on documents and commentary furnished by immigrant associations, antiracist organizations, and political parties. Additional data includes a comprehensive press analysis conducted of Parisian and regional newspapers for the years 1980 through 1990 as well as the relevant scholarly documentation, including books, articles, and unpublished analyses.

I have organized the analysis to follow the chronological contests over French citizenship leading to its revision and re-envisioning. After providing an overview of contemporary immigration and citizenship prior to the 1980s in chapter 2, I focus my analysis on the processes of French citizenship politics. In chapter 3, I examine the politicization of citizenship in French immigration politics, highlighting the role of political agency. I show how conflicts over pluralism and the national identity constituted the initial phases of the new politics of citizenship, while the extreme right played only a partial role in shaping these debates. In chapter 4, I examine the emergence of a conservative attempt to revise the nationality code through an analysis of the debates propelling the reform. I argue that despite the dramatic polarization between the Right and Left over the reform, there were important commonalities in the re-visions of citizenship, arguments, and justifications articulated by both sides. These commonalities were rooted partly in ambiguities of French ideologies of nation and nationalism.

In chapter 5, I address the question of the failure of the Right's restrictive politics of citizenship in 1986, by identifying both institutionalist and political process factors that constrained the Right's politics. Next, I examine the work, televised hearings, and final report of the government appointed national "commission of experts," which was greeted with near unanimous acclaim. I argue in chapter 6 that this final phase of the reform process enabled the emergence of a nationalist politics of citizenship. What were the consequences of this new nationalist politics of citizenship? Analyzing the "l'affaire des foulards" or Islamic scarves crisis of 1989, I argue in chapter 7 that the impact of the reform politics and the new nationalist citizenship politics have been visible in the changing politics of immigrant incorporation.

To what extent was a nationalist citizenship institutionalized in French nationality policy? I conclude in chapter 8 with an analysis of the two French nationality reforms, which do emerge from this decade of membership debate and immigration conflict. The 1993 conservative revision, following many of the recommendations of the National Commission on Nationality (the committee of experts), diminished access to citizenship on territorial criteria. In contrast and in response, the 1997–98 Socialist revision rhetorically aimed to "reestablish the territorial right" to citizenship in France (though it had not been abolished) and in fact only partially rescinded the 1993 restrictions. In arguing that we need to look beyond these reforms as products of partisan politics or reflections and rejections of specific citizenship traditions, I suggest that the two reform cycles are part of the ongoing patterns of divergence and convergence in citizenship politics visible in France, and increasingly consequential in the wider European context.

CHAPTER 2

The New Immigrants and
Citizenship

Contemporary Immigration in France

In 1987, passions rose and public divisions grew over the rightist attempt to pass a restrictive revision of the French Nationality Code. Finally, in late Spring, the conservative government led by Prime Minister Jacques Chirac established a multipartisan Commission of Experts (Commission des Sages), a "National Commission on Nationality," to review the need for a reform. The Commission held a series of public, televised hearings—the first of their kind in France—at which numerous immigrant activists, religious leaders, community representatives, intellectuals, and anti-immigrant advocates presented their views on French citizenship, the integration of immigrants, and the prospective reform. One of the most revealing episodes of the whole drama was a near nonevent.

The Commission had neglected to invite representatives of the Portuguese community to the televised hearings. In fact, the Commission had to add on another, nontelevised session to accommodate them. Yet according to the 1982 census, the Portuguese population was the second largest foreign group in France (21% of the foreign population), barely less numerous the Algerians (22%).[1] In fact, by the 1990 census, the Portuguese once again constituted the largest foreign population, 17.9 percent, while the Algerians accounted for 17.1 percent of foreigners in France (see Table 2.1: The Evolution of Foreign Population in France, 1921–1990). Despite the popular rhetoric during the whole reform politics that targeted above all North Africans, the government's proposed reform actually affected Portuguese youth much more than it did Algerian youth. Why were the Algerians and the other Maghrebis—Tunisians and Moroccans—at the center of the new politics of citizenship, and not the Portuguese? This chapter provides a brief portrait of contemporary immigration in France. My aim here is to clarify the linkage between the new immigrants and issues of citizenship and so lay the groundwork for the following analysis that discusses the initial emergence of the new citizenship politics.

In the sixties, the phrase, "foreigners in France" evoked images of "invisible," solitary, Southern European (Italians, Spaniards, Portuguese) migrant workers, living in hastily built hostels and inadequate conditions (Berger 1968; *Esprit* 1966). By the eighties, the term, "les immigrés" evoked images of marginalized Algerian and African workers, North African Islamic girls wearing veils, rooms crowded with African women and children, with large cooking pots simmering in the background (*Esprit* Mai 1985; *Les Temps Modernes* 1984; Chebel 1988). The evolution of terms, from foreigners to immigrants, from migrants to settlers, is just one indicator of the changes that occurred in the postwar immigration in France.

France is not a traditional country of immigration, in the fashion of the United States, Canada, or Australia. In contrast to those countries, France does not consider itself to have been formed demographically or culturally by successive waves of immigrants. Nonetheless, France is a country with a long history of immigration, including large waves in the latter half of the nineteenth century, then between 1921 and 1931, and most recently from 1956 to 1972 (Noiriel 1988).[2] In the postwar era, France recruited and attracted massive numbers of foreign workers. This postwar immigration to France began as a labor migration, whose stay was generally assumed to be transitory; when unemployment arose, the workers would be sent home (Tapinos 1975; George 1986).[3] By 1968, foreigners accounted for 5.3 percent of the resident population in France; this contrasts to 1946, when foreigners accounted for 4.4 percent of the population (*Hommes & Libertés* 1985:7). This population was composed largely of transient, male migrant workers; over a majority of whom were from Spain, Italy, and Portugal (see Table 2.1).

When the economic crises of the early seventies arrived, France, along with other West European states, officially closed its borders to labor migration in 1974. But, despite efforts to encourage the return of migrant workers to their countries of origin, the effect of the economic downturn and new immigration policy was the stabilization—and not the return—of the foreign populations. In fact, immigration in France increased substantially from the early sixties into the seventies. The reasons for this were several. The prospering economy of the sixties led to more demand for foreign labor. Anticipation by foreign workers of the changing policies and then the formal border closure led to an increase in family reunifications and other forms of "social" migration. Overall, the proportion of foreigners in France rose to 6.5 percent of the resident population by 1975.[4]

During the conflicts over immigration and citizenship in the eighties, the French extreme Right consistently contended that the postwar immigration into France was becoming a growing "invasion" of immigrants. However, the proportions of the foreign population and naturalized French remained stable from the early seventies through the eighties.[5] Whereas the 1975 census showed 6.5 percent foreigners and 2.7 percent French by acquisition in the general population, the 1982 census registered 6.8 percent foreigners, and 2.6 percent French by acquisition in the resident population.[6] The 1990 census actually registered a drop in the number of foreigners to 6.4 percent of the total population, while the proportion of naturalized French rose to 3.1 percent.[7] This proportion of foreigners in France was not unprecedented, as it paralleled figures of the 1930s, when foreigners accounted for 6.6 percent of the resident population (see Table 2.1).[8]

Certain French historians have pointed to the modern parallels with the thirties to undercut the argument that contemporary waves of immigration featured unique characteristics that sparked the current conflicts over citizenship (Milza 1985; Noiriel 1988). Nationalist and anti-immigrant sentiments flourished in the thirties. According to these historians, the contemporary anti-immigrant sentiments are a manifestation of "old demons." In these explanations, the Algerian is the "bouc émmissaire" of today while in the 1930s Polish and Italian immigrants had been the scapegoats.[9]

Nonetheless, the closure of the French borders in 1974 marked an important turning point in the demographics and economy of French immigration that in turn helped change the nature of immigration politics in France (Tapinos 1988; de Wenden 1988b; Weil 1988b). It was at this juncture in France that the foreign population evolved into the settled, feminized, young, and increasingly, non-European population of the late seventies and eighties. Family reunifications increased after 1974, especially among the North Africans and Africans from the sub-Sahara. From a population of mainly male, transient guest workers, the foreign population in France diversified and settled. Of those foreigners present in France in 1985, over 80 percent were residents for at least ten years, over 43 percent were women, and 23 percent were actually born in France (*Hommes & Libertés* 1985; Ministry of Social Affairs 1986). Because of these changes, the realization that the immigrants came "to stay" gradually grew through the late seventies and early eighties (Rogers 1985; Tapinos 1988).

With the changes in the composition of the foreign population came a concurrent trend of a shift in the national origins of immigrants, from predominantly European to non-European. In 1968, Europeans accounted for 72 percent of the foreign population. In 1975, Europeans still accounted for approximately 60 percent of the population. But, by 1982, Europeans accounted for only 48 percent while non-Europeans accounted for over 50 percent of the foreign population; and by the 1990 census, European Community nationals only accounted for 36 percent of the foreign population (see Table 2.1).[10] According the 1982 census, The North African or Maghrebi immigrant groups constituted nearly 40 percent of the foreign resident population in France; broken down, the largest foreign group were the Algerians, accounting for 22 percent of the foreign population, while the Moroccans (12%) and Tunisians (5%) constituted significantly smaller

TABLE 2.1.
Evolution of Dominant Nationalities in Foreign Populations in France, 1921–1990

	Belgians	Spaniards	Italians	Poles	Portuguese	Algerians	Moroccans	Tunisians	Turks
1921									
Number × 1,000	349	555	451						
percentage	22.80%	36.20%	29.40%						
1931									
Number × 1,000	254	325	808	508					
percentage	9.40%	12.90%	29.80%	18.70%					
1954									
Number × 1,000		289	508	269		212*			
percentage		16.40%	28.70%	15.20%		12.00%			
1968									
Number × 1,000		607	571		291	474			
percentage		23.20%	21.80%		11.10%	18.10%			
1975									
Number × 1,000		497	463		759	711	260		
percentage		14.50%	13.14%		22.00%	20.60%	7.60%		
1982									
Number × 1,000		321	334		765	796	431		
percentage		8.70%	9.10%		20.80%	21.60%	11.70%		
1990									
Number × 1,000		216	254		645	620	585	208	201
percentage		6.00%	7.04%		17.90%	17.20%	16.20%	5.70%	5.60%

*French Muslim Algerians were counted as foreigners during this period.

Sources: Costa-Lascoux (1989a:19); Hollifield (1991a); George (1986); *Hommes & Libertés* (1985:7); INSEE (1992).

proportions of the total (Voisard and Duscastelle 1988; Lebon 1988). By the 1990 census, Algerians accounted for only 17.2 percent of the foreign population; the decline in numbers perhaps indicates the increase in naturalizations among Algerians due to the reform conflicts of the decade. Otherwise, the 1990 census indicates an increase in the number of Moroccans to 16.2 percent of the foreign population, while Tunisians accounted for 5.7 percent. In general, the 1982 census underscored the growing diversification of immigration to France: other growing non-European populations include those from Turkey (3.7%), from sub-Saharan Africa (3.4%), and Southeast Asia (2.9%); and by 1990, foreigners from Turkey accounted for 5.6 percent of the foreign population (SOPEMI 1985).

The formal closure of the border and the economic crises of the early 1970s shaped the economic participation of the foreign population in France after 1974. However, the impact of the labor market problems differed among non-European and European groups. The border closing led to the preoccupation by the state and political classes with "clandestine" immigration, a preoccupation that continued through the seventies and eighties (Marie 1988; Tapinos 1988). There was an overall decline in the active (registered) foreign population, despite its increased feminization. Of those (registered as) unemployed, the overlapping categories of non-Europeans, youth and unskilled workers constituted the majority (Ministère des Affaires Sociales 1986). So, the marginalized, unemployed worker was more likely to be a non-European than a European.

By the early 1980s in France, the postwar immigrant populations were undergoing a variety of changes. Demographic shifts, increased social and economic settlement, and new kinds of immigrant activism were visible across immigrant communities. In 1981, over 70 percent of immigrants in France had been settled there for at least ten years. There were several ways in which the demographic and economic changes increased the visibility of the foreign populations. The youthfulness of the foreign populations in contrast to the native French populations was striking. Already, in 1982, it was estimated that there were approximately 2 million youths of foreign origin in France (Marangé and Lebon 1982). While youths under twenty years old account for only 27 percent of the French population, by the early eighties, they accounted for a approximately 40 percent of the North African populations (Tribalat 1986, 1995). Overall, foreign students accounted for 8.9 percent of the French school population in 1989 (Perotti et al. 1989).

From the sixties onward, immigrant activist organizations and support networks, notably unions, human rights associations, and church groups began to establish substantive infrastructures across immigrant populations.[11] The political activism of immigrant groups in France in the seventies did not focus as much on the extension of civic or political rights as on social and economic rights, and struggles against discrimination and for equality (Miller 1981; de Wenden

1988b:256–275, 305–309). Beyond instances of discrimination, cultural and social factors contributed to increasing the specific visibility of non-European, and
especially North African populations in France. Religion, color, food, family
habits, and dress all served as distinguishing marks of the growing North African
populations in France. By the late seventies, Islam had become the second largest
religion in France behind Catholicism. North Africans and those of North
African origin account for the majority of the 2.5 to 3 million Muslims estimated
to live in France (*Le Monde* 11/30/89; Voisard and Ducastelle 1988). Accordingly,
the number of Mosques and Islamic associations in France burgeoned in the seventies and eighties; from a few mosques to over a thousand, from a few organizations to over 600 associations. Islam also played a significant role in organizing
Muslim immigrant communities in French public life. From the seventies onward, the number of Koranic courses, new Islamic organizations, and demands
for religious rights increased substantially (Kepel 1987).

Another dimension of the growing visibility of the non-European immigrant
populations by the 1980s was the fact that the category of *foreigner* no longer cap-
tured the extent of the new *immigrant* populations in France. Even before the
conflicts over immigration and citizenship grew, it was clear that many immigrant
origin populations were legally French, but identified themselves and were identified by others as immigrants (Sayad 1981–1982, 1984). For the new immigrants
and especially second-generation immigrants, the label of immigrant and non-
French was both self-definition and external description. For example, during the
1982 census, youth of Algerian origin defined themselves as Algerian, even
though many were attributed French nationality at birth. At the same time, often
those who were French of immigrant origin were classified under "immigrant
population" in surveys, studies, and interviews. This kind of classification was especially true in the case of those of North African, Muslim origin.

The seeming visibility of the new non-European immigrants (often defined
as in contrast to the previous flows of European origin immigrants) has also been
part of the racialization of immigration policy and political debate in France.[12]
For example, in 1993 as part of conservative legislative efforts to tighten immigration controls, one provision introduced in the National Assembly authorized
giving the police more leeway to run on the spot identity checks. The provision
read that police could run identity checks on a person presumed to be a foreigner
as long as the basis was something "other than racial appearance (*Le Monde*
6/22/93)." The implication of course was that certain racial appearances would
inevitably invoke the presumption of foreignness.[13] Though the term "second-
generation" (or third-generation) immigrant youth applied to all youth of immigrant origin, it was used most often as a reference to those of North African or
Maghrebi origin (Marange and Lebon 1982; Gonzales-Quijano 1988).[14] The majority of these were of Algerian origin, and the remainder of Moroccan and
Tunisian origin. A significant proportion of these populations held French na-

tionality. In the 1980s, scholars estimated that there were 1.5 million Franco-Maghrebis, of which 1 million were Franco-Algerians. By 1987, youth of North African nationality, origin alone, or both probably reached close to 2 million (Jazouli 1986:20–21; Leveau and de Wenden 1988b; Gonzalez-Quijano 1987).[15]

Immigrants and Citizenship Status

The dominant linkage between immigration and citizenship has been a dynamic one. France's general history of immigration helped set the stage for much of the nationality reforms there since the nineteenth century. There are several key provisions or articles in the French Nationality Code — certain of which would be modified in the 1993 reform — that pertained to those born in France of immigrant origin. Article 23 of the French nationality code attributed French citizenship at birth to a person born in France of noncitizen parents when at least one parent was also born in France.[16] The presumption was that after two generations in France, the process of "francization" or assimilation had taken place. The principle underlying this provision, called in France *double jus soli*, dated back to nationality reforms of 1851 and 1889. The 1889 law, considered a central reform in French history, clarified that children attributed French citizenship at birth through Article 23 could not simply repudiate French nationality. The impetus behind the expansionist Article 23 derived in part from nationalist demands that the youth of immigrant origin serve in the French military (Brubaker 1992). The socialization wrought by two generations of living in France was not to be easily undone.

Episodes of nationality reform continue in the twentieth century. In 1927, amid demographic pressures due to the losses of World War I, a nationality reform decreased the waiting period for naturalization eligibility. Several years later, however, the Vichy regime instituted vastly restrictive criteria for citizenship access and rescinded citizenship rights from Jewish immigrants. The postwar French political order annulled the Vichy regime legislation. The government passed a new law in 1945, which reconstituted the French nationality code by essentially reincorporating the 1889 regulations governing citizenship attribution and acquisition. These regulations included the modified version of the principle of *jus soli*. Article 44 of the nationality code permitted the acquisition of French citizenship "without formality" at the age of majority by individuals born in France, of noncitizen parents, and residing there for the preceding five years, as long as they fulfill certain conditions, including the absence of criminal convictions listed under article 79 of the code.[17] Article 44 was categorized as "automatic" or "semi-automatic" access to French citizenship, although several specific conditions clearly still needed to be met. It applied to second-generation youth of immigrant origin, other than those covered by Article 23 of the nationality code and law.

Beyond the demographic pressures for more French, which certainly contributed to these reforms, France's ideological traditions, statist institutions, and long history as a colonial power were all central to understanding these nationality practices. The French Revolution, Jacobin state, and French republican traditions encouraged territorial understandings of citizenship and the conceptualization of citizenship as membership in a specific nationally oriented political and cultural community. Actual citizenship and nationality policies underwent many changes, but several trends resulted in further territorial criteria. The 1889 reform took place amid nationalist movements and the exigencies of war during the during the late nineteenth century. The provision of *double jus soli* (Article 23) was instituted to apply to those of immigrant origin in France, translating into an expansionist move for French regulations.[18] In contrast, other nationalist periods in France, such as early twentieth century, featured restrictive nationality practices toward foreigners and immigrants. Throughout, French ideological traditions and institutional practices operated as important resources and sites of change (Noiriel 1992; Leca 1985; Gallisot 1986; Brubaker 1992).

Certainly, a complicating factor for the contemporary immigrants, and in particular for the non-European immigrants from former French colonial territories, have been the differentiations and ambiguities in their legal and political status. For ex-colonial and other immigrant populations in France, the regulations governing their citizenship and nationality acquisition were linked to their historical experiences with French national membership. The colonialist and post-colonial experiences continued to promote extensions and modifications of French nationality policies in several important ways. France's vast colonialist ventures meant that specific linkages were established for the migration of colonial and later postcolonial populations. The process of decolonialization brought with it an extended application of *double jus soli*. Unlike other second-generation youth who acquired French citizenship (automatically) at their majority, many second-generation youth from former French territories were attributed citizenship at birth. Young immigrants of Algerian origin in France were automatically attributed citizenship at birth if at least one of their parents had been born in Algeria before its independence in 1963, because Algeria had been considered an integral part of France, one of the French *départements*.[19] A 1973 reform of the Nationality Code extended the provision of *double jus soli* (Article 23) to immigrant populations from certain sub-Saharan countries which had been former colonial territories of France.[20] From 1963 through the mid-eighties, an estimated 290,000 persons born in France of Algerian parents were attributed French citizenship at birth through this article (Long 1988). In 1985, there were approximately 15,184 attributions of citizenship to second-generation Algerian origin youth.[21]

Many long regarded the extension of Article 23 to those of Algerian origin as deeply ironic, it being the automatic attribution of French citizenship to those whose parents fought a difficult and deliberate war of independence against France. The reactions of these parents—"How, as an Algerian, could I produce French children"—were part of the more general confusion, bitterness, and conflict over the issue (Sayad 1981–1982; GISTI 1983). Such reactions were perhaps one of the first indications of how the linkage between contemporary immigrants and citizenship could be formulated as problematic, for immigrants and French society. Already in 1981, the sociologist Abdelmalek Sayad argued, "If each period of the history of immigration had its own manner of coming to terms with the (political) illegitimacy that is fundamentally attached to the immigrant, and each crisis period, its manner of revealing to itself this illegitimacy . . . this is betrayed today through" the manner in which immigrants and their children were automatically nationalized and naturalized into French membership (Sayad 1981–1982).

Overall then, the acquisition of French citizenship at the age of majority (Article 44) rarely applied to the children of Algerians, and (given the smaller size of their populations) the numbers of second-generation Moroccan and Tunisian youth also constituted a minority of the total number of acquisitions based on it. Instead, Article 44 applied most significantly (in terms of actual numbers) to the second generation youth whose parents were Southern Europeans (Portuguese, Italian, and Spanish). The numbers of youth acquiring French citizenship by this route can only be estimated, since they were not formally registered. From 1973 through the mid-eighties, more than 225,000 persons have become French through Article 44.[22] In 1985, an estimated 17,607 did. These youth also had the right to refuse French citizenship in the year before the age of majority, but the numbers to do so were below 10 percent of those eligible.[23]

In the postwar period, decolonialization and mass labor migration ushered in new institutional practices and reforms, including the granting of more economic, social, and civil rights to foreigners. As the new immigrants and their families settled in France, their experiences as foreigners and members, immigrants and citizens, French nationals and postcolonial populations in France raised questions about citizenship. In what ways does citizenship matter? What ought to be the definition of citizenship? What constitute the boundaries of citizenship? Postcolonial experiences and linkages complicated such questions. For example, during the summer of 1996, a national crisis erupted in France when the government strove to deport hundreds of African immigrants while the immigrants took shelter in Paris churches and undertook hunger strikes. The legal status of many of the immigrants had become complicated following the restrictive citizenship and immigration revisions of 1993. On the one side, the government aimed to frame their expulsions as an effort to control the national boundaries. On the other side, the African immigrants framed their protests in terms of human rights. But these immigrants also framed their right to stay in France in terms of their membership within the French national boundaries. As one Mali immigrant argued, "We're here to stay . . . for us, we're not immigrants. We are in our native land" (cited in Rosenblum, AP newsbrief, 8/16/96).[24] Contemporary immigrants in France as elsewhere have raised questions about citizenship because they expose certain of the assumed boundaries of national membership. By their dualistic presence in one state and absence in another, by their ambiguous legal and social status, immigrants seem to straddle the boundaries of national membership, while showing how the parameters of citizenship in the modern world are changing (Sayad 1984).

In many respects, citizenship in the postwar period in Europe has become more extensive and layered. An array of studies of postwar Western Europe has demonstrated the increasing gradations in membership status and practice for foreigners and immigrants. These gradations ranged from formal citizenship, dual citizenship, denizenship, or legal residency to more precarious categories for foreigners without long-term residency permits and for those who remain undocumented (cf. Hammar 1989; Layton-Henry 1990; Bauböck 1994; Soysal 1994). The formal closure of the borders and the settlement of immigrants after 1974 brought into sharp focus broader changes in the rights and obligations traditionally associated with citizenship.[25] In 1977, when the conservative French government halted the increasing influx of family reunifications, the Conseil d'Etat (Council of State) declared the ban illegal. According to the council and courts, the individual rights of migrant workers had primacy.[26] The longer duration of residence in France prompted other actions as well, by foreign worker solidarity organizations and immigrant associations, to ensure the rights of immigrants as residents and workers in France (FASTI 1987; Miller 1981). In other trends, citizenship would gradually come to matter less for the nationals of the European Community (EC) member states, who enjoyed the freedom of movement under EC regulations. By 1992, the continuing process of European integration included the establishment of a European citizenship for all European Union nationals. The status of non-European nationals under the EC regime however has remained ambiguous and contested.

Throughout the seventies in France, links between immigration and citizenship issues appeared noncontroversial or even dormant (cf. Freeman 1979; de Wenden 1988b). Before the 1990s, the last major reform of the French nationality code took place in 1973. Led by a rightist government, the National Assembly passed an expansive reform of the French Nationality Code, whose main goal was to equalize treatment of men and women under nationality law. At the same time, it also extended the application of Article 23 to other former colonial territories. Immigration was presumed as a historical experience, not problematized as a challenge. Likewise assimilation was assumed as inevitable, not questioned as a practice or outcome. "France, which is known to be for all time a land of immigration, affirming her character in the search for foreigners to espouse our nationality, must follow in the same spirit of generosity of complete assimilation," proclaimed the young Gaullist deputy Pierre Mazeaud, who would later become one of the more outspoken supporters of restrictive citizenship reform.[27] In 1979, ministers of Giscard D'Estaing's government held meetings to discuss strengthening the automatic provisions of the nationality code, whose effect would be to increase attribution of French citizenship to those of foreign origin. As late as 1981, Jean Foyer, the architect of the 1973 nationality reform, defended the existing code. By 1985, however, he would be an ardent supporter of a new, restrictive attempt to revise that code.

When conflict over citizenship and immigration does arise in the eighties, the debates involve ideological boundaries of national membership, historical contexts of migration, postcolonial immigration, and immigrant settlement, and the shifting institutional rights and obligations that had traditionally been associated with formal national status. Challenges to French ideologies and institutional patterns become simultaneously resources for and constraints on conflict over citizenship as diverse political agents with dissimilar aims strive to re-invent French citizenship. For the conservatives and socialists, nativists and multiculturalists, the relationship between immigration and citizenship becomes problematical. The meaning of pluralism in France is publicly at issue. French national identity, civic rights, and nationality and citizenship policies are at issue. And at the crux of the conflict appears to be the integration of Maghrebi, Muslim immigrants.

CHAPTER 3

Politicizing Citizenship in French Immigration Politics

Until 1983, citizenship was not a salient issue in contemporary France. Despite presidential campaign promises by the Socialists in 1981 to extend municipal voting rights to immigrants, the newly victorious Mitterrand government was otherwise preoccupied. In actuality, economic and social policies rather than civic rights were the more pressing issues for most of the immigrant associations as well. Nor was citizenship a concern in extreme Right discourse. Nationality and immigration were clearly distinctive issues in public opinion and the press.[1]

By the time restrictive Nationality Code reform proposals turned up on the political platforms of far Right and rightist parties in 1985, it would seem natural to many that anti-immigrant forces would turn to citizenship as another front to wage their attacks. But, citizenship concerns and the question of citizenship reform did not emerge overnight in France. In fact, a whole series of processes and factors led to citizenship being constructed as an issue for political strategies, as a stake in national debates, and as a focus for mobilization. The purpose of this chapter is to reconstruct those processes that led to the politicization of citizenship. In other words, my aim is to uncover the initial stages of the politicization process, which I argue in turn shaped the latter stages of the conflicts.

In this chapter, I trace two phases of the politicization process. The first phase was defined by debates and conflicts over pluralism, whose roots could be found in the politics and policies of the sixties and seventies. The debates then resurface in a second phase marked by a surge of contestation around national identity issues. These series of conflicts, one redefining pluralism and the other contesting national identity, laid the groundwork for reformulating French citizenship as problematic.

In the analysis, I also address the question of the far Right's role in politicizing citizenship and particularly within the context of France's intensified immigration politics. Were Le Pen and the National Front responsible for politicizing citizenship in France? Were the conflicts around citizenship a product of the immediate immigration politics? At first look, the ways in which citizenship issues became framed does suggest the strong influence of the anti-immigrant, extreme Right.[2] While in the 1970s immigration policies were primarily defined in economic or social terms (Freeman 1979; Tapinos 1975), in the 1980s they were issues to be contested in French elections at every level (Schain 1988; de Wenden 1988b; Weil 1991).[3] Concerns about citizenship became politicized in the context of an increasingly polarized immigration politics and the electoral rise of a far Right party.

The first electoral success of the Jean-Marie Le Pen and his party, the National Front (FN), coincided with highly charged debates over the settlement of the non-European, and in particular, Maghrebi or North African immigrant populations. Le Pen and the National Front appeared to crystallize public concerns over the immigrants' cultural, religious, ethnic and racial diversity and the challenges that immigrants posed to the French national identity (Perotti 1985, 1986). Simultaneously, numerous immigrant associations strove to become a visible political force with marches and protests. Conflicts over citizenship were considered struggles between racist and humanist tendencies.[4] As a result, Le Pen has at times been given nearly sole credit for imposing the tone and themes of the political debates, politicizing citizenship, and generating the rise of racial politics (Hollifield 1986, 1989; de Wenden 1988b).

Contrary to such perspectives what I stress here is that the extreme Right played an important but only partial role in the politicization of citizenship. Other political agents, including state representatives, the classic or majoritarian Right parties (RPR and UDF), the Left Socialist (PS) and Communist (PCF) parties and the immigrants' association movement shaped the processes as well. I suggest that the politics of citizenship during this period can not be reduced to a product of polarized immigration politics or generalized racial politics. The rhetoric and actions of the far Right and others were clearly racist. But the categorization of "racial politics" became more a political ploy in France than a useful analytical tool. The unfolding of the complex and multiple political processes that led to the politicization of citizenship is central to the story of this chapter. To start, I trace the transformations in the concept and practice of pluralism. French debates and policies moved from reconsidering notions of pluralism in the context of regional activism to redefining pluralism in the context of immigration politics.

The Transformations of Pluralism in France

In the sixties and seventies, a resurgence of French regional and ethnic activism marked a challenge to the Jacobin, republicanist model in France.[5] The traditional model entailed the defense of universalist aspirations, the refusal to recognize differences among the citizenry, and an insistence on a nationally convergent political and cultural community. The regional activists, however, rejected notions of national unity that could "transcend class, region, and ideology" (Wahl 1980). Regional movements drew on the emergence of supranational political entities, including the array of European international organizations and more global organizations, and on trends toward subnational regionalization. Their demands for political and cultural rights relied on a justificatory discourse which combined references to emergent regimes of transnational human rights and subnational collective identities and loyalties (Beer 1980:39; Safran 1985).

In a similar fashion, other ethnic minorities, immigrant communities, and parts of the Left joined in rejecting the traditional constraints on pluralism by calling for the "right to difference." As articulated by these groups, the call for a right to difference was a separatist demand for egalitarian treatment. It was a demand for the right to be culturally, socially, religiously, or nationally different from the French majority. Such demands encompassed linguistic, cultural, media, educational, and citizenship policies. In the late seventies, for example, Left and immigrant activists advocated (unsuccessfully) for a voluntarist revision of the French nationality code so that those of Algerian origin would not be made "French despite themselves" (Costa-Lascoux 1987b).

In response to the regional and ethnic activism, the Right government under Valery Giscard D'Estaing was, at least in rhetoric, more accommodating to minorities than previous administrations. Public officials seemed to show a "willingness to accommodate the cultural aspirations of native ethnic minorities which . . . in turn spilled over into accommodationist attitudes toward other subcommunities," including immigrants (Safran 1985:41). At one point, Giscard D'Estaing asserted that France had become a pluralist society. In 1979, the Giscardian government proposed a series of immigration policies under the rubric of improving the life of "installed ethnic minority communities." The proposals included the formation of extramunicipal councils for "giving immigrants a say." Within this context, Jacques Chirac, representing the Gaullists (RPR) declared his party was favorable to giving immigrants the right to vote in municipal elections (de Wenden 1988b:257–258). But in actuality little was done by way of concrete policies (Safran 1984:42).

For many observers, it was the arrival to power in 1981 by François Mitterrand and the Socialist Party that signified the milestone in the movement toward pluralist policies and "ethno-cultural accommodation" (Safran 1985:41–42). On a stop in Brittany (one of the centers of regionalist activism) during the presidential election, Mitterrand declared: "It is to wound a people to the deepest of itself to limit it in its culture and language. We proclaim the right to difference." Soon after the election, the new government passed legislation giving immigrant groups the legal "right to association," which helped generate a new proliferation of immigrant activism and associations (Loi No. 81-909, 10/9/81). In contrast to the previous governments, the Socialists were more explicit in their rhetoric promoting ethnic diversity, and in their policies developing more pluralist and decentralized practices. Not surprisingly, their efforts were considered a significant "rupture" with the past (Lochak 1987:63; Safran 1985; de Wenden 1988:276–278).

The Socialist government made its most concerted efforts to move away "from traditional Jacobinism" and embrace pluralist policies in the early eighties (Safran 1985:43–50). A celebrated report, commissioned by the Ministry of Culture and entitled *Cultural Democracy and Right to Difference* (Giordan 1982), supported the right to difference for "all minority cultures." Included in the category were not only traditional regional ones, but also minority workers, political refugees, and national or religious communities, such as the Armenians and Jews (50–56). The report dismissed efforts of previous French governments. It cited both international recognition of the need to ensure pluralistic accommodation of "ethnic, religious, or linguistic" minorities, and specific French commitments to promote the "right to difference":

> The one and indivisible French Republic recognizes and protects the diversity of cultures, mores, and ways of life. Everyone has the right to be different and to be manifest as such . . . the taking into account of linguistic and cultural differences by the state carries in it the seed for a new cultural citizenship (nouvelle citoyennete culturelle), breaking with the secular tradition. (16–17)

The Socialist policies encompassed immigrant groups. A 1981 reform gave foreigners the right of association. Under the slogan of "to live together with our differences," the Socialist government reworked some programs and created others. In 1982–1983, the FAS (Fonds d'Action Sociale)—the French government agency organizing the settlement and insertion of immigrants—was regionalized. In 1984, the government established the National Council of Immigrant Populations as a new national advisory body under the direction of the Directorate of Migrant Populations in the Ministry of Social Affairs (*Journal Officiel* 7/20/84:2363). The goal of the changes was in part to enable representation by immigrants at all levels (Safran 1985:54–55).

Immigrant Associations and the Right to Difference

The immigrant association movement would emerge as a forceful pressure in French politics most strongly after 1983. But support for the right to difference was already an important component in immigrant activism in the seventies and early eighties (*Autrement* 1977; Verbunt 1977). In fact, scholars have considered the differentialist activism as the first phase of the association movement's emergence in French society (Jazouli 1986; Leveau 1988; Sayad 1981–1982). A 1982 conference on the political rights of immigrants was typical of such activism. As one participant, K. Muftari summarized, "By not requiring the renunciation of our past, isn't that to recognize positively and not negatively the right to difference, the right to a cultural identity" (*Les Cahiers de la Pastorale des Migrants* 1982:17).

Immigrant activism surged in the early eighties. It came in the context of increased racial attacks and a seeming rise in racial politics. The riots during the "hot" summer of 1981 and wrenching automobile strikes involving immigrant workers in 1982 and 1983 were interpreted in part as a response to such racism and in part as a precursor to later activism (de Wenden 1988b:287). Beyond antiracist organizing, immigrant activists invoked visions of a right to difference, pluralist polity, and differentialist egalitarianism. As Paul Gilroy pointed out in his analysis of blacks in Britain, "the dimensions of oppositional practices . . . are not reducible to the narrow idea of anti-racism" (1987:154).

Identity politics operated as a component of immigrant activism.[6] Diverse North African associations, for example, organized themselves around a shared Arab identity. It was during this period that second generation youth of North African origin became known as *Beurs*. It is a term connoting Arab that was created by immigrant youth and only used in the French context (Gonzalez-Quijano 1988). Indeed the popularization of the term *Beurs* in this period recalls the description of ethnic group identity formation by Donald Horowitz, a scholar of ethnic conflict. Horowitz has noted that context and contact form the basis of ethnic group identity: "ascriptive identity is heavily contextual . . . and it changes with the environment" (1987:118).

In a highly publicized 1983 "March for Equality and Against Racism," immigrant youth and especially *Beurs* traversed across France. One of the primary slogans of the marchers was "Let us live equally with our differences."[7] A major aim of the march was to bring together the "different communities living in France" and "to assemble in the largest way possible the habitants of France in order to make known our desire to construct a pluralist and solidaristic nation" (*La Croix* 10/9–10/83). The demands for the right to difference were not only demands for the "right to cultural identity," but more important for "the conditions of putting into place equality of their differences" (Perotti 1983:5).

When taken altogether—the differentialist demands of earlier ethnic and regionalist groups, the changing political rhetoric and policy practices of successive governments, and the emergent activism of immigrant associations—these movements in French politics seemed to be leading to a transformation of French notions of pluralism. However, the expanded understandings of pluralism did not go unchallenged. By the mid-eighties, definitions of pluralism in France were being publicly contested. Competing interpretations of what pluralism meant in France helped frame struggles over immigration and immigrants. One interpretation defined pluralism as the respect for diversity, another as the defense of French particularity. The first interpretation could reject the national terrain, the second depended on it.

The debates over pluralism were not partisan struggles. Nor were they easily divided along pro-immigrant and anti-immigrant lines. Competing notions of pluralism spanned the political spectrum, as the far Right, Right, Left, state officials, and immigrant movements advanced their various visions of French pluralism. Some understood pluralism to be the active tolerance for a range of diversities, regardless of their basis. This definition was manifest in endorsements for a differentialist and pluralist polity. Others expressed a clear wariness about differentialism, and called for a return to the visions of the French model as the articulation of national unity. They understood pluralism as the defense of national particularities, the features that were constitutive of the national unity. The aims, rhetoric, and modes of integration of these conceptions of pluralism stood in evident tension with each other.

By 1985, most interpretations of pluralism in France would be dramatically re-anchored to the national level (and to the level of the nation). In contrast to the earlier pluralist rhetoric and differentialist demands, the predominant discourse would rely on references to the national identity, national community, national membership. What provoked this return? What happened to the right to difference and an expansive pluralism? A popular view blames both the extreme Right, and immigration. For example, "The short response to (the) question (why "the right to difference is clearly out of favor in the current political climate") is immigration and Le Pen" (Vichniac 1991:40).

The Pluralist Debates and the Extreme Right

An attack on the more diverse definitions of pluralism was a long-standing feature in French far Right discourse (Taguieff 1987). For the far Right, the aim was twofold. The first was to appropriate the differentialist discourse from a defense of diversity to a justification for French particularity. That is, turn the right to difference into a demand for the right to be French. As Le Pen argued, "We not only have the right but the duty to defend our national personality, and we also have our right to difference" (cited in *Le Monde* 9/21/82). Likewise, the club GRECE elaborated an "antiracist" strategy as early as 1974 (Taguieff 1987:579). The second was to reject the egalitarianism evident in the new pluralism. The French scholar Pierre Taguieff has traced how the denunciation of egalitarianism was the "central argumentative act" of the National Front, and the "new Right" intellectual clubs against the Left from 1978 to 1984 (1988:50; 1986:91–128).[8]

To what extent does the far Right attack on pluralism explain the changes in pluralist discourse during the eighties? In order to assess the influence of far Right discourse, we need to consider the rise of Le Pen and the National Front. Le Pen and the National Front did not suddenly emerge in the eighties, rather they became electorally visible during this period. Their same discourse and platform failed in the seventies. Anti-immigrant rhetoric was also not greatly successful for the French Communist Party (PCF) in the seventies, when they attempted to propel immigration themes into electoral issues (de Wenden 1982; Schain 1988). Yet the proportion of immigrants in France did not change dramatically from one decade to another.[9]

What did change? Many interpretations of the National Front's success in the 1980s suggest that a disillusioned, "anomic," insecure electorate, part of whose resentment was manifest in hostility toward immigrants and generous immigration policies, led or strongly contributed to its rise (Mayer and Perrineau 1989; Jaffre 1986; Charlot 1986; cf. Husbands 1988). According to this view, Le Pen was a key situational figure who shaped the substance and direction of immigration politics (Hollifield 1986, 1989; de Wenden 1988a).[10] Political process models, however, assume that we need to examine the interplay of several factors in order to understand the successful rise of a movement. These include organizational resources and infrastructure, favorable changes in the "structure of political opportunities," changes in the "collective assessment" of those inside the movement and out, and the interpretative context (McAdam, McCarthy, Zald, eds. 1996).

I do not seek to provide here an exhaustive account of the rise of the National Front using a political process approach. Rather, my point is trace the interactions between Le Pen's rhetoric on pluralism and changes within the political process so that we can understand the far Right's influence on the pluralism debates. In the French case, the growing appeal of Le Pen's platform needs to be situated within the changing political opportunities in the party system and the shifting context for framing or interpreting issues of immigration and pluralism. The combination of these changes helped ensure a reanchoring of French notions of pluralism.

The logic of the far Right's new right to difference pervaded the discourse of Le Pen and his movement. The basis of the "principle for the National Preference"—one of the National Front's founding themes—was "France for the French" (Le Pen 1984:170, 239). The radical exclusion of foreigners deemed inassimilable was sought in the name of respecting national identity. Rhetoric denounced the mixture of cultures and races because "we are observing a true invasion that is in the process of making the French nation disappear before the next twenty years" (Le Pen in *Le Monde* 11/2/82; Taguieff 1986). Or, as one National Front leader put it, "They (our adherents) know that the western civilization is in peril. The white race risks submersion by the third world, and one shouldn't defend oneself?"[11]

The National Front's discourse was not explicitly about the French nationality or citizenship. Although the logic of extension to such themes was evident. When the right to vote for immigrants did come up in 1981, the National Front declared the project would lead to "the process of defrancisation of France" (*Le Monde* 8/12/81). Nonetheless, in the early eighties, the core components of Le Pen's political rhetoric were arguments focusing on the French nation and its "personality," on western civilization and the white race (Taguieff 1988, 1989; Schields 1987). Le Pen would consistently claim, "There is a racism I detest more than all other: the anti-French racism that tends to consider the French in their own country as people who ought not to have the same rights as others" (cited in Llaumett 1985:11).

Le Pen contributed to transforming the pluralist debates through the ways in which the far Right finally succeeded in appropriating the pluralist logic. However, that success depended on the rising visibility and legitimation of Le Pen and his party. Le Pen's visibility was intertwined with the emergent politicization of immigration issues while his party's legitimation was closely connected to changing party strategies and state practices (Schain 1988). After the Socialist victory in 1981, the majoritarian Right parties turned to their intellectual clubs and the "new Right" in their search for new political issues. These conservative intellectual and political clubs played a significant role in disseminating and legitimating extreme Right discourse (Lochak 1987; Taguieff 1986, 1987). In 1982, the club, "Avenir et Liberté," one of the many associations created by the right after 1981, declared that the "opposition goes from M. Stasi (a progressive moderate) to M. Le Pen. It is necessary to play down our differences." The President of the Club de l'Horloge, Y. Blot (RPR), stated in 1984, "The opposition can in effect have only one strategy: the union of all its constituents (including the National Front) against the Socialists, the primary adversary" (*Identités et Egalités* 1986:36).

From 1982, the far Right's themes of a "savage" or primitive and uncontrolled immigration and their amalgam of clandestine immigration, terrorism, delinquency, and the economic crisis began to surface in the political talk of Majoritarian Right parties. These parties moved beyond their prior calls of "assimilate or go home" to more radical anti-immigrant stances. Linkages between immigration and security preoccupations appeared as well within Left discourse and the Socialist government (de Wenden 1988b).[12] Even as Socialist policies and immigrant activism were promoting pluralist, inclusive policies, and the use of a differentialist logic, other segments of the Left voiced concerns about immigration.

The politicization of immigration issues was in sharp contrast to a few years earlier when the major parties in Right and Left were largely in agreement over keeping immigration depoliticized. During the 1981 presidential campaign, for example, François Mitterrand and Giscard D'Estaing agreed not to debate immigration issues during their televised debate (Lochak 1987).[13] Both the changing pluralist politics regarding immigration and the resurgent anti-immigrant rhetoric shaped the politicization of immigration issues. Public opinion polls were indicative of public uncertainty about the ongoing shifts. A national French annual survey in 1983 showed a public decline in confidence in Mitterrand, disillusionment with the Socialists, rejection of the communists, confusion about the Right, and strong concerns about unemployment and security (SOFRES 1983). The new context was one of a crisis of legitimacy over Socialist governance coupled with the transformations taking place among the major Right parties (Schain 1987).

The structure of political opportunities had changed to favor the rise and legitimation of Le Pen and the National Front in several ways. Le Pen's initial electoral success helped propel the French parties, in particular the majoritarian Right, to elaborate electoral strategies regarding immigration issues (Ysmal 1984). The linkage between the National Front and growing politicization of immigration played a role in shifting the collective assessment of Le Pen. For many analysts, the electoral successes of the anti-immigrant National Front platform in Paris and nearby Dreux in 1983 marked the first successful politicization of immigrant issues and the initial legitimation of the Le Pen's rhetoric. The elections and their aftermath were seen as a turning point in French immigration politics (Hollifield 1986; de Wenden 1985). But the causal role of the National Front has always remained ambiguous in these analyses, which refer to Le Pen as instigating, benefiting from, and crystallizing the politicization of immigration:

> The rise of the National Front coincided with—and was both cause and a product of—the politicization of the immigration issue. The particular terms in which what has previously been considered a social and cultural problem were what they were because they were framed by the peculiar nationalism of the extreme right; they proved explosive for the same reason. (Lavau 1987)

During the campaigns, Le Pen and the National Front were joined by those on the Right and Left in anti-immigrant rhetoric. Numerous candidates of the mainstream conservative parties, the RPR and UDF, as well as some segments of the Left, asserted, "It is necessary to stop this invasion (of foreigners)." Politicians linked "clandestine immigration, delinquency and criminality" (*Le Monde* 3/12/83).

The legitimation of extreme Right themes extended to the denunciation of egalitarianism and the appropriation of the differentialist logic (Taguieff 1984, 1986; Plenel and Rollat 1984). The conservative Gaullist politician Alain Griotteray published *Immigrants: the Shock* (1984), a book promoting a differentialist defense of the French national identity. Club 89, a political club with links to the

RPR, argued in *A Strategy of Government* (1985) that the large portion of the immigrant population did not want to assimilate or go home and that they menace the French cultural identity that "the French have the right and duty to preserve." In response to the Right's distortion of their arguments, those on the Left and in immigrant associations became wary of using differentialist justifications for fear that they would backfire. Thus, the Right effectively succeeded in appropriating the right to difference from its earlier proponents.

The Right's appropriation was understood in two distinct ways. One was to suggest that the differentialist discourse was in itself susceptible to distortion. In other words, it was a perverse effect of differentialist egalitarianism that it could easily be turned around against itself. The other suggested that differentialist logic interfered with the incorporation of French immigrants as potential citizens. It encouraged Anglo-style "ghettoization" or an ethnic citizenry and not equality according to the French model. This too was seen as an inevitable, perverse effect of this kind of pluralism (Taguieff 1986). Interestingly, such interpretations recall Alan Hirschman's insights regarding the usage of the perversity thesis in successful reactionary rhetoric (1991). Hirschman argued that "according to the perversity thesis, any purposive action to improve some feature of the political, economic or social order only serves to exacerbate the condition one wishes to remedy" (1991:7).

The visible transformation of the pluralist debates in the aftermath of the elections in 1983 constituted a critical point in the politicization of citizenship concerns. Until 1983, the core of the pluralist debates could be considered in terms of the terrain in which changing understandings of pluralism were to be defined. Do pluralist practices entail a rejection of the traditional French model or an elaboration of a variant of it? Does pluralism mean an acceptance of a range of diversities and identities or a defense of French national particularisms. The Right's constriction of pluralism helped delimit the scope of the terrain. After 1983, the debates would be contested on a specifically *national* terrain. The next phase would be the emergence of an explicit focus on national identity and national membership concerns.

The Contested National Identity

To be sure, the previous conflicts over pluralism and the "right to difference" implicated competing visions of the French national identity. Questions about what it meant to be French were implicit in such debates. But until 1983, these questions were not explicit. From 1983 to 1985, however, the successful appropriation of the right to difference by the far Right combined with several other factors to lay the groundwork for framing French immigration politics in terms of national identity conflicts. The other factors included the spread of "national-populist" discourse, the continuing construction of a bifurcated politics by the major parties, and a growing stress by immigrant associations on active integration and new forms of political rights. This new phase would lead to the direct focus on citizenship reform.

Rooted in the French conservative nationalist tradition, national-populist discourse was voiced foremost by Le Pen and others in the extreme Right during the 1983 campaigns (Taguieff 1988). According to the French scholar, Pierre Taguieff, Le Pen's anti-immigrant rhetoric was couched as part of a denunciation of modern decadence, an expression of antistate bias, and as an "ostentatious defense of the 'national identity'" (1988:22–24). These themes enabled Le Pen to attract a cross class, populist mobilization (Ibid.; also see Taguieff 1984; Schields 1987). Le Pen's rhetoric moved from defending Western culture and the French "soul" to defending the French nation and identity. His was above all an essentialist conception of the national identity (Perotti 1985; Plenal and Rollat 1984).

Beyond Le Pen, aspects of national-populist discourse appeared in the rhetoric of the majoritarian Right, and parts of the Left as well (Lochak 1987; Taguieff 1985; Schain 1988). In the rhetoric of the Majoritarian Right, the organic conceptualizations of French nationhood and the antistate bias were largely dropped. Instead the focus shifted to the threat posed by immigrants to the French nation and national community, understood as a political and cultural project of the state. These claims were manifest in the proliferation of books by Rightist politicians and clubs, including *Les Immigrés: Le Choc* (1984) by Griotteray, *La Préférence Nationale: Réponse à l'Immigration* (1985), and *l'Identité de la France* (1985) issued by the Club de l'Horloge, and *Les Immigrés, Pour ou contre la France* (1985) by Bariaini (UDF). These books argued that immigrants were menacing the French national identity.

The rightist charges were not a simple rejection of pluralism or diversity. In its most expansive form, the rightist arguments reanchored French pluralism as a vision of Francization. Former president Giscard D'Estaing, for example, affirmed that France must continue to integrate foreigners who "wished" to integrate, "all in keeping their traditions of origins." He claimed that "the central problem of immigration is the question of the menaced identity of French society . . . it is necessary to define the rights and duties of foreigners in an open and inclusive France, but where they have specific rights and duties" (*Le Quotidien de Paris* 6/22–23/85). In more restrictive fashion, the rightist parties, including the RPR, UDF and FN, denounced a "multiracial society where France loses its identity" (*Le Figaro* 6/6/85).

The rightist press contributed to the new pluralist debates with a continuous flow of special magazine issues and journal articles devoted to the ominous challenges of immigration to the French national identity, notably by Muslim Maghrebi immigrants. An issue on the demographic future of France published by *Figaro Magazine* was entitled "Will we be French in thirty years?" "Conserve this dossier on immigration," began the issue, "You will find here, revealed for the first time, the secret numbers that, in the thirty years to come, will put in peril our national identity and determine the destiny of our civilization" (10/26/85).[14]

The polarization of immigration and the popularity of Le Pen led the Right to radicalize their rhetoric and stances. The legitimacy of the immigrants' presence in France, and their relation with French society became appealing targets. Yet, simultaneously, the majoritarian Right was grappling with the durability of long-term legal immigrant settlement in France. By 1984, about 80 percent of immigrants were living in France for at least ten years. During this period, all three major political parties in France (PS, RPR, and UDF) converged on three major axes of immigration policy, namely the need to control the flow of immigration, to introduce integration policies for those already settled in France, and to reinstate some form of return aid for immigrants (Weil 1991; *Le Monde* 6/8/85 and 11/5/85; Cercle Pierre Mendez 1988). In conceding the permanence and the de facto incorporation of many of the immigrants, the Right was forced to reformulate their ideas about the integration of immigrants.[15] The debates over national identity reconstituted previous policy disputes over the "integration," "assimilation," or "insertion" of immigrants in France (Costa-Lascoux 1987a, 1989a:9–12).

The Left, National Identity, and Citizenship

Like Right politicians and clubs, those on the Left began to focus on national membership and identity concerns. The reasons for the shift on the Left paralleled those for the Right in several ways, including the need to respond to the far Right and the polarization of immigration issues (Weil 1988a; de Wenden 1988b; Lochak 1987). On one level, the Socialists responded by encouraging greater polarization since it pushed the Right to radicalize their views further and align with the far Right (Lochak 1987). On another level, the Socialists' pursuit of policy convergence necessarily led to its retreat from earlier support of differentialist policies. The process of changing directions and interactions propelled those on the Left, as it did those on the Right, to elaborate their own views on the French national identity.

On the other hand, one of the Socialist strategies was to reintroduce their support of municipal voting rights for foreign residents. The right to vote for foreigners had been part of Mitterrand's 1981 presidential platform, but was dropped soon after the elections.[16] In 1985, Mitterrand restated his support for it. The move was quickly interpreted by the press as another attempt to polarize the Left and Right. Certainly, Mitterrand's move was not an appeal for public support.[17] Public opinion data continued to indicate that a clear majority of French were against giving this right to foreigners. In one poll, SOFRES-MRAP, 63 percent of the respondents disapproved of giving immigrants the right to vote under any conditions, while 33 percent approved, with conditions attached; while the Left was more tolerant (47% approved), a majority supportive of the right to vote (56%) was found only in the extreme Left (SOFRES 1985).[18]

Socialist support for the right to vote, however, did find an attentive audience among immigrant associations and their social support networks, including human rights organizations and clergy. For most of these groups, the right to vote became a high priority after 1983 (de Wenden 1988b:306–308). By 1985, support for civic rights for foreign residents was an important factor in leftist electoral strategies aimed at attracting immigrant groups and the new immigrant vote. Though the links between the leftist parties and immigrants groups were not new, both Socialists and Communists began vying specifically for the potentially powerful electoral clout of immigrants (Interviews, *IM'media*, CAIF, MRAP, and France-Plus). In 1985, the PCF, which had long refused to support the right to vote, finally issued a revised stance, and became a strong proponent for the municipal voting rights and an active supporter of immigrant associations.[19]

The Socialists' pursuit of convergence, on the other hand, meant a retreat from their initial generous and experimental policies toward immigrants. After 1983, the Socialist government changed the focus of the state political agenda from social reform to national integration. From advocating policies that were experimental forms of ethnic accommodationism, the Socialists shifted to support policies of cultural pluralism, as can be best seen in the latter part of the "vivre ensemble" campaign (Safran 1985; Ministère des Affaires Sociales 1986). It is useful to see the Socialist's shift in institutional terms. The policies of ethnic accommodationism had necessitated institutional reform while the new cultural pluralism policies simply insisted on celebrating existing diversity.[20] The government's earlier reforms had clashed with predominant French institutional practices which externalized ethnicity or relegated it to the private sphere. In contrast, the new policies complemented existing institutional configurations (Soysal 1994; Safran 1985). In celebrating existing diversity, the new policies situated cultural features of the immigrant populations in "the essentially private realm of family and belief" (Castles 1989:99).

Not surprisingly, the policy shift led to numerous contradictions in Socialist political discourse (Weil 1988a; de Wenden 1988b). Forced to create a new justificatory discourse for their changing orientation, the Socialists turned their attention to emergent national identity rhetoric. After 1983, the Socialist antiracist campaigns appealed to French humanist and republicanist traditions without invoking differentialist logic. Leftist politicians elaborated their own visions of the national community. Identified as Left-wing French Jacobins and republicans, a majority of politicians and commentators sought to reaffirm the "founding myths" of France (Safran 1990; Krulic 1988a). They contended that the assimilationist French model and its confluence of political and cultural community should make France an efficacious "melting-pot" for integrating immigrants ("le génie

de la France"). But from their new vantage point, they were also to define contemporary immigration as a challenge to be handled. Some were optimistic. Immigration is "a challenge to French society on all levels," declared the Socialist
minister, G. Dufoix in an interview, but it should also be "a chance for
France . . . I believe sufficiently in the identity of France . . . so as not to fear the
contributions of immigration" (*Le Monde* 6/6/85). Others were reflexive. In a colloquium entitled "the foreigners who are also France" (one of many held during
this period), several speakers called for a "new social contract."[21] Such calls were
meant to evoke Ernest Renan's famous definition of a nation as "the desire to live
together" (Costa-Lascoux, 1987b). Others were clearly concerned. They called
for a renewal of the classic integrative institutions in France, such as the school.[22]
They demanded the separation of public French citizenship from the private religious and cultural particularities of Muslim, North African communities
(Schnapper 1987). For the most part, they rejected any disassociation of citizenship and nationality (de Wenden 1988a; Safran 1990).

These understandings of the national identity and national membership
combined an inclusive agenda with a model that conflated public membership
with political-cultural membership. The model relegated all group particularities
to the private sphere and thus constructed immigrants as a potential challenge.
This in turn led to the need to strengthen the national identity and modes of national integration. These views upheld pluralism. But it was a pluralism that had
to be compatible with the specific French identity (cf. Schnapper 1987). The Left
views overlapped with positions held by moderate Right and centrist politicians,
who contributed to the national identity debates with their own books and articles. The centrist politician Bernard Stasi (UDF) wrote *Immigration: Une Chance
pour la France* (1984), Michel Hannoun of the RPR wrote *Français et Immigrés
au Quotidien* (1985) and *l'Autre Cohabitation: Français et Immigrés* (1986), and
Michel Noir also of the Gaullist party advanced a new "moral contract" in 1985.[23]

The Left and centrist press and intellectuals moved from promoting ethnic
pluralism to focusing on national identity concerns. In August of 1983, for example, the French newspaper *Le Monde* published an article entitled, "The challenge of the Maghrebi Immigration," which sparked a series of public debates.
The author argued that the contemporary wave of North African, Muslim immigrants challenged the French national identity because of their cultural and religious particularities, and that the resultant non-assimilability threatened the
coherence and foundations of the French national community (8/23–24/83).[24]
The Left sociologist, Alain Touraine, who would later become an important figure in the debates over revising French citizenship legislation was quoted approvingly by the rightist journal, *Le Figaro*, for asserting that the French were not
racist. Touraine argued that if the French were xenophobic, it came "from a loss
of identity" (6/6/85).[25] The Socialist prime minister Laurent Fabius epitomized
the shift in the Left's rhetoric and logic when he declared in 1984 that the posi-

tions of the "the extreme right (. . . are) the false answers to real questions" (cited in Lochak 1987:73). To borrow a phrase from cultural studies scholar Richard Handler, these interactions of analytical commentary and political agendas reinforced French "naturalistic—and decisive—images of society and nation" (1988:14).[26]

The Left's newfound focus on national identity issues met with support in public opinion. Surveys showed a public concerned about the presence of immigrants in France and their cultural integration. They showed a public increasingly supportive of the themes if not the political persona of Le Pen, and most hostile to the North African populations (SOFRES 1985). A BVA–*Paris Match* poll of November 1985 showed that more than two thirds of the respondents agreed that "if one does nothing to limit the number of foreigners, France risks losing its national identity" (cited in Hannoun 1987). SOFRES-MRAP polls of 1984 showed that the French consistently overestimated the number of foreigners in France. Forty-two percent of the respondents thought the proportion of foreigners in France was over 11 percent (when it was between 6.8% and 8%). A majority of French (58%) found the presence of immigrants in France "too much" (SOFRES 1985).

For the French, the integration of immigrants was not inevitable. Nearly half of the respondents (49%) in the SOFRES-MRAP poll thought that "most of these communities can not be integrated into French society because they are too different." Integration meant integration into a specific French model. A *Le Nouvel Observateur* poll reported that 64 percent of the respondents judged that children born in France of noncitizen parents, but who hold French citizenship themselves should "adopt as much as possible the customs, and values of French society." Only 28 percent believed these children should "conserve, if they want, the customs and values of the country of origin" (11/30/84). Other surveys demonstrated that of all the immigrant populations, North Africans were still by far the most signaled out as "too numerous" (*Hommes et Migrations* 1/15/85), and in terms of "ethnic proximity" were the least accepted. In the SOFRES-MRAP survey, 70 percent estimated the Portuguese to be "well-integrated" while the same percentage thought Algerians to be "badly integrated" (SOFRES 1985).[27]

The multiculturalists or more substantive pluralists among the Left also engaged in the national identity debates. Their endorsements of pluralist conceptions of the French national identity were less insistent on national political-cultural membership and more sympathetic to a disassociation of citizenship and nationality. They too contributed to the evolving politicization of national identity. These pluralists represented a minority among the Socialists and were usually tied to the immigrant association support network. For example, the Socialist-linked Club 89 published a volume of essays entitled *L'Identité Française* (1985). A central question for many of the contributors to *L'Identité*

Française was "Is our national sentiment sufficiently strong so as to be able to be enriched by a grand diversity of cultures?" (76). Club 89's goals were to combat racism, and "strengthen our national identity in a spirit of tolerance and pluralism." It invoked at once a vision of France as a "multicultural society," the principle of "the right to difference," and the past "patriotism of 1789" (85, 90, 94). Its members celebrated a pluralist identity defined as a defense of national unity and French ideas of nationhood. Their articulation of a French model of pluralism reflected the continued transformation of the pluralist debates.[28] While Club 89's discourse contrasted with more confined and limited definitions of pluralism, it was not advocating the pluralism of the seventies and early eighties. That earlier pluralism defined partly in terms of subnational loyalties and transnational rights had been in many ways independent of a specific French national model (Giordan 1982:13–17; Beer 1980; Safran 1984).

Immigrants, National Identity, and the New Citizenship

Not surprisingly, immigrant associations and immigrant support organizations became actively engaged in the growing debates regarding the national identity and pluralist politics. The aftermath of the municipal elections of 1983 in fact signified for many commentators the effective political emergence of these "second generation" associations. This period saw a proliferation of new associations, new political elites, and new directions for immigrant activism. For the first time, such associations responded in a concerted fashion to the increasing negative usage of immigration and anti-Arab themes. Both older (e.g., FASTI, CAIF) and newer (e.g., TEXTURE and Memoire Fertile) groups promoted new or at least newly emphasized themes, including that of "the new citizenship."[29] Their emergence therefore not only affected the political strategies of the parties, but also played a role in the politicization of the national identity and citizenship.

It is important to stress that the immigrant association movement was not monolithic. Consider the contrast between three organizations established during this period. SOS-Racisme was an antiracist, media-oriented organization appealing to a cross section of second-generation immigrants and other French youth. France-Plus was an electorally oriented integrationist organization that targeted Franco-North Africans. TEXTURE, an association based in the industrial north of France, was more innovative and transnationally oriented, attracting second-generation immigrants, mainly of North African origin. These different orientations reflected the internal tensions of the association movement, and the diverse often competing associations categorized under its rubric. It was heralded on one level as a sign of an emergent "ethnic politics" or communitarian approach in France. On another, many of the associations were described as contained within and not challenging the ideological bases of the French republicanist model (Leveau and de Wenden 1988a, 1998b; Leveau 1990; Pinto 1988; Kastoryano 1989b).

From the early eighties onward, the immigrant associations functioned increasingly as replacements for the traditional integrationist institutions in France. In doing so, they generated a new generation of immigrant political elites and cultural intermediaries. These included those heading radio stations, magazines, and community centers, and later the leaders of the political, social, and cultural associations, like France-Plus, SOS-Racisme, FASTI, TEXTURE, and JALB. The emergence of these elites, coupled with changes in state policy and decentralization of power to the local levels in the 1980s, increased the strategic efficacy of their demands. Through their organizations, these new elites began to negotiate with the state, social institutions, and political groups at local and national levels (de Wenden 1988).

From the perspective of the political process, the changing "interplay" among the state, parties and immigrant groups situated the immigrant associations as both "members of the polity" and "challengers" (McAdam 1982). The growth of these associations, with their particularist priorities, helped constitute a "network . . . linking immigrant associations, antiracist organizations, public agencies in charge of immigrant "insertion" policies, and Left parties. It was a network that could be "neither reduced to the associative life nor to actions of the state" (Dubet 1989:123). The network reflected in part how certain differentialist aspects of immigrant activism were extended through the eighties. According to some observers, the Franco-North African or Franco-Maghrebi associations engaged in deliberate "ethnic lobby" and "ethnic-style" politics. Franco-Maghrebi groups used their culture, national origin, and religion to mobilize their constituencies for political stakes. They partly centered their identity around the Muslim, Maghrebi culture (Leveau and de Wenden 1988a; Leveau and Zghal 1989; Leveau 1990). For those second-generation activists, membership in the Muslim, Maghrebi community served as a functional entry into the sphere of French politics.

Several common aims did bind the diverse immigrant association movement. First, the associations aimed to organize themselves as a pressure group in French politics. This aim eventually moved most of the organizations to turn from differentialist strategies to integrationist, French-centered emphases. Like the Left's re-articulation of pluralism, the immigrant associations' shift reflected the transformation of pluralism going on around them, which led many of the associations to embrace the redefined notions of pluralism. Second, immigrant associations sought to positively politicize immigrant issues. As the Right used notions of national identity to attack immigrant groups, immigrant activists responded with their own defense of French national identity. Naming an organization "France-Plus" suggests a vision of France in which immigrants are both an addition as well as an enrichment. It is useful to recall that earlier the extreme

Right appropriated the differentialist arguments of immigrant activists, regionalists, and others as part of their own strategies. Such a cycle of appropriation and counterappropriation is part of social movement strategies to generate growth, ensure legitimacy building, and manage conflict. The immigrant association strategies and interaction contained implications for the general direction and logic of the movement. It was during this period that many in the association movement visibly moved from a differentialist pluralism to embrace different forms of political and cultural pluralism and engage in French-centered integration. To contextualize this evolution, it is useful to consider three national marches (organized by the immigrant associations) that took place between 1983 and 1985. The 1983 march "for equal rights and against racism" carried as one of its slogans "let us live equally with our differences." The 1984 "convergence for equality" proclaimed "let us live equally with our similarities (resemblances), whatever are our differences" (*Hommes et Migrations* 1985:4). By the 1985 "march for equal rights and against racism," a *CAIF Informations* editorial (a newsletter representing numerous immigrant groups) wrote that the march shows how much immigration must be "a social and political movement within the framework of the French society . . . (it is) a question of defining a true project of insertion . . ." (12/85:1, 2).

Immigrant association strategies reflected the growing integrationist orientation of the period and the tensions entailed in the pluralist-national identity debates. On the one hand, when SOS-Racisme was created in 1984 as a self-labeled antiracist organization of French and immigrant members with close financial ties to the Socialist party, it situated itself as the progressive alternative to the ethnic "Beur" groups of the previous years. It broke with the "ambiguity of a right to difference" to privilege a "right to resemblance" (Desir 1987:36). Building on images of diverse youth, social consensus, and cultural integration, SOS-Racisme fashioned a model of pluralist national integration to counter the false homogeneity of Le Pen's France.[30] Desir and others in his organization defined this model in terms of the French national terrain, invoking justificatory images of a pluralist republicanist lineage, though they also referred to a transnational antiracist human rights network. France-Plus, on the other hand, was created in 1985 as a counterpoint to SOS-Racisme. With a Franco-Maghrebi constituency, France-Plus was an electoralist organization, whose goals were to empower its constituency in the French political system through voting, electoral leverage, and office holding (Interviews, France-Plus). While SOS-Racisme rejected the ethnic basis of the earlier movement, France-Plus's pluralism was situated in the Maghrebi, Muslim context, from which it derived its legitimacy.[31]

Another association, Mémoire Fertile, was also created in 1985. Its members overlapped with the CAIF, the long-standing umbrella organization of immigrant groups. For Mémoire Fertile, the goal was the elaboration of the immigrants' "collective memory," a memory necessarily rooted in both France and the countries of origin, whose implications, according to Mémoire Fertile's members, would re-define the French national community. Mémoire Fertile explicitly rejected any type of differentialist approach: "It must not be ethnic politics . . . above all not a lobby (like France-Plus)." The point of departure for the association was a plural-ist "multicultural space," not a communitarian one (Interview, Mémoire Fertile). More than SOS-Racisme and France Plus, Mémoire Fertile situated itself in terms of transnational ties and discourse.

In general, however, most immigrant associations anchored their varied re-definitions of pluralism on a specifically *national* terrain. Their stances on inte-gration resisted going beyond a national French model. By the mid-eighties, immigrant associations termed the struggle to "reappropriate the collective in the large sense of the word" as "several 'Bastilles' to take."[32] Older immigrant organi-zations, such as CAIF or FASTI (umbrella immigrant support associations), iden-tified this movement explicitly. In 1985, CAIF members agreed on the need to "occupy and invest in new spaces of expression, and all particularly in the youth issuing from immigration, the problems of women and family, political rights and the right to vote, the cultural road" (CAIF 1985:9). At the same time, the CAIF identified "demarginalization and institutionalization" as one of its priorities. By which it meant that integrationist activities were "especially needed for the possi-bility of the state financing organizations." The state agency, FAS, was its "princi-ple financier" (CAIF 1985:17). In contrast to the earlier stress on articulating particularist interests within the state, immigrant associations' activities after 1983 reflected the more traditional French institutional process in which "interests compete to achieve institutionalization in the state apparatus and categories, and thereby to define a general will" (Jepperson and Meyer 1991; cf. Berger 1981). The state's own emphasis after 1984 on the national integration of immigrants and cultural pluralism (and not ethnic reformism) clearly contributed a great deal to limiting the notion of pluralism and turning attention to national integration.

The positive politicization of immigration themes by immigrant associations arose in the aftermath of the 1983 local elections and the subsequent European elections of 1984 when Le Pen's National Front gained electoral ground again. Immigrant associations countered anti-immigrant rhetoric with their own pro-motions of a "new citizenship" and a pluralist national identity. Regardless of their different orientations, groups such as SOS-Racisme, FASTI, France-Plus, TEX-TURE as well as MRAP (an antiracist organization) and the League of Human Rights called for municipal voting rights for immigrants, a "new citizenship," and an enlarged national identity (de Wenden, 1988b:338–344).

Immigrant activists argued that politicizing alternative notions of citizen-ship and identity was a necessary project. Julian Dray of SOS-Racisme wrote, "we act politically . . . because we take up problems that are essentially political ones, that is to say, related to the life of citizens in the city" (Dray 1987:145–146). The concept of "Nouvelle Citoyenneté" (new citizenship) became increasingly appealing in the debates over the national identity in which competing notions of the French national community were presented. As part of its mission in 1985, Mémoire Fertile expressed the goal to construct and defend a "new citizenship." The aim was to redefine citizenship as participation of all sorts—social, political, economic, cultural—in the community, and to separate this membership or citizenship from formal nationality. This would enable its proponents to incorporate immigrant communities, whether legally French or not, into the national community.[33] A Portuguese activist, Albano Cordeiro described the promotion of "la nouvelle citoyenneté" as a step toward "plural France" (Interview, A. Cordeiro 1987).

Though it featured some aspects of the earlier differentialist approaches, the discourse around "new citizenship" was inscribed in the transformed pluralist approach of the mid-eighties. Even if it disassociated national origin from citizenship and relied on local participation, the concept did not necessarily recall the transnational or subnational pluralist arguments of the seventies.[34] Rather, it appeared rooted in the national terrain. Its proponents invoked French republicanist antecedents and rejected differentialist interpretations. FASTI organizers claimed, "Our action does not consist of demanding rights for a minority, but to struggle for a transformation of the definition of the exercise of rights for all" (FASTI 1987:17). An organizer of Mémoire Fertile stated, "It is an . . . end in so far as it strongly actualizes the very ancient aspiration of a France more just and more equal."[35] Like others engaged in the pluralism and national identity debates, these immigrant activists sought to retrieve what Eric Hobsbawm has called the "constructed and 'invented' component(s)" of French ideologies of nation. In subsequent years, the fervent activity by immigrant associations for the French bicentennial became another opportunity for them to elaborate a pluralist collective memory and new citizenship from the "materials" of revolutionary republicanism (Hobsbawm 1983:14).

Certainly, the complementary emphasis by immigrant groups on republican themes and principles was as significant as their integrationist goals. Immigrant groups deliberately assumed a republicanist national orientation as part of their collective memory. The immigrants' socially constructed, multiculturalist understandings of the French national community and identity opposed essentialist views of these issues. They sought to situate themselves as the true inheritors of the Republican tradition and delegitimize the extreme Right and its interpretation of history (Mémoire Fertile 1987; FASTI 1987).[36] In other words, these immigrant groups operated on a parallel national terrain to their opponents.[37] Even as the Right called for a reexamination of the linkage between immigrants and the French "national community," so too did these immigrant activists. Both the "differentialists" and "new pluralists" had come to interpret this linkage as problematic. At the same time, for those engaged in the debates around the national identity, each project was articulated as no more than "self-assertion" (Hobsbawm 1983) of the true roots of French traditions of nationhood. If the differentialist arguments of the 1970s and early 1980s had proven ambiguous, the integrationist and redefined pluralist arguments were to prove ideologically slippery (Gallisot 1985).

On the one hand, the "Left-wing Jacobins," republicanists, more self-proclaimed "pluralists" and immigrant supporters appealed to the French tradition of nationhood. On the other hand, the different Rightist movements also proclaimed that they were articulating the true idea of French nationhood. Regardless of their competing platforms, all these groups laid claim to being the true inheritors of the French revolutionary, republicanist traditions. What such a seemingly contradictory picture points to is the paradox about the concept of nation itself. Modern nations and all their impedimenta generally claim to be the opposite of novel or constructed. Nations claim to be rooted in the remotest antiquity, human communities so "natural" as to require no other definition than self-assertion. Yet, whatever the historic or other continuities embedded in the modern concepts of "France" and "the French," these very concepts themselves include constructed or "invented" components (Hobsbawm 1983:14).

The simultaneous appeals to French nationhood by those on the Left and Right underscore the ambiguities involved in the discourse on national identity. Nation and national identity are malleable concepts. The French historian Gerard Noiriel has noted that the view of French history as founded "on a fecund pluralism, under the sign of republican ideals" is not borne out by French history (1984:74). Until Vichy, Noiriel argued, "the dominant point of view in the matter of immigration remained the negation of the identity of the other" (75). At their most expansive, ideologies of nation are still very limited pluralist visions. As Paul Gilroy has written, nations are necessarily exclusionary in so far they are constructed against the "other."

> Nationhood is not an empty receptacle which can be simply and spontaneously filled with alternative concepts according to the dictates of political pragmatism. The ideological theme of national belonging may be malleable to some extent, but its links with the discourses of classes and races and the organizational realities of these groups are not arbitrary. They are confined by historical and political factors which limit the extent to which nationalism becomes socialist at the moment that its litany is repeated by socialists. The intention may be radical, but the effects are unpredictable, particularly where culture is also conceived within discrete, separable national units coterminous with the boundaries of the nation state. (Gilroy 1987:55)

The national identity debates that emerged in France after 1983 demonstrated that elaborations of the nation and national identity could not be easily separated from nationalist discourse. The Left responded to the rise of the extreme

Right and its anti-immigrant rhetoric by shifting away from differentialist politics and toward national integrationist politics. Leftist politicians and intellectuals focused on re-articulating the national identity and national community. French scholar René Gallisot lamented this move when he commented that the Left countered rightist racism with a rhetoric "in terms of nationalism" (1985:5). This phase in politicizing immigration, which was marked by a return to a more confined pluralism and the growing preoccupations with national identity and unity would in turn lay the groundwork for the explicit politicization of citizenship.

The spread of national identity concerns and its subtext of nationalist logic does raise questions regarding the degree to which the conflicts over national identity (and later citizenship) should be defined in terms of racist and antiracist politics. After the 1983 elections, scholars and the press used the term, racial politics to describe the rise and effect of Le Pen. There is no doubt that Le Pen's and the National Front's rhetoric were racist, despite their disclaimers. Studies also documented that the number of "violent acts directed against immigrants or their property for apparently racist motivations" or at least the reporting of such acts clearly rose from the seventies to the eighties.[38] But the categorization of "racial politics" became a misleading one. During the debates over the national identity, the Left, on the one hand, frequently accused the extreme Right and Right of being racist or racially motivated. The Right, on the other hand, defended its actions as patriotic and not racist, and accused the Left of using the charge of racism to better its electoral chances (*Le Monde* 11/23/85).

National Identity Debates, Racial Politics, and Nativism

The use of the term, "racial politics" to capture the emergent trend of national identity politics often ignored how previous divisions between the Right and Left became blurred. It masked the emergence of a variegated nationalism in France. During the 1980s, strong or exclusive conceptions of the national identity were increasingly found across the political spectrum. Most commentary on national identity debates, however, employed the term *nationalism* to exclusively describe the xenophobic, national-populist rhetoric of the extreme Right (Taguieff 1988; Hollifield 1986). Nationalist sentiments were attributed to the racists and not to the humanists. Other catchphrases, including "lepenism" and "l'effet Le Pen" also pointed to a bifurcated politics between a "racist" Right and a "humanist" Left.

In fact, defining the extreme Right's politics—including their national-populist rhetoric, anti-immigrant sentiments, and nationalist stance—in terms of racial politics does not even capture that movement's appeal in French politics. A more accurate characterization of the National Front is that of a nativist movement. Although the American historian John Higham has defined nativism as "distinctively American," that distinctiveness, like other features of American "exceptionalism," shares important commonalities with the European experience (1988:3). Nativism, as a specific form of nationalism, regards people and ideologies of foreign origin as sources of disloyalty and threats to the national identity; nativism is the "intense opposition to an internal minority on the grounds of its foreign (i.e., un-American) connections . . . seeing or suspecting a failure of assimilation (the nativist) fears disloyalty. Occasionally the charge of disloyalty may stand forth naked and unadorned, but usually it is colored and focused by a persistent conception about what is un-American" (Higham 1988:4–5). Pre–Civil War nativism in the United States has been described in terms remarkably similar to the preoccupations aroused by the National Front:

> [It] reflected a fundamental concern with national identity, The question that bothered the Native Americans and Know-Nothings might be expressed in colloquial fashion as "whose country is this, anyhow?" They were disturbed and angry because the vast influx of Catholic foreigners not only challenged the hegemony of Protestantism, but seemed to threaten republican principles, the political process, the educational system, and prevailing cultural and behavioral norms.[39]

Though nativism has often been associated with a rejection of pluralism, it actually expressed more a refashioning of a particularist pluralism. In his review of the study of American nativism, the American historian Bergquist described this pluralism as "a distinct set of values and beliefs about American society and culture. The nativist was first of all assimilationist, believing that society should be organized to integrate new groups on the basis of conformity to older established cultural values. This assumed a strong belief in the necessary homogeneity of society; the Republic would be threatened if its citizens did not have standards of behavior agreed upon to rather fine details" (1986:138). Le Pen's appeal in the majoritarian Right, and more broadly in French politics, reflected in part the ambiguities of predominant French republicanist and Jacobin ideologies. Le Pen's rhetoric functioned in some ways, as a subtext—and not as a countertext or "counternationalism" as it has often been depicted—of French ideologies of nationhood.

Conclusion: From National Identity to Citizenship

The culmination of the focus of national identity in French immigration politics was said to mark a "new stage in the uncontrolled slippage of the French political class" (Lochak 1987:74). The widespread stress on the national identity combined with the changing usages of pluralism resulted in blurred divisions between the Right and Left. This chapter began with the efforts by regionalist and ethnic movements in the sixties to move the definition of pluralism beyond the French model. This chapter ends with French notions of pluralism once more firmly anchored into French national terrain and notions of national integration. But it is not simply a return to the old players and discourse.

What changed included both the contributors and contributions. Consider the array of those engaged in the pluralism and national identity debates—Le Pen and other extreme Right activists, Right Politicians, state officials, Socialist politicians and others in the Left, emergent immigrant activists and supporters. The malleability of past French nationhood traditions was proving great. Moreover, this resurgence of the nation revealed, as Eric Hobsbawm has put it, how "ancient materials (are used) to construct invented traditions of a novel type for quite novel purposes." Hobsbawm went on to note the pervasiveness of such practices: "A large store of such materials of any society, and an elaborate language of symbolic practice and communication, is always available" (1983:6).

The language of nation and national identity was rediscovered by all as a way of articulating the debates over immigration, pluralism, and the far Right. While the Left and immigrant groups operated explicitly as antiracist groups, their strategies for a pluralistic national integration and national identity were constructed as defenses for a contested national unity. René Gallisot accurately argued that the "antiracism of the left was caught in the trap of national identity" (1985:10). The implications go beyond rhetoric to logic. By using different ideologies of nation and national identity to justify their strategies, policies, and new orientations, leftist politicians and immigrant activists began to pursue what I call a nationalist politics of citizenship.

The growing controversies over membership exposed the implicit and problematic acceptances of nationalism in French society. Gilroy's observations about Socialists and nationalism in British politics are applicable in the French case as well: "It is as if the only problem with nationalism is that the Tories have secured a near exclusive monopoly of it . . . the types of subjectivity which nationalisms bring into being and put to work pass unquestioned. The problem has become how socialists can (re)possess them from the right" (Gilroy 1987). The causes for a resurgent nationalist politics were not confined to the immediate instance of immigration. George Lavau has noted, "The political community in postwar France had been sitting atop a fault line created by the way the political class had handled the national identity questions generated by the occupation and decolonization." Crediting the National Front for shifting this fault line, Lavau adds, "Little wonder that the shockwaves affected the entire political system" (Lavau 1987).

The emergence of a variegated nationalist discourse around the national identity set the stage for the explicit politicization of citizenship, nationality, and national membership. In 1985, the emergence of conflicts around the French nationality code constituted this next phase of the new citizenship politics. It marked the emergence of citizenship concerns in their formal sense as interchangeable with nationality. It continued to feature renewed contestation over pluralism and the integration of the Muslim, Maghrebi "second-generation" immigrants in France. The conflicts reaffirmed for many commentators the political class's resurgent preoccupations with the national identity. The next chapter traces the emergence of the efforts to reform the nationality code conflicts. What were the ideological and strategic sources for the various reform proposals and counterproposals? How did the contemporary interpretations reconstruct citizenship?

CHAPTER 4

Re-envisioning Citizenship

The Debates Over the Nationality Code

On June 5, 1985, during a special National Assembly debate on immigration, a moderate Right politician, Alain Mayoud (Union pour la Démocratie Française [UDF]) introduced a restrictive proposal to revise the French Nationality Code. His proposal was only one of several supported by all the rightist parties. While conflict over the Nationality Code and attempts to restrict access to citizenship were not novel in France, what was new in this attempt was the target and its comprehensiveness. Most of the proposals called for an unprecedented elimination in the French nationality legislation of all automatic attributions of citizenship on the basis of territorial connection, of *jus soli*, a key principle in the French tradition of citizenship.[1] The proposed reforms aimed, above all else, to restrict access to citizenship to those born within French territory of noncitizen parents. While justifying their proposed revisions by the principle that the acquisition of French citizenship ought to be more voluntaristic, the Right targeted second-generation youths of Algerian and other North African origin.

The proposals immediately became an "anathema" for the Left, and an effective electoral "battle-horse" for the Right during the 1986 legislative elections (*Le Monde* 6/8/85). "No racism, but no more French despite themselves" was the Right's self-described position. The immigrants needed to "merit" citizenship. "To be French, you need to earn it," asserted the blunt, National Front slogan (*Libération* 6/7/85, *Le Monde* 6/8/85). This chapter is about the political debates surrounding the Nationality Code reform in 1985 and 1986. The restrictive efforts to modify the code relied on three kinds of arguments. The first were voluntarist arguments that stressed the centrality of individual choice in the acquisition of French citizenship. In other words, to be French meant to act and choose to be French. Communitarian arguments stressed the centrality of collective choice and communal membership. According to this logic, to act and choose to be

French only comes (naturally) to those who are French, or who at least belong to the national community. Finally, nativist arguments stressed the suspect assimilation and loyalty of North African immigrants.[2]

The aim here is to show that despite the strong opposition by the Left and immigrant associations to the Right's proposed reforms, the Right and Left did share a common logic and discourse. The commonalities are obscured when the nativist aspects of the proposed reforms are highlighted. Yet the voluntarist and communitarian arguments on reconstructing citizenship evinced wide appeal and common articulations. The commonalities point out the need to reexamine the debates and their impact on French citizenship politics. I suggest that the usage of voluntarist and communitarian arguments enabled the construction of a broadly based nationalist citizenship politics. The new nationalist politics of citizenship was not defined by an exclusively rightist nativism. Rather, it entailed a variegated and cross-cutting nationalism, shaped by the earlier debates over pluralism and national identity and informed by the varied strands of French nationalist ideologies.

My analysis contrasts with much of the commentary on the nationality debates. When scholars have defined the attempts of 1985–1986 in terms of a "new nationalist critique" of citizenship, they have referred exclusively to the efforts of the French Right to implement a closed, restrictive politics of citizenship (Brubaker 1992; Perotti 1986). According to this view, the impetus for the legislative revision and symbolic reenvisioning of citizenship has been associated largely with the Right. The closed nationalist perspective has also been advanced in more sociopsychological terms, as a "racist, fascist-nationalist response to the accelerated transformations of modernity" (Balibar 1988b). Commentary on the conflicts have focused on why a restrictive politics of citizenship emerged, and subsequently, why it failed in 1987–1988; with the failure often being understood as proof of the more predominant republicanist, political-cultural understandings of citizenship. From a political process perspective, however, the nationalist politics is not a product, but is a process to be reconstructed.

From National Identity to Nationality Code

Many have credited Le Pen as being the small, sharp voice that reverberated in a great booming echo, to borrow a phrase from Eugene Weber.[3] Commentators traced the proposals to the discourse on immigrants menacing the national identity as advanced by New Right clubs in the seventies, and popularized by Le Pen in the eighties (Perotti 1985, 1986; Delorme in *Témoignage Chrétien* 10/13–19/86; de Wenden 1985a). The press claimed Le Pen, "first opened fire," starting the debate over the code in 1985 and "leading right parties to align with his views" (*Le Monde* 3/14/86, 12/22–23/85). The Socialist and Communist parties and immigrant associations emphasized that, in the words of one immigrant activist, "We didn't choose (this) combat" over the code, "it was imposed on us (by) the extreme right, Le Pen" (interview, CAIF).

The impetus to revise French citizenship, however, was not an innovation of extreme Right agendas. A questioning of French nationality practices, including the automatic attribution of citizenship to second-generation immigrants, can be traced to concerns of immigrant and Left activists, and to administrative discussions within the state. Left and immigrant activists during the seventies demanded the loosening of the Code provisions that transformed second generation Algerian immigrants into becoming "French despite themselves." As discussed in chapter 2, the Left stance was part of complex historical phenomena involving the postcolonial Franco-Algerian and Algerian populations in France. Rightist politicians in the seventies generally advocated the restriction of choice in nationality on the basis of their natality and demographic concerns.[4]

Since the last reform of the French Nationality Code in 1973, there were also pressures within the state to revise the code. From 1975 to 1985, there were three periods—1975, 1979, and 1982—during which series of discussions took place in the state aimed at revising the nationality code, and numerous revisions were actually implemented. Issues of automatic attribution of citizenship, dual nationality, and marriage all came under interministerial discussion. The discussions reflected tensions between the idea of voluntarism or choice and nationality practices. In some cases, the aim was to enlarge choice and in others to restrict it (Interviews, Bureau of Nationality). Until 1986, the issue of the nationality code was not really politicized and such internal state discussions and revisions were defined as "technical" issues and not political stakes (Interview, Directorate of Population and Migration).[5]

In contrast, the new questioning of citizenship practices on the part of both the Right and Left during 1985 to 1986 was generated by the ongoing debates over the national identity. The impulse to revise the code accorded "perfectly with the new problematic centered around the national identity" (Lochak 1987). Though the visions varied according to their divergent aims and ideological commitments, many participants in the national identity debates from 1983 to 1985 claimed that the links between national membership, contemporary immigrants, and the French nation were deeply problematic (Krulic 1988a; Lochak 1987; Brubaker 1992). The major lines of the debate—the voluntarist, communitarian and nativist arguments—reflected the changing political temper in France, as discussion focused increasingly on questions of national membership, identity and community.

Besides the groundwork laid by the national identity and pluralism debates, the 1986 national elections proved to be an opportune context for restrictive nationality proposals. The Socialist immigration policies, labeled lax by the Right, were set against the politics of the Right, labeled racist by the Left, while the extreme Right was set against emergent immigration association movements. The reform of the nationality code was associated with a larger group of immigration policies advocated by the Right and rejected by the left, including the restriction of certain social welfare policies for immigrant families. Concerns about second-generation immigrants and the role of Islam were increasingly voiced by the French parties (regardless of their divergent political agendas). Finally, public opinion surveys buttressed concerns over immigrants (SOFRES 1985). Within this context of polarization, an attack on French citizenship practices, already expansive in comparison with other continental European countries, became electorally profitable (Weil 1988b; Costa-Lascoux 1987b).

By late 1984, the far Right parties had proposed the complete elimination of the *jus soli* provisions, and the suppression of "automatic access" to citizenship — not based on *jus sanguinis* — in the French nationality code.[6] As set out by the National Front (FN) and the Parti des Forces Nouvelles (PFN), the proposals called for replacing territorial modes of attribution with the naturalization procedure. Furthermore, they aimed to modify the requirements for naturalization, expanding the conditions needed to demonstrate the candidate's "assimilation to the French community."[7] Claiming that "knowledge of French language does not suffice," they added the criteria of knowledge of "the culture and history of France, and the respect of French customs and civil law" (see *Le Monde* 3/14/86).

The Voluntarist Arguments

At first glance, the voluntarist and communitarian arguments for reforming the nationality code may seem incompatible. The former places priority on individual choice, and the latter on communal identity. But all three of the arguments to be examined — voluntarist, communitarian, and nativist — have historically been expressive of different strands of nationalist logic. There is an individualistic basis to many nationalist ideologies, which define the nation as "in principle two things at once: a collection of individuals and a collective individual" (Louis Dumont cited in Richard Handler 1988:32). At the same time, nationalist ideologies insist that "however individual members may differ, they share essential attributes that constitute their national identity; sameness overrides difference . . . an individual, human or collective (can not) be two things at once. To divide one's allegiance, affiliation, or identity is to court disaster" (Handler 1988: 6, 49).

The conservatives' stress on *volonté* was not simply an argument that the acquisition of citizenship ought to be based on an individual and deliberate choice. Despite their slogan of "no more French despite themselves," the voluntarism of the restrictive proposals implied more. It implied selectivity, assimilation, and the revalorization of citizenship. Pierre Chaunu, a conservative historian who would later sit on the National Commission on Nationality, argued "It is good that their demand is submitted to a jury. It is good that they have to undergo a probationary period. To give French citizenship freely was to devalue it" (*L'Express*, 10/24–30/86).

In *La Préférence Nationale: Une Réponse à l'Immigration* (1985), a book published under the auspices of the Club de l'Horloge (a club with ties to both the National Front and the Gaullist party—the RPR), the authors argued that "the law on nationality must aim to retain as French only those people who are proud to be it and of whom France could be proud" (Le Gallou 1985:82). In order to achieve a "real revalorization of French nationality," these conservatives claimed the need to eliminate automatic access to French nationality.

> The suppression of automatic access to French nationality; [and] naturalization for those who manifest intensely the desire to become French and who are deserving of it; requirement for those to master our language, but also to know our history, culture, and our institutions, limitation on instances of binationality. (Le Gallou 1985:90)[8]

In a subsequent book, *Être Français Cela se Mérite* (Le Gallou and Jalkh 1987), written as a defense of the proposed Code revision, the position was simplified to two principles. First, French nationality ought to be attributed solely on the basis of *jus sanguinis* (filial ties). Second, others can become French if they ask for it, merit it, and renounce their nationality of origin. These two principles constituted the political position of Le Pen and the National Front.

The Right's voluntarist arguments effectively articulated the double-edged ambiguities that *volonté* has expressed in French nationalism. The desire to participate and the imperative to assimilate, the manifestation of individual choice and the overriding homogeneity of the collective will were all raised in the demands to eliminate automaticity and substitute voluntarism. Club 89, another conservative club with ties to the RPR and UDF, issued its own proposed revisions in 1985. In some respects, their proposals were harsher than those of the National Front, given that they required both parents be French for an automatic attribution of citizenship (Lochak 1986). Club 89 asserted that acquisition of citizenship must be the result "of a personal choice, founded on the desire to integrate oneself, to adopt to the laws and value system of the host country . . . to become a French citizen must be considered like an enthronement." Their proposal enumerated a substantial list of conditions to be satisfied to be eligible for naturalization (to be permanently conferred at the end of a probationary period), including "mastery of the language," "Francization of names," and "sponsorship by nationals." The proposal concluded with an ultimatum for second-generation immigrants: "Second-generation immigrations must opt for this naturalization or for the return" to their parents' country of origin (Club 89 1985).

Many of the restrictive proposals seemed to imply that there were those who were French who didn't deserve to be so. They were illegitimately French or "faux Français." A leading official of the National Front, J-P Stirbois, elaborated the retroactive loss of French citizenship. Evoking memories of the Vichy regime for many, he said in an interview that "the people who are today French by naturalization may not be any more after the arrival of the Right into power because they will no longer satisfy the conditions with the retroactive effect that we will enact" (*Le Monde* 6/19/85; cf. *Témoignage Chrétien* 10/13–19/86). Provisions for the retroactive loss of nationality also appeared in the reform proposed by P. Mazeaud of the RPR in June 1986 (Mazeaud 1986:6, see Appendix B).

By Spring 1985, the major parties of the Right all adopted the calls to revise the nationality code as part their political-electoral strategies. In its spring Congress, the RPR endorsed the call to "revise the Nationality Code so that becoming French no longer results in certain cases of an automatic procedure with no control nor manifestation of reciprocal desire (volonté)" (*Libération* 5/18/85). The RPR-UDF electoral platform, *Plateforme pour Gouverner Ensemble*, stated the French nationality "must be demanded (by the candidate) and accepted (by the state), and its acquisition ought not to result from purely automatic mechanisms." Other segments of the Right concurred. The Parti Republican (PR) asserted "the acquisition of French nationality should be a voluntary act." The CNPI argued that "only naturalization will permit accession to French nationality." Like the far Right, the Majoritarian Right parties' endorsement of a reform was not based solely on the rejection of automaticity and the affirmation of individual choice.

Their arguments intertwined the voluntarist themes with those of selectivity, assimilation, national identity, and revalorization of French citizenship. Jacques Toubon, the Secretary General of the RPR claimed that the revisions would ensure that "foreign youth born in France don't become French at their majority without having asked for it, sometimes, without even knowing it. To be French, is not nothing. It isn't only a paper, a formality, but also a value" (*Le Monde* 11/5/86).[9] The moderate Right party, the UDF issued the Bariani report which stressed that "the acquisition of French nationality ought to be the adhesion to the homeland . . . (immigrants have to) take French nationality and assimilate in linking themselves closely to the destiny of France, all in conserving from their cultural specificity the elements compatible with French culture." The only alternative listed in the Bariani report was for immigrants to refuse and leave French society (cited in *Le Monde* 6/8/85). The choice between Francization or return was not a new immigration stance for the Right. But its articulation differed from the seventies when such calls were still accompanied by efforts to ease and not restrict access to naturalization.[10]

The Right's preoccupation with the national identity was a leitmotif of the National Assembly debates in June 1985. Rightist politicians asserted that the acquisition of nationality based "on voluntarism" would strengthen the national identity. Mayoud of the UDF justified his proposed revision on the grounds that he wanted to "preserve our national identity" (*Le Figaro* 6/6/85, 6/7/85; *Libération* 6/7/85, *Le Monde* 6/8/85). Later, in the RPR-UDF combined electoral platform, the Nationality Code reform was cited as a means to "strengthen our national identity" and to achieve a primary objective of making the "national community more confident (stronger) in its identity" (RPR and UDF 1986).

Public opinion surveys showed wide approval for the reform, in particular for its voluntarist cast. In a *Le Monde-IPSOS* poll of March 1986, a majority of all respondents approved of a reform, and even 46 percent of Socialist-identified voters were supportive (*Le Monde* 3/25/86). The substitution of voluntarist procedures in place of the existing automatic provisions gained the most clear cut support. A 1986 BVA survey published in *Paris-Match* showed that 61 percent of respondents believed (and 32% disapproved) that "children born of parents who are foreigners should no longer become France automatically at age eighteen." Moreover, 68 percent of the respondents approved (and 25% disapproved) that "foreigners born in France wishing to acquire French nationality must make an 'express' demand for it between 16–23 years." On the other hand, only 48 percent approved and 39 percent disapproved of a conservative proposal to give the state "a year and a half to oppose a foreign spouse of a French demanding naturalization" (cited in *Le Monde*, 12/5/86).

What was the import of such polls expressing approval of a restrictive reform? Certainly, as with much poll data, the results may not reflect what is ostensibly being polled. Pierre Bourdieu has remarked on the nature of polls as "an instrument of political action," and as such, they can be indicative of different preoccupations (Bourdieu 1980; Llaumett 1985). For example, the approval of voluntarism in 1985 to 1986 was perhaps more reflective of a long-standing opinion among the French public that immigrants acquire French nationality too easily than of immediate support of the Right's new initiatives. A much earlier 1966 survey of immigrants and French (when immigrants were mainly Southern European) had indicated that "many of the French surveyed thought that naturalization is accorded too easily; this opinion is held with a complete ignorance of the procedure" (Schreiber 1966:820).

Nevertheless, the stress on voluntarism enabled moderate right politicians, who otherwise could not countenance far-Right-linked proposals, to support the reform. The moderate politician, Bernard Stasi (UDF) who wrote the book *Immigration: La Chance*, claimed that "to replace an automatic by a voluntary step, that's what gives sense to the admission in the French nation . . . it is to become conscious of a history and an ensemble of values . . . to measure the rights and duties of the citizen . . . to enter into a true moral contract." Michel Hannoun (RPR), a strong antiracist advocate, declared that "everybody admits nationality acquisition should be voluntary." Evoking the famous lectures on the nation by the French author Ernest Renan, Hannoun asserted that the French cultural identity is enriched by integrating those groups "accepting its rules of living" because acquisition of citizenship is "marriage with the nation" (*L'Express* 10/24–30/86).

Voluntarism and the Left

The appeal of voluntarist arguments for the Left was unmistakable. The Socialist already had espoused voluntarist revisions of the code in the seventies and early eighties. In 1981, the Socialist Interior Minister Gaston Deferre declared on a visit to Algeria, "I will make some proposals in this direction [toward a voluntarist revision] to the government. If they are realized, young people born in France of Algerian parents would no longer automatically have French nationality. They would have to ask for it."[11]

Yet it would be a mistake to equate the Left's earlier stances toward voluntarism with their position during the conflict over the code. Those earlier demands for immigrants' "right to difference" and their right to avoid being "French despite themselves" reflected a negative voluntarism in so far as the aim was limit the right of the government to impose what it meant to be French.[12] In the new context—where conservatives effectively transposed voluntarist arguments into justifications for a revalorized, selective membership—segments of the Left began to voice a positive voluntarism. For example, in the Socialist party, divisions appeared between those who supported a "voluntarist, active policy of integration," including the Socialist ministers Maurice Chevènement and Jean Poporen, and those who supported "integration with respect of differences," including Michel Rocard and Lionel Jospin (*Libération* 12/3/85).[13] The development placed the Left in an ambiguous and ambivalent position. While they flatly rejected the elimination of *jus soli*, the selective "triage" and exclusionary tone of the conservative proposals, Left politicians generally admitted that voluntarism was a "seductive idea" (*Le Monde* 3/13/86).

The Left and centrist press struggled over the implications of voluntarist arguments. "The (reasoning for the reform) has conquered the right, it could please part of the left" (*Témoignage Chrétien* 10/13–19/86). An editorial in the leftist newspaper, *Libération*, argued that while voluntarism "seems superficially good," it was not because the motives are "marked by the fear, almost pathological of the foreigner." Notably, the editorial did not reject defending the France national identity: "Why not defend the national identity," the article concluded, the exclusionary reform is just not the way to do it (9/4/86). The liberal Magazine, *Le Nouvel Observateur*, claimed that while the government's proposal was "restrictive," the "whole of the political class was ready for a reform done gently." It quoted an aide to President Mitterrand as saying "voluntary acquisition of nationality is discussed . . . but the project of the government is totally inopportune and dangerous" (10/24–30/86). The conservative paper, *Le Quotidien de Paris*, also stated indignantly,

> in private, the majority of political leaders is in effect in agreement, this is including the left, on the principle of "voluntary" and not longer "automatic" acquisition. But in public, it's another song. (11/13/86)

The ways in which voluntary acquisition could contribute to a revalorization of the national identity, an identity seemingly "challenged" by contemporary immigrants, was an issue for those on the Left. The President of LICRA, an antiracist organization, favored some form of voluntary acquisition because "it is an honor" to be French. The antiracist organizations, MRAP and LICRA, the Socialist club, Espace 89, and the immigrant association, France-Plus all proposed alternative reforms of French citizenship in 1985–1986.[14] All these proposals firmly defended *jus soli*, and planned the expansion and facilitation of citizenship accession in France. At the same time, concern for the national identity was moderated in response to the Right's proposals. The MRAP proposal declared that "it is up to the immigrants to decide when they want the same rights and duties as nationals; immigrants should not automatically and obligatorily be dual nationals, that is neither normal nor wished for. It seems legitimate to recognize the immigrants' right to become citizens fully if they have the desire for it" (MRAP 1986:5).[15] The LICRA and France-Plus versions supported a "voluntary act" or "positive step" that constituted a "symbolic request" for citizenship (i.e., one that had no conditions attached, and simply meant addressing a request to acquire French citizenship to the local mayor, and not to a judge, as the Right advocated).[16]

The Communitarian Arguments

The Right's communitarian arguments complemented their emphasis on *volonté*. Their arguments stressed the necessity of the citizenry's attachment to a community embedded in French culture, mores, political values, and history. Communitarianism focuses on "communities of character, historically stable, ongoing associations of men and women with some special commitment to one another and some special sense of their common life" (Walzer 1981:32). Although American communitarianism has often been identified as a defense of local community in contrast to the vagaries of the national level, for the French conservatives communitarianism was defined in terms of national, community and nation:[17]

> The nation is constructed by the communal will to live together, concretized by the national service and acquisition of nationality, rests on a more political and cultural identity, acceptance of identical values and

*rules, education, language, and the putting to rest, or in the back-
ground, all particularities. (Le Quotidien de Paris 12/3/85)*

The conservatives effectively used the national communitarianism engendered in
French republicanist ideology, often evoking Ernest Renan's writings on the nation. In *Qu'est-ce qu'une Nation* (1882), Renan wrote, "a nation is a soul, a spiritual principle . . . one is in the past, the other in the present. One is the shared
possession of a rich legacy of memories; the other is the mutual consent, the desire to live together, the will to continue to valorize the heritage that one received
individually." Likewise, the Right's communitarianism denounced the commodification of national membership, advocated its resacralization, and insisted that
the citizenry must foster homogeneity.

The rightist communitarians were shaped by the different currents in the earlier debates on pluralism and identity. Immigrant rights proponents of a New Citizenship had called for the disassociation of citizenship and nationality and a
communitarianism defined by local identities, participation and choice. In clear
contrast, the conservative communitarians argued that citizenship required exclusive, sacred loyalty to the state. They drew on traditional conceptions of citizenship
and on the statist and assimilationist expressions of French nationalism. They also
qualified the role of individual choice further.[18] Conservative organicist conceptions of the nation implied that choice was subordinate to essence, "a homeland,
this chooses itself" (Pierre Chaunu cited in *L'Express* 10/24–30/86). Other conceptualizations focused on the kind of code of conduct that must define the relationship of the immigrants to the French national community.[19] The moderate
Right politician, Michel Noir (RPR) called for a new "moral contract" between the
French and those immigrants whose "desire (*volonté*) to share the values of the national community is manifested" (*Le Monde* 6/8/85). The conservative *Aspects de
La France* was more explicit: "To become French means to integrate into a community which possesses a long history and which is charged with a rich physical,
spiritual, and cultural patrimony . . . (immigrants) ought not to acquire nationality
as an escape or as a simple commodity, or still less, by fraud" (11/13/86).

The Right claimed that citizenship was being increasingly commodified and
that this development menaced the national community. Their targets were so-
called "paper marriages" (where foreigners marry French simply to acquire
French nationality), dual nationality, and what they saw as a general increase in
fraud, all of which were indicative to rightist politicians of how the nationality
code was in fact a sieve, a "code passoire." They blamed the phenomena of commodified citizenship on Franco-Algerians in particular. The Right characterized
Franco-Algerian and Franco-Maghrebian attitudes toward French citizenship as
utilitarian and hostile, which proved that they were not French "at heart."[20] In *La
Préférence Nationale*, Le Gallou denounced the Franco-Maghrebis, who treated
French nationality as a "commodity," as a "carte orange" (the Parisian public

transportation pass). He argued that "every candidate for bi-nationality must bring proof that he is totally attached to France and to the values which found it" (Le Gallou 1985:79, 81, 89).

A highly charged attack on dual nationality was one of the most visible targets of the Right's communitarian arguments. Dual nationality was already seen as suspect when uncontrolled. It now was denounced for the ways in which it desacralized and commodified citizenship to "engender a rejection of the national identity" (Darras 1986:953).[21] Once again, the conservative historian Pierre Chaunu:

> Because of the automatic naturalization, many people find themselves with dual nationality: these are the false citizens, citizens of nowhere. When it suits them, they call themselves French. When this no longer suits them, they call themselves Algerians or something else . . . This is detestable . . . these people don't necessarily share our values. If they don't feel themselves French, we don't want to have anything of them. (*L'Express* 10/24–30/86)

Conservatives feared that the dual national status engendered an ambiguous loyalty if not disloyalty to the national community. In the National Front's *Dossier Migration*, J. P Stirbois and J. F. Jalkh stated, "It could be difficult to be faithful to two homelands at the same time" (cited in Perotti 1986: 211). An oath of allegiance, one of the new provisions found in some of the reform proposals, addressed such concerns. One oath called for the person to "renounce all allegiances to states of which I could have, even involuntarily, the nationality" (Mazeaud 1986; see Appendix B).

Franco-Algerians were an especially charged target. In the late seventies, as the post-1962 war Franco-Algerians began to reach the age of majority, the realization grew that they were indeed French, thus obligated to serve in the French army. At the same time, as Algerians, they were bound to serve in the Algerian army. Until 1984, no agreement on military service existed between the two countries.[22] The 1984 accord gave these binationals the rare option of choosing the country in which to complete their military service, regardless of their place of residence. The accord suscitated much controversy, in particular, among the Right, who saw the option of choice as an affront to French nationality and patriotism. In 1986, the National Front proposal asserted "It will be necessary to enlarge the possibility for the loss and forfeiture of nationality . . . Franco-Algerians must choose one nationality" (*Le Monde* 3/14/86).

In part, this conservative communitarianism equated the country to a club, where dual nationality and other abuses denigrated membership practices.

> Before admitting someone into a club, one verifies if he is capable of exercising its rights and fulfilling its duties One will accord French

nationality in 98 percent of cases But we will turn away those who den-
igrate us I say this in the name of those who died for this country.
(Chaunu quoted in *L'Express* 10/24–30/86)[23]

In part, this communitarianism claimed that the citizenry must foster homogeneity. During the debates in the National Assembly in June 1985, the Right emphasized the impossibility of a "pluriracial," "pluriethnic," or "pluricultural"
society: "We exclude from our talk any conception of pluri-ethnic or multi-faith
society which would end ineluctably in the shattering of the national community" (*Le Monde* 6/8/85).[24]

Rightist politicians often defined their motivations to revise the code in communitarian terms. When Socialist President Mitterrand denounced the conservative project as being "inspired by a philosophy that he didn't share," referring to
its selective and exclusionary character, politicians on the Right quickly responded. They stressed their understanding of the national community as the fusion of the political and cultural communities, and the need to reaffirm the state's
control over national membership. The rightist party newsletter, *La Lettre de La
Nation*, asserted "a nation is culture . . . When foreigners, 50 years, 100 years ago
integrated themselves in France, they integrated into the culture in a very clear
manner. But, today, there were youth who want to live in France without adher-
ing to the culture, without doing their military service, without accepting the
obligations" (no. 2659, 11/13/86). The republicanist and statist components of
such assertions resonated with many on the Left. Many identified with Renan's
definition of a nation, an entity based not only on political consensus but also on
historical and cultural homogeneity, where the national state, and not any type of
local community, defined membership.

Communitarianism and the Left

Richard Handler has described nationalists as those who agree on the "existence of a nation which is taken to be bounded, continuous, and at least min-
imally homogenous, but there is disagreement and confusion regarding the
content of national existence" (1988:32). During the early eighties, the Left's
efforts organize their antiracist politics and responses to immigration could be
characterized as having "fallen into the trap of the national identity" (Gallisot
1985:10). The debates over the code further developed the articulation of a
Left communitarianism. Opposition to restrictive nationality proposals were
often framed in reference to the French nation: "It is certain that the insertion
of immigrants gives (them) the right to retain their way of life and their culture. But, they also have to integrate themselves to the French nation" (*La
Croix* 10/30/85).[25]

Reflecting on the presence of Franco-Maghrebis, those on the Left asked, "Does the attachment to one's community of origin exclude the attachment to the national community" (Perotti 1986:5)? As the Right elaborated communitarian arguments, defending their revisions of the code, the Left voiced a parallel, even overlapping, communitarianism, condemning the revisions themselves as menacing the national community:

> Isn't is to profoundly devalue the French nation and its vitality by reducing it to a mother incapable of producing children after entire centuries? Would only blood [ties] alone be capable of engendering worthy children of France . . . a nation does not choose its citizens; it must recognize those which it has engendered. (Perotti 1986:5)

> (The reform threatens the) French nation . . . a project lived together, a spirit, an aspiration . . . [it] seriously compromises the national identity. (*Témoignage Chrétien* 11/10–16/86)

> (The reform) touches at the heart itself of the constitution of the nation. (*Libération* 11/13/86).

Like rightist communitarians, those on the Left defined adhesion to the national community in terms of a pluralism bounded by French particularisms. Their more inclusive versions invoked the "republican tradition of openness and integration" and situated adhesion as matter of "a language, a culture . . . a way of living together" (*Témoignage Chrétien* 11/10–16/86, *Réforme* 11/22/86).[26] Their arguments against the reform emphasized a pluralist content to the national community. President Mitterrand proclaimed, "France is a plural society . . . and it has been for centuries" (*Le Monde* 10/23/85).[27] But for the most part, this was a pluralism defined by the existing community. For the majority of the Left republican communitarianism was inclusive within limits. The boundaries were delimited by a political-cultural membership, separation of public and private, an espousal of universalist, assimilationist themes.

The Nativist Arguments

The voluntarist and communitarian arguments underlying the restrictive proposals in turn complemented the nativist components of the extreme Right's and part of the Majoritarian Right's proposals. In each of the major axes of the Right's restrictive reforms—voluntarism, decommodification of citizenship, revalorization of national membership—Franco-Maghrebis often appeared as the crystallization of what was "un-French." In each of these areas, the loyalty and assimilation of second generation North African immigrants became broad and highly visible targets in the rhetoric promoting a restrictive politics of citizenship.

It is perhaps not coincidental that France's contemporary nativist movement was in the forefront of the movement to reform the code. The historical study of political nativism in America has shown a close relationship between it and social reform movements. The "nativist-as reformer" has been identified as one aspect of the nativist mentality.

> The nativist mentality and the reform mentality which historians de-
> fined over the quarter-century after 1855 thus converged in a struggle to
> preserve the necessary homogeneity of American society, without which,
> it was thought, the Republic could not operate. This nineteenth-century
> assimilationist view insisted upon the acceptance of a certain core set of
> values—generally evangelical Protestant ones—as a standard of confor-
> mity. (Bergquist 1986:135)

From this perspective, the situational centrality of Le Pen and the National Front in the new politics of citizenship lies not simply their articulation of a nationalist critique of citizenship. Rather, it lies in their more determined impulse to reconfigure the arguments in terms of a sweeping social reform.

Nativist components were not a necessarily explicit part of the Right's other arguments and reform proposals. Many analyses sketch a portrait of the Right as articulating an exclusionary, nativist politics in the early period of trying to reform the code (responding to Le Pen), then retreating into a much more inclusive idiom as they encountered political difficulties and highly charged opposition (cf. Brubaker 1992; Perotti 1986). This portrait is too reductionist. Certainly, explicit nativist arguments were highly visible in some Rightist campaign rhetoric. But even in the early stages of the efforts to revise the code many of the reforms' proponents found the nativist rhetoric too disruptive and politically dangerous (e.g., Noir, Stasi, Hannoun, and Chalandon) and stressed more inclusive rationales and idioms.

The nativist arguments, however, were a powerful subtext of the voluntarist and communitarian arguments, evoking and transforming a combination of themes. It permitted the articulation of French desires for assimilation, social cohesiveness, and cultural homogeneity. To borrow a phrase from Michael Rogin (1990), these desires could be understood as "historically acceptable but contemporaneously problematic." In claiming the central necessity for choice, the conservatives recalled Renan's famous definition of the nation. More subtly, and even if many of their audience were not aware of Renan's history, the conservatives also evoked Renan the "orientalist" (Said 1979), and through him the history and myths of French assimilationism, colonialism, and ideological superiority. They employed the particular communitarianism of French republicanism that previously had surfaced as a defense of the nation against internal or external dangers. In this regard, the proposals were articulating a closed politics of particularism and difference as a voluntarist, communitarian politics of citizenship.

Nativism and the Left

The Left highlighted the nativist arguments as part of their electoral opposition to the reform, opposition fostered by the polarized context of French immigration politics and encouraged by strategic electoral considerations. An attack on the nativist arguments formed the emotional nexus of the Left's protest against revising the code. Nativism was primarily defined as racism. The reform opposition contrasted the Right's exclusionary politics of race with the Left's "firm, humanist politics" (*La Croix* 12/28/85). Unquestionably, this stark opposition helped obscure the underlying links between nativism and the assimilationist communitarianism of republicanist traditions, whose reference was a mainstay for the reforms' opponents.

The denunciation of nativism gained activist support from its association of the reform with other nativist aspects in the Right's entire package of immigration policies. "Wake up, my pal, they've gone crazy" ("Réveille-toi mon pote, ils sont devenue fous"), proclaimed an SOS-Racisme slogan (*Libération* 11/15–16/86). The reform's opponents decried the efforts to "fabricate foreigners," and categorized the revisions as part of a "war against youth" (*Im'media* 1987). In the electoral campaigns of 1986, the reform proposals were connected with a larger package of anti-immigrant policies advocated by the Right, such as efforts to restrict certain welfare benefits to French nationals, and to restrict entry and resident requirements for foreigners (Perotti 1985; de Wenden 1988).

The Constraints of French Ideologies

Nearly all the participants in these debates to re-envision French citizenship argued that their positions were most reflective of classical French understandings of membership. They embedded their arguments in French ideologies of nationhood, "political-cultural" membership, or nationalism.[28] The French ideologies at once provided important resources for both the Right and Left and constrained the scope of redefinitions of pluralism, national identity, and citizenship. In other words, French ideologies—including French republicanism, Jacobinism, and other strands of French nationalism—operated simultaneously as a malleable resource and a "nationalist trap" during this period (Gallisot 1989:34).

On the one hand, the classic republicanist and Jacobin model of French membership is considered to have strongly shaped French political thought about citizenship (Vernon 1986; Tilly 1996). Scholars have defined French republicanism by its convergence of the political and cultural communities so that national political membership necessarily implies acceptance of French cultural values and bases (Schnapper 1987; Weber 1976; Safran 1990; Higonnet 1988). French republicanist citizenship refuses the existence of an ethnic citizenry. Likewise, the centralized, unitary Jacobin system has been defined by its insistence on an individualist relation between the state and people so that no intermediary bodies ought to represent particular groups within society (Lochak 1989b).

On the other hand, French republicanism and Jacobinism have been malleable precisely because historically their contents have been contradictory, their definitions elusive, and their references changing over time (Noiriel 1988; Gallisot 1989; Citron 1988). Republicanist conceptions of the nation and citizenship are ambiguous. Revolutionary conceptions of citizenship were individualist and voluntarist (e.g., E. Sieyes 1982:32).[29] The privileged components were *jus soli*, birth and residence in the territory as much as *jus sanguinis* (Lochak 1988:80). At the same time, the passage from the more "open and universalist conception of the nation" present at the beginning of the French revolution, to a more "territorial and 'nationalist' conception" has also been traced to the revolutionary era (Lochak 1988:82; Guibert-Sledziewski 1988:175; Gallisot 1989).[30] René Gallisot has described this passage as the confusion of citizenship and nationality, a confusion that accorded with republican ideas and complemented its potentially communitarian aspects (1989:31). The internal ambiguities of French republicanism were extended as it became an essential component of the "patriotism of the left" during the nineteenth century (Ibid.).[31]

The Jacobinist tradition too has been questioned from several perspectives. While the idea of a "Jacobinist model" has been frequently appealed to, scholars have begun to question even if there is a Jacobinism to be identified (Gallisot 1989:33; de Wenden 1988). Despite the association of Jacobinism with the centralized state system in France, it has been argued that "the exemplar of French centralism belongs more to the history of nationalism, and not to the original declaration of human rights" (Gallisot 1989:29). This questioning has also been part of a broader inquiry of the extent to which the notion of a "one and indivisible France" is actually borne out by French history.[32] The ambiguities in French republicanism and Jacobinism have enabled successive, and competing interpretations of French citizenship since the Revolution, all appealing to the revolutionary heritage. It is not surprising then that in the mid-eighties Jacobins, pluralists, assimilationists, communitarians, and proponents of a New Citizenship (the disassociation of citizenship and nationality) all refer to aspects of French traditions. During the debates over the national identity, both the Right and Left referenced French conceptions of national community, and used such references in widely different arguments. Parts of the Left framed conceptions of national identity in terms of a more open, inclusive republicanism that admitted to a limited universalism and curtailed pluralism. Likewise, the immigrant associations who proposed New Citizenship reforms harked back to the 1789 definition of citizenship, arguing that in privileging birth, residence, and participation in the territory, their new redefinition complemented most authentically the original definition, which also disassociated nationality from citizenship.

The usage of French ideologies of nation and ideas of a "political-cultural" nationhood have been inextricably intertwined with the history of French nationalism.[33] The contestation over citizenship drew on, and were shaped by key ambiguities of French nationalism, ambiguities about voluntarism, universalism, and republicanism. These ambiguities were constitutive of the traditional, and still largely predominant, interpretations of the French nationalism that divide the history of French nationalism into two major strands of competing ideologies. Both contain assimilationist themes. One rests "upon the equality and fraternity of the races, the other upon their opposition and antagonism" (Joly 1863:22–23, cited in Jennings 1990:1). In his history of French nationalisms, Winnock characterized the split as the "nationalism of the patriots versus nationalism of the 'nationalists'" (1990).

Emerging as a force during the French revolution of 1798, French nationalism was first defined as an ideology of the Left, an "open, republican" nationalism, based on popular sovereignty and *volonté* (voluntarism), and expressed through a unified state and a universalizing mission.[34] Merline de Douai in 1790 voiced this emergent nationalism when he said, "The Alsatian people are united with the French people because they wanted it."[35] This republican nationalism "articulated the state, the society, and the nation into a patriotic synthesis" (Nora 1984:61). Thus, while it made "the nation a supreme value," it has been defined as "open to other people, other races, other nations" (Winnock 1990).[36]

By the latter part of the nineteenth century Left nationalism was opposed to another strand of French nationalism (Jennings 1990:1). French conservatives had developed their own "counternationalisms," or "closed" versions of republican nationalism (Girardet 1983; Weber 1959; Sternhall 1983).[37] Epitomized by such slogans as "France for the French," this nationalism has been defined as "closed, frightened, exclusive" organic, "invariably pessimistic," antidecadence, and often, racist, xenophobic, and anti-Semitic (Winnock 1990; Nora 1984; Taguieff 1988). Within this perspective, the voluntarist and "open" aspects of the French nation recede, and are subordinated to an organic conception of the nation based on race and filial ties. Often understood in pathological terms, this strand of French nationalism is seen as Jean-Marie Le Pen's lineage; Nora remarked that the appeal of Le Pen signifies "a new malaise in our civilization" (1984).

Despite the emphasis on their dissimilarity, these two strands of French nationalism are overlapping ideologies of the nation.[38] The historian Girardet remarks on "a certain unity to French nationalism," found in the sense of "nostalgia," and a "dynamic of refusal" (1983). Exclusion, assimilation, and defense against otherness are properties of both nationalisms. "It is possible to say that French nationalism has been essentially a culture of exclusion" (Manin 1984:7).[39] Gallisot has traced Left nationalism as the beginning of the pattern which would culminate in the "consensus of today over the French identity from the Left to the Right" (1989:32).

In studying French "lieux de mémoire nationale," Pierre Nora concluded that republican nationalism "obtained its coherence from that which it excluded" (1984).[40] It did not define the social contract as the reconciliation of interests, but as "the expression of the general will which necessitates its excluded (exige ses exclus)" (Ibid.). Though the nature of the assimilation insisted on differs across the two nationalisms, it has played a central role in both (Jennings 1990:4). Birnbaum has argued that "even if the nationalisms of the Right and Left diverge upon certain crucial points they merge together in a common defense of the French nation, partially occupied and threatened by the foreigner" (cited in Jennings 1990:5).

Such commonalities signal the fact that both nationalist versions are ideologies "concerned with boundedness, continuity and homogeneity encompassing diversity" (Handler 1988). The fluctuating meaning of *volonté* for the Left and Right can be understood in this context. *Volonté* refers both to the individual's manifestation to participate, and to the imperatives of the collective will which dictates that "sameness override(s) difference" (Ibid., p. 6). It is telling that both the Right and Left in France invoked Ernest Renan's famous lectures at the Sorbonne, in which he defined *volonté* as an essential component of a nation, as a "plebiscite forever." In that same lecture, Renan situated *volonté* within a context of closed continuity and cultural homogeneity. Such placement was not coincidental. As Edward Said has written, Renan's intellectual persona, as an orientalist was imbued with his understandings of the natural and moral superiority of the Occident over the Orient (Said 1979).[41]

The commonalities between open and closed French nationalisms extend beyond ideological suppositions to their expression as political responses. Historically, the priority of strengthening the national unity and identity has cross-cut the two nationalisms, constituting periods of "passages, convergences, even compromises between" the two nationalisms (Winnock 1990; Weber 1959; Sternhall 1983).[42] These ambiguities also have had forceful implications in the periodic debates over immigration and citizenship, which have taken place in France over the past centuries. The "well-established dominant style of thinking and talking about citizenship in relation to migration" in France has reflected the "rhetoric of inclusion," "weakness of ethnicity," and "ambiguities of nationalism," by which is meant the confusion between assimilationist and exclusionary nationalist concerns (Brubaker 1992). Both the expression of the two distinctive nationalisms, and the overlapping between these strands have been highlighted for past revisions of citizenship (Lochak 1985).[43]

The politics of immigration and national identity in the eighties reinforced and appealed to the ambiguities in French nationalism on several levels. The debates over the national identity were marked by warring conceptions of the nation. The extreme Right's nativist, racist conceptions of the nation confronted the themes of an inclusive, political-cultural republicanism. Yet the debates also contained implicit if not explicit agreements on the assimilationist priorities of the nation. Both those on the Left and Right conflated concerns of social and national integration.[44] Differentialist politics (on both the Right and Left) provoked the majority of the political class to affirm a distinctively French assimilation and a necessarily limited universalism and pluralism.[45] The immigrant's association movement in France also aligned themselves in the tradition of the French revolution and so submerged their own communal identity demands into the communitarianism of French republicanism. Likewise, the far Right aligned their nativism to be effectively the belly of the republican, Jacobin beast. These ambiguities of French nationalism were part of the process that legitimated and made meaningful views that the French national identity being threatened by the challenge of Muslim, North African immigration.

In the new politics of citizenship during the eighties, the ambiguities about nation and national community became even more central as political debates became preoccupied with re-envisioning citizenship and actually revising French nationality. Eric Hobsbawm (1983) has written that the "invention" of tradition occurs "more frequently when a rapid transformation of society weakens or destroys the social patterns for which 'old' traditions had been designed, producing new ones to which they were not applicable, or when such old traditions and their institutional carriers and promulgators no longer prove sufficiently adaptable or flexible." In the context of intensifying polarization and convergence in French politics, the debates over the national identity were the initial phase of this process to redefine the citizenry. The move in 1985 toward explicit questions of citizenship was a turning point toward reinventing citizenship. References to France's historic past in the debates recall Hobsbawm's remark that "the peculiarity of 'invented traditions' is the continuity with it is largely factitious" (1983). French republican, secular traditions, and the French "genie" of assimilationism were appealed to by all sides of the debate. As Left intellectuals argued for a "forceful republicanism" to combat Le Pen (Winnock 1990), the concept of *volonté* slipped between its exclusionary and assimilationist meanings.

The identity politics of French nationalism became increasingly important as the so called challenge of the North African immigrant populations began playing a more integral role in both immigration and citizenship policy conflicts. Edward Said has argued that "European culture gained in strength and identity by setting itself off and against the Orient as a sort of surrogate and even underground self" (1979). As provocative and revelatory figures, set off against the ambiguities and limited universalism of French nationalism, Islam and "Maghrebinite" began playing a parallel role in the debates over revising the code.

Conclusion

The shift of attention to the nationality code enabled both the proponents and opponents of the reform to raise nationalist concerns more explicitly than they had
in the previous debates over the national identity. Participants invoked key themes
of French nationalism, including double-edged voluntarism, national communitarianism or republicanism, and limited universalism. Proponents of the reform
aimed to center the debate around a seemingly simple question of voluntarism or
volonté versus automaticity. They sought to define the reform as the defense of
voluntarist and communitarian ideals, appealing in part to French conceptions of
nationhood and in part to the need to re-envision those conceptions because of
the specific challenges of the contemporary immigrants.

The reform's opponents fought to recenter the debate around the far Right's
and Right's exclusionary nativism. These opponents on the Left firmly defended
an inclusive politics of citizenship based on the principle of *jus soli*. At the same
time, they articulated their own voluntarist and assimilationist (re)visions of citizenship, again by appealing to republicanist and universalist French traditions. If
the participants disagreed over the methods by which a "Jacobinist" perspective
linked citizenship and immigration with centrally regulated state membership,
the majority still resisted efforts to displace the issues from a statist perspective to
a more local or differentialist one which could advocate a New Citizenship based
on local participation.

The voluntarist and communitarian perspectives, embedded in the traditional French ideologies of nation, complemented the different emphases of
French nationalism as they were variously expressed by the Left and Right. The
Right's call for the complete elimination of the principle of *jus soli* constituted a
break with the predominant understanding of citizenship based on the criteria of
jus sanguinis and *jus soli*. The Left's positive voluntarism and assimilationism
constituted a break from their earlier articulation of a negative voluntarism and
more diversified pluralism. The voluntarist and communitarian arguments are
not easily divided into a bifurcated politics, even though the Left and Right tried
to portray them as such.[46] The overlapping between the different sides was indicative of an emergent politics of citizenship that could be neither conflated with
a restrictive, racial politics nor contrasted to a republicanist, humanist politics. In
brief, beneath the disagreements between the proponents and opponents of the
reforms ran an emergent nationalist discourse of citizenship.

CHAPTER 5

The Reform, the State, and the Political Process

The Right's efforts to reform the French Nationality Code (CNF) began with an assertive, confident push in the spring of 1986. The promise to reform the code was a prominent issue in the legislative campaigns of many rightist politicians. It was considered central to Jacques Chirac, the leader of the Gaullist party (RPR), and his strategy to win over the electorate drawn to the views of Le Pen and the National Front. After the UDF-RPR won a majority in the legislative elections of March 1986, Chirac as the new Prime Minister reaffirmed his determination to reform the code, stressing the voluntarist and communitarian motivations.[1] He proclaimed to other legislators, "all in pursuing an active policy of the insertion of youth, we will submit the acquisition of French nationality to the demonstration of a real desire [*volonté*] of adhesion and belonging. To this end, we will propose to you the modification of the Nationality Code" (Sénat *Journal Officiel* du 16 Avril 1986).

Under consideration in the National Assembly were three versions of a restrictive reform of the nationality code which were formally deposited by the beginning of summer. They were the legislative propositions of Mayoud (UDF), Le Pen (FN), and Mazeaud (RPR) (see Appendix B). Le Pen and Mazeaud proposed the complete elimination of *jus soli*, and automatic access to French nationality, not based on *jus sanguinis*. Mayoud proposed only the modification of the acquisition of French nationality at the age of majority. Despite its association with a larger package of anti-immigrant policies and the attempts to depict it as a "new form of discrimination," many predicted that a nationality code reform would enjoy a successful passage through the state (*Le Monde* 7/2/86; *Le Matin* 11/13/86; *Le Témoignage Chrétien* 10/13–19/86).

But the conservative attempt to revise the code failed. By the following winter of 1987, the Right's efforts had unraveled into a series of successive retreats. This chapter is about the failure of the Right's proposed reform. The reform process was shaped by a series of constraints, some contingent on institutional priorities and configurations and others conjunctural, linked to the specific po-litical processes surrounding the reform attempt.

State citizenship practices and bureaucratic agendas constituted the institu-tionalist constraints. While certain administrative goals did reinforce aspects of a restrictive reform, other state practices undermined efforts to eliminate the *jus soli* principle and contradicted central parts of the proposed revisions. The varied agendas in the state simultaneously influenced the reform process even as the in-ternal conflicts heightened the dissension around the reform. A negative decision by the Council of State—the highest administrative review body—provided a po-litical nexus for the reform's opponents.

Political process constraints were generated foremost by the organization of protests around the reform. The protests, their resources, the shifting political align-ment of groups, and the changing collective assessment of the participants in the re-form conflict contributed to diminishing the reform's appeal. Interactions among immigrant associations, social and religious groups, the parties, and the state in the reform struggle dramatically overlapped with social conflict involving French stu-dents. Overall, the constraints severely limited the possibilities for the passage of the Chirac government's proposals as they were laid out and pursued in 1986 and 1987.

State Constraints on a Reform

The proponents of the revision confronted a specific set of institutional configu-rations that mediated their political efforts at reform. The French scholar Pierre Birnbaum has characterized the French state as an exemplar of the "highly insti-tutionalized, differentiated, and autonomous" state (1988:69). To a degree more than in other state orders, scholars argue that French state sovereignty resides in its centralized administrative institutions, so that the administrative order consti-tutes an "area of autonomous action" and pursues "distinctive goals" (Nettl 1968:592; Skocpol 1985:22). From the French revolution, the bureaucracy in France developed into a "system of specialized roles . . . and the administration (has) thereby developed into a highly institutionalized and autonomous organi-zation" (Badie and Birnbaum 1983:112).

The statist features of the French polity have shaped the processes by which groups can make claims or reforms imposed on the state (Birnbaum 1988; Jep-person and Meyer 1991). In the "Republic of functionaries," the "ideology of the general interest reigns supreme . . . it is common for officials to regard themselves as agents of the state" (Badie and Birnbaum 1983:112; see also Suleiman 1974). Birnbaum recounts that "civil servants openly admit to a feeling of complete con-tempt for pressure groups, and for deputies who are supposed to be acting in the name of particular groups" (1988:187). Given that particularistic interests can threaten the universalistic claims of the state, argues Birnbaum, pressure groups in France "are virtually illegitimate . . . The representatives of private interests are refused access to the state apparatus" (1988:187). Not surprisingly, as scholars of reform and interest groups have noted, reform pressures in France traditionally have been expressed in collective action aimed directly against the state.

The universalistic claims of the French state, the specialized roles of its administrative institutions, and the nature of French reform processes all combined as constraints on the Right's proposed revisions. State bureaucrats played a decisive role in the policy process. The autonomy of the administrative institutions, their distinctive goals, and their adherence to an ideology of the general will all became forceful determinants in shaping the state's politics of citizenship. These factors were constraints not only in and of themselves, but also in the ways in which they were in tension with each other.

It should be stated at the outset, however, that French state bureaucrats were certainly not adverse to a nationality code reform. Even before Chirac came to power in March 1986, the Bureau of Nationality in the Ministry of Justice began preparing for a possible revision of the nationality code. Soon after Chirac's arrival, a revision of the code was, as one Bureau official put it, the "order to the day."[2] As with previous reforms of the Nationality Code, it was the task of the Bureau of Nationality to research and formulate the text of the government's legislative proposition. The Bureau was a seemingly strong ally for the conservative forces. Since the 1973 nationality code reform, the Bureau had grown increasingly supportive of reforming the code, in particular, of tightening up the provisions against fraud, eliminating the provisions that reflected colonial and postcolonial priorities, and clarifying the provisions governing citizenship acquisition (Interviews, Bureau of Nationality).

Instead, the Right encountered unexpected obstacles. The major thrust of their revisions, including the elimination of the *jus soli* principle, clashed with important aspects of the state's citizenship practices. The territorial principle of citizenship constituted the most prominent aim of most of the conservative forces. The target was actually the practice of *double jus soli*, which covered persons born in France of noncitizen parents who were born themselves in France (i.e., Articles 23 of the CNF and Article 23 of the 1973 law, which constituted *double jus soli*) and that of the qualified *jus soli*, which gave persons born in France of noncitizen parents not born in France (i.e., Articles 44 and 52 of the CNF) quasi-automatic access to French citizenship. In his proposition, Mazeaud argued that the *jus soli* principle had "lost its utility . . . its justification" (Mazeaud 1986:3). Conservatives pointed out that the original military and demographic impetus for the territorial principle was no longer applicable in the contemporary situation, especially given the "incapacity" of France to assimilate the new immigrants (Mazeaud 1986:3). Its removal would have affected nearly half of the approximately 100,000 persons (cases in which neither of the parents are French nationals) acquiring French citizenship each year.[3] (See Table 5.1: The Evolution of the Acquisitions and Attributions of French Citizenship, 1975–1986, Targeted by the Reform Proposals of 1985–1987.)

TABLE 5.1.
Evolution of the Acquisitions and Attributions of French Citizenship, 1975–1986,
Targeted by the Reform Proposals of 1985–1987

Article	Year						
	1975	*1980*	*1982*	*1983*	*1984*	*1985*	*1986*
Article 23 of the French Nationality Code*	15,775	17,173	18,695	17,303	16,460	15,184	13,750
Article 23 of the 1973 Law*	2,294	4,585	6,091	7,262	7,582	8,033	8,308
Article 44*	9,759	15,708	15,966	16,378	17,456	17,607	17,949
Articles 52 and 55	5,348	13,767	14,227	13,213	10,279	12,634	15,190
All *jus soli* based attributions and acquisitions†	33,176	51,233	54,979	54,156	51,777	53,458	55,197
Article 84	7,647	9,324	8,037	5,220	4,822	11,978	10,344
Article 37-1	8,394	13,767	14,227	13,213	10,279	12,634	15,190
Articles 153 and 155	372	1,371	1,238	1,216	69	979	622
Total Acquisitions and Attributions‡	73,052	95,168	96,467	87,991	85,124	110,024	105,193

Note: Article 23 of the French Nationality Code (CNF) attributes French citizenship at birth to a person born in France of noncitizen parents, when at least one parent was also born in France (double *jus soli*); Article 23 of the 1973 Law extended double *jus soli* to certain former French colonies and territories; Article 44 of the CNF enables the acquisition of French nationality "without formality" at the age of majority by individuals born in France of noncitizen parents born elsewhere as long as certain conditions are fulfilled (qualified *jus soli*); Articles 52 and 55 provide children born in France of noncitizen parents born elsewhere the right and opportunity to become French before the age of majority through a declarative process by the parent (qualified *jus soli*); Article 84 enables acquisition of French nationality by declaration by a minor through "collective effect" when the parent naturalizes; Article 37-1 enables acquisition of French nationality by declaration through marriage to a French national; and Articles 153 and 155 enable reintegration into French nationality by declaration, and often based on past colonial ties.
*These totals are only estimates.
†This total is the sum of Articles 23 (CNF and the 1973 law), 44, 52, and 55.
‡This total is the sum of all acquisitions, including those not listed in this table and all *jus soli*–based attributions of citizenship (by children of noncitizen parents).

     Many on the Right denounced the practice of the *double jus soli* as part of their efforts to restrict access to French citizenship by second generation Algerian immigrants. As noted in chapter 2, second generation Algerian youth were often covered under Article 23 because Algeria had been considered part of France before its independence. In 1985, there were around 15,184 attributions of citizenship to second generation Algerian origin youth. Although there was opportunity to decline French nationality if only one of the parents were also born in France, the number of repudiations was very small (Lebon 1987).

Despite their political support for rescinding the principle, Rightist politicians soon learned that French state practices effectively ruled out the elimination of Article 23 of the nationality code. From the perspective of the Bureau of Nationality, the logistical and substantive ramifications of the elimination of *double jus soli* were too costly. From the perspective of the "general interest," the complete removal of a fundamental organizing principle of citizenship was too risky. The conservatives had ignored that the rule of *double jus soli* was the "mode of proof for the immense majority" of the French, and formed an integral part of the administration's citizenship procedures.[4] From October 1985 through the spring of 1986, the Bureau of Nationality of the Ministry of Justice prepared documentation detailing the impossibility of eliminating Article 23 of the CNF.[5] The Bureau argued that "suppression of article 23 . . . was not desirable . . . (it was) one of the two fundamental modes of attribution of French nationality . . . very useful in the matter of proof (of French citizenship) . . . it is technically preferred to the long and delicate demonstration" required for proving citizenship on the basis of filial ties.[6]

At the same time, the Bureau was in favor of rescinding Article 23 of the 1973 Law, which had extended the right of *double jus soli* to certain postcolonial territories and populations. Moreover, the Bureau's reports also show that the officials there did attempt to formulate revisions of Article 23 of the Code that would specifically "exclude(e) the application of Article 23 of the CNF for only children of Algerians."[7] That in itself was not objectionable to the Bureau. They concluded, however, that modifications of Article 23 of the CNF "risk not satisfying the expected objectives of the reform." What were their concerns about a revision that would target only immigrant origin youth from Algeria? If it were written broadly they argued it would also affect all those from Algeria, including those of European origin, and not only those of North African, Muslim origin, and make proof of nationality for all more difficult.

At the same time, state officials in the Bureau of Nationality did not believe that state practices and priorities stood in conflict with the second major axis of the Right's desire to eliminate the territorial principle: the abrogation of Article 44 of the nationality code. To recall, Article 44 of the CNF permitted the acquisition of French citizenship "without formality" at the age of majority by individuals born in France, of noncitizen parents, and residing there for the preceding five years, as long as they fulfil certain conditions, including the absence of criminal convictions listed under Article 79 of the code.[8] It applied to those second generation youth of immigrant origin not covered by Article 23 of the nationality code and law. As part of their voluntarist and communitarian arguments for nationality reform, the Right claimed that these youth were acquiring French citizenship "without their knowledge, and at times against their desire, without (the state) having exercised in fact the least control over their effective integration" (Mayoud 1986:4). While conservatives always stressed the automaticity of this acquisition, opponents to the reform stressed that it was only quasi-automatic given the conditions that needed to be satisfied.[9] In 1985, there was an estimated 17,607 acquisitions of French nationality via Article 44 (see Table 5.1). The youth covered under Article 44 did have the right to refuse French citizenship in the year before the age of majority, but the numbers to do so have always been below 10 percent of those eligible.[10]

The differences in the ease of abrogation of Articles 23 and 44 soon caused a contradiction in the Right's rhetoric. Their political rhetoric highlighted the problem with second-generation youth of Algerian origin. But the actual Article of the Nationality Code that rightist politicians in late 1986 began to target in their rhetoric was Article 44. Indeed public opinion polls indicated that many thought Article 44 covered the majority of the "Beurs" or second-generation Maghrebi youth. This was of course a mistaken perception. Article 44 rarely applied to the children of Algerians. In actual numbers, it was mostly second-generation youth of Southern European origin (Portuguese, Italian, and Spanish) who became French via Article 44. Thus, despite the intensity of their rhetoric, the Right's proposals in fact applied to those who were very visibly not the targets of their revisions (e.g., Mayoud 1986:3).

While explicitly noting the limited scope of Article 44—in light of the Right's objectives—the Bureau of Nationality formulated a substantial modification of Article 44. It was largely based on the earlier restrictive proposals. The Bureau's text proposed replacing article 44 with a provision that called for candidates to make a request for citizenship between the ages of sixteen and twenty. It inserted an oath of allegiance, copying the text from Mazeaud's proposition, a formal condition of assimilation, as well as a much expanded Article 79. But, the Bureau did not eliminate the territorial principle of citizenship. It refused to touch Article 23 of the nationality code. As a Bureau report noted, "All the ministries concerned by problems of nationality have expressed the most extreme reservations regarding the opportunity to abrogate Article 23 of the nationality code."[11] By refusing to eliminate the *double jus soli* principle, the state greatly constrained the radical import—in substantive and symbolic terms—of the Right's revisions. It meant that the most prominent, remaining target for the Right's voluntarist, and communitarian arguments was Article 44, which encompassed no more than 20,000 youth each year, the majority of whom were not of North African origin.

Other provisions in the Right's proposed revisions contradicted existing state's practices of citizenship as well. In trying to establish a reform text in the spring of 1986, the Bureau searched for "guidance" in the RPR-UDF's electoral platform and in Mazeaud's formal proposition (Interviews, Bureau of Nationality). During the following months, the Bureau formulated a dozen drafts of a nationality reform. In doing so, the Bureau underlined the "points of divergence" between their drafts and the previous proposals, where the Right's revisions "appeared too radical." The Bureau's key criticisms of Mazeaud's proposal included its complete elimination of the declarative procedure, which interfered with numerous existing provisions, its introduction of a system of the retroactive loss of French citizenship, which "clashes with several principles" of French law, and its naturalization option for the spouse of a French national, which could pose a "problem for the French abroad." The Bureau's report also rejected the renouncement of dual nationality that appeared in Mazeaud's "oath of allegiance" as "incompatible with the actual state of our legislation." The report critiqued "the conditions of naturalization," in so far that the institution of an exam for naturalization candidates "did not seem opportune," and the expanded "assimilation" provision fell under the "regulatory domain," and not the domain of law.

The Right's suspicion of dual nationality in particular clashed with the existing and emergent practices within the French state. Many French officials were actually promoting an increasing tolerance for dual nationals and indifference about the problems traditionally associated with the dual nationality. From the state's distinctive viewpoint, dual nationality was decreasingly seen as a problem or threat to state sovereignty or obstacle to integration.[12] Since the 1973 nationality code reform, French state bans on dual nationality had been substantially loosened. The position of the Bureau of Nationality reflected the evolving positions: "Our problems are not the dual nationals; we don't care about other nationalities" (Interview, Bureau of Nationality).

The issue of dual nationality was especially salient in 1986 to officials at the Ministry of Justice and the Ministry of Foreign Relations. These two ministries were engaged in discussions with other European countries regarding the usefulness of the 1963 Convention of Strasbourg, whose aim has been to discourage the incidence of dual nationality. In that context, French officials were beginning to question this convention's principles and application.[13] Thus, when Bureau of Nationality officials included an "oath of allegiance" in their legislative drafts, these other officials removed the phrase requiring the candidate "to renounce" all other nationalities. Not only did it contradict existing practice, but it also undermined their evolving administrative priorities.

The Four Objectives of the Bureau of Nationality

If the Bureau of Nationality operated as a constraint on several major elements of the restrictive revisions of the code, it also increased the pressure for other aspects of the restrictive reform. In overall terms, the Bureau of Nationality had no quarrel with the voluntarist and communitarian imperatives of the Right's politics of citizenship. During the summer of 1986, the Bureau set out to formulate the "motives" for a proposition of law: The Bureau identified four objectives for the reform of the nationality code, of which one was the elimination of automaticity:

> To impose on all children of foreigners born in France (20,000 cases per year) who wish to become French a positive step in the form of a declaration before a judicial authority. Submitted to a control, whose efficacy will be reinforced but in the conditions strictly defined by the law and respectful of individual liberties, this voluntary act will constitute a real engagement of the candidate to our nationality of the nature to reinforce the cohesion and unity of our national community. (Bureau of Nationality. Untitled. Dated 28 July 1986. 2 pp.)

The three other objectives were "to reform the conditions of acquisition of French nationality by right of marriage," "to adapt the legislation to the actual preoccupations attached to immigration," and "to put in place measures to fight against fraud" (Ibid.).

According to Bureau officials, these objectives would reinforce statist prerogatives, focus priorities on abuses in nationality legislation, eliminate provisions derivative of colonial and postcolonial ties, and permit a "general cleaning" of the code. Certainly, their preoccupations about fraud had been reinforced by the arrival of the Chirac government, which placed priority on the distinctive concerns of the Ministry of Interior in France. Officials in the Ministries of Justice, Foreign Affairs and Social Affairs all noted the growing predominance and visibility of the Ministry of Interior's priorities to fight against fraud and abuse in a variety of areas, among them immigration and nationality (interviews with officials).

The Bureau's proposed nationality code reform was to conform to the four stated objectives—rescind automaticity, combat marriage fraud, other provisions susceptible to fraud, and target immigration-related issues—and the general institutional goals. Concerns about substantive inconsistencies in the text as well as fraud underlay much of their reasoning for modifying specific provisions covered by the *jus soli* principle. Thinking to "profit by the occasion," officials there sought to reinsert specific mention of the French civil majority, to clarify and expand the list of convictions falling under Article 79, and to limit the possibility of fraud. A declarative procedure would make the process more "clear-cut, clear, and precise" (interviews, Bureau of Nationality).

In their proposed legislative text, the Bureau eliminated Article 23 of the law of January 1973, which extended the provisions of Article 23 of the code to those born in France to parents born in the former French territories in Africa.[14] Article 23 of the 1973 law was considered by the state more easily revocable than Article 23 of the code. The Bureau's notes highlight the "actual difficulties" of Article 23 of the 1973 law: "young women . . . taking the airplane in order to give birth in France and obtain the resident card for themselves and their husbands."[15] Likewise, the Bureau recommended modifying Articles 52 and 55, through which children born in France of noncitizen parents have the opportunity to become French automatically or by full right before they reach the age of majority[16] (see Table 5.1). A major impetus for reforming these provisions was to prevent parents from using those procedures to benefit themselves, a practice that these state agents considered significant (interviews, Bureau of Nationality).

Its specialized role and priorities led the Bureau of Nationality to complement more than constrain the second major aim of the Right, namely, the elimination of other types of privileged access to French citizenship, which were based neither on *jus sanguinis* nor on *jus soli*. The arguments underlying this strand of the conservatives' revisions combined voluntarist imperatives with concerns about the commodifying and desacralizing of citizenship, including the proliferation of fraud. In the French nationality code, the provisions that enabled this type of privileged and quasi-automatic access were the acquisition of citizenship through marriage to a French national (Article 37-1), through a "collective effect," as a minor when a parent is naturalized (Article 84), and through "reintegration" into French citizenship, which often was based on past colonial ties (Articles 153 and 155) (see Table 5.1).

A restriction of these routes to French citizenship largely complemented past trends and priorities in the state, priorities not only of the Ministry of Justice, but also of the Ministries of Interior, Foreign Affairs, and Social Affairs. For example, the phenomena of so-called paper marriages and the procedure of reintegration for those with colonial ties were both subjects of reform discussions and actual revisions since the 1973 reform of the nationality code.[17] In its preparations of a reform text, the Bureau highlighted abuses in Article 37-1, Article 84—which was not specifically mentioned by most conservative proposals—as well as Articles 153 and 155. Throughout the reform process, officials at the Bureau were aware of the political explosiveness of their modifications; after listing a series of modifications that ought to be done but were "politically tainted," an internal memo acknowledged that "it would be necessary to make an effort to present this reform as only technical."[18] By September 1986, the Bureau presented for interministerial discussion a reform text that (1) modified Article 44 by instituting a positive step, and making its acceptance conditional on an expanded set of exigencies, which included an oath of allegiance, a formal assimilation requirement, and a lengthier Article 79; (2) replaced the declarative procedure in the acquisition by marriage with a naturalization procedure; (3) eliminated Article 23 of the 1973 law; and (4) restricted the "collective effect" of Article 84.

Agendas, Autonomy, and Dissension Within the State

The Bureau's agenda was not fully shared by other ministries and parts of the state also involved in nationality concerns. The major institutions in the reform process were the Ministries of Justice, Interior, Foreign Affairs, and Social Affairs, and the Council of State. Other institutions included the Ministry of Defense, the Commission on Human Rights, and the High Council of the Population and the Family. The divisiveness within the state over the reform could be attributed to several factors. On one level, the conflict reflected long-standing and ongoing priority and policy differences in the state. Not surprisingly, functionaries in different parts of the state expressed the particular viewpoints of their institution. "[State functionaries] act or so they believe, not in accordance with their class background, or as dictated by their political beliefs, but rather in keeping with the role they play in the governmental institution. Such behavior is essential to the operation of the institutionalized state" (Badie and Birnbaum 1983:114).

On another level, the conflicts reflected the growing trend of what has been called the "dedifferentiation" of the French state (Birnbaum 1988:184; also see Berger 1981; Hall 1986).[19] Dedifferentiation refers to the process by which societal interests and pressure groups have become quasi-institutionalized within the French state. Since 1981, when the Socialists first came to power, the trend toward "dedifferentiation" has been particularly noted. A confluence of Socialist practices diminished some of the presidentialist bias and centralized bureaucratic authority in the state. Some Socialist decentralization reforms shifted authority to regional political, economic, and social structures and other reforms incorporated quasi-public bodies within the state (Schmidt 1991). Certain of these voices, now heard to a degree within the administrative regime, protested against the reform.

This process was exacerbated by the conflictual realities of what the French call "cohabitation." Cohabitation describes a split partisan executive, the coexistence of a president from one party and a prime minister from another party or bloc. The victory of the Right RPR-UDF coalition in the 1986 parliamentary elections had ushered in a period of cohabitation for the first time in France. Chirac called for President Mitterrand's resignation in 1986, but Mitterrand refused. Mitterrand and Chirac more or less carved out distinctive areas of jurisdiction, with Chirac holding responsibility over most domestic policy domains. But, in several important policy areas, including immigration, Mitterrand and Chirac clashed (Feldblum 1996:133–143). During this period, Mitterrand used different sites within the government to stake out his opposition to Chirac and his policies.

Mitterrand's influence could be seen in two state-led councils, which early on expressed their disapproval of the reform proposals. The short-lived National Council of Immigrant Populations (created under the auspices of the Directorate of Population and Migration) was the product of Socialist government's efforts in the early eighties to institutionalize representation of immigrant groups within the state. The High Council of the Population and the Family was a quasi-institutionalized group created in 1985 by the Socialist government and presided over by Mitterrand himself. In October 1985, the National Council of Immigrant Populations approved a resolution, upholding the principle of *jus soli* in order to "affirm a desire (*volonté*) for insertion, if not integration of populations issued from immigration . . . to prepare for a future where the French Nation can find an equilibrium between its historic traditions and their necessary evolution" (Conseil National des Populations Immigrées 1985:4). In January 1986, the High Council also recommended against the reform, and argued it was its "duty to be on guard against certain solutions sometimes advanced concerning notably the reform in a restrictive sense of our traditional law of nationality" a measure that "would be contrary to the historic evolution of" that law, one that would have a "unfavorable effect on the insertion of foreign families."[20] As the press understood it, President Mitterrand and the High Council had stated bluntly no immigrant insertion without French nationality (*Libération* 9/4/86).

Finally, the conflicts within the state coincided with dissension in the Chirac government and rightist parties over the strategic and political features of the reform. There were numerous conflicts between hard liners and moderates. For example, the Minister of Justice Albin Chalandon was nominally in charge of the text yet seemingly opposed to a very restrictive reform. In discussing the progress on the government's reform proposal during the summer, Chalandon mentioned only three of his Ministry's objectives, leaving unsaid the objective to adapt the legislation to "preoccupations" linked to immigration. Instead, Chalandon stressed that "it appears necessary to simplify the nationality code while maintaining the spirit of openness and welcome that has always been characteristic of France's attitude in this respect, all in fighting against fraud" (*Le Monde* 7/26/86). Early on, Chalandon aimed to dampen the protests against the reform by incorporating immigrant representatives in the reform process. On October 16, 1986, Chalandon met with Harlem Desir of SOS-Racisme, informing him that he would reconsider the insertion of the oath of allegiance. Indeed, throughout the reform process, Chalandon, was manifestly ambivalent about the motivations and methods driving the reform. His ambivalence seemed to grew during the reform process when he stressed that the government's text was not overturning the *jus soli* principle and evinced little enthusiasm for the restrictive aspects of the reform.

The division between the hardliners and moderates was confirmed with the advent of interministerial meetings to discuss the government's legislative reform draft. The proposal on the table was the one formulated by the Bureau of Nationality. At the first meeting on September 15, representatives from Ministries of Justice, Foreign Affairs, Interior, and Social Affairs and Work, as well as from the Secretaries of State in charge of Human Rights and Repatriates were present. Representatives of Chirac's cabinet led the discussion.[21] The meeting revealed the moderates (Ministries of Social Affairs and Foreign Affairs) and hard-liners (Ministries of Justice and Interior, and Chirac's representatives). Representatives from the Ministries of Interior and Justice dominated the discussion with their preoccupations over fraud and administrative sovereignty.

In contrast, representatives from the other Ministries voiced a series of concerns. Representatives of the Ministry of Social Affairs proposed a more lenient modification of Article 44. Though they supported revising Article 37-1, they also contended that the phenomenon of "paper marriages" was a "marginal problem." These officials expressed their reservations about an oath of allegiance, as "little conforming to our traditions." At least in part, the Ministry's disapproval of the reform proposal reflected its own administrative priorities and substantive agenda. Immigrant integration and the process of "Francisation" were the ongoing tasks of agencies under the Ministry of Social Affairs. The Directorate of Migrant Populations within the Ministry of Social Affaires was particularly concerned about naturalizations and the processing of citizenship acquisitions (Interview, Directorate of Migrant Populations). During the meeting, representatives from the Ministry of Social Affairs feared that the proposed revisions "risk(ed) to slow down acquisitions" or be a "source of delay" for the date acquisitions took effect.[22]

The Ministry of Foreign Affairs and the Secretary in charge of Human Rights expressed disapproval for other aspects of the reform draft. The Ministry of Foreign Affairs was most concerned about how the reform would affect French living abroad, and French who intermarried with foreigners. Officials from Foreign Affairs argued against the substitution of a naturalization procedure for the existing declarative process for the foreign spouses of French nationals. Dual nationality was at issue as well. The Ministry of Foreign Affairs supported a loosening of the regulations governing dual nationality.[23] Anticipating the role of the Superior Council of the French Abroad (CSFE), the Ministry asked if it could submit the reform draft to the CSFE for its recommendations. The CSFE was a quasi-institutionalized lobbying association that represented French abroad, and had risen in prominence in the eighties. It was increasingly influential in the Ministry of Foreign Affair's deliberations on questions of citizenship.

Despite the dissenting opinions, the reform draft prepared by the Bureau of Nationality was largely approved. The text, for the most part, coincided with hard-liner positions within the Chirac government, such as those expressed earlier by Pasqua, the Minister of Interior (*Le Quotidien de Paris* 9/6–7/86). Prime Minister Chirac's representatives firmly endorsed the recommendations of the Ministry of Justice, including the inclusion of an oath of allegiance, and the naturalization procedure for foreign spouses. At the same time, they acknowledged the Ministerial consensus that Article 23 could not be amended.

The government's legislative proposal still faced internal state obstacles. A critical rejection of the reform came from the state's administrative and jurisdictional review body, the Council of State (Conseil d'Etat). As a governmental institution, the Council of State is concerned with "legality in the widest sense of conformity with the law, with desirability, and with efficacy" (Rendall 1970). For many scholars, the Council of State epitomized the French "republic of functionaries." A "very autonomous" institution, whose presiding official (the vice-president of the council, not the Justice Minister, who was only a nominal head) is the "highest functionary," the Council's most distinctive administrative role was its broad concern for the general interest and administrative order (Massot and Marimbert 1988:15–19). In the reform process, it fell to the Council of State to review the legality and opportuneness of the reform proposition.[24]

The government's reform proposition arrived at the Council of State on October 7, 1986. For the following three weeks, the council's sections on the Interior and Social Affairs examined it, each of which issued a negative recommendation on the draft. Finally, at the end of October, largely based on their sections' recommendations, the full assembly of the Council submitted a mostly negative decision on the reform to the government (Interview, Council of State). In the decision, which was leaked to the press, the Council firmly rejected the major axes of the state's revisions, including modification of Article 44 (the automatic acquisition of citizenship at the age of majority by persons born in France of noncitizen parents), substitution of a naturalization procedure for the declarative procedure in Article 37-1 (acquisition of citizenship by foreign spouses), and institution of an oath of allegiance" (*Libération* 11/5/86; *Le Figaro* 11/3/86; *Le Quotidien de Paris* 11/3/86; *L'Humanité* 11/3/86).[25]

The Council of State prefaced its decision by claiming that the government's project was inopportune and against the "republican tradition." In significant ways, the disagreements between the Bureau of Nationality (Ministry of Justice) and the Council of State reflected the conflicting administrative priorities of the two parts of the state. The Justice's reform draft had expressed a primarily individualist focus. In contrast, the Council aimed to represent the "universalist" France. According to a "counselor" in charge of formulating the Council's recommendations, the Council's concerns were for the "public interest . . . and administrative order." The Council of State appeared wary of any revision of the nationality code, even if it admitted the need for a "general cleaning." From its perspective, "form and substance" were inextricably linked in the code. The Council was aware of its role as the liberalizing institution, and supporter of the collective interest, which included the rights of immigrant populations in France (de Wenden 1988b; Weil 1988a). Thus, it explicitly rejected the nativist motivations of the Right's proposals, the "measures of exclusion of populations already in France." For the Council, a "judicial system was placed in peril" by the proposed reforms. In particular, its own role in the nationality process was displaced in the state's reform draft. From the perspective of the Bureau of Nationality, the Council's decision was motivated less by grand concerns than specific bureaucratic battles. Bureau officials argued that it was the displacement of the Council of State from the nationality process which really motivated the negative decision on the legislative proposal. In their eyes, it was largely a matter of bureaucratic conflicts and maneuvering for power (interviews, Council of State and Bureau of Nationality).

In response to the Council of State's decision, the Chirac government re-treated on a few provisions but ignored the gist of the Council's recommendations. On November 7, 1986, Chirac's Council of Ministers met to review the govern-ment's "projet" or legislative draft for reforming the code. Their new text dropped the oath of allegiance, permitted a longer period for the acquisition process for Ar-ticle 44, dropped the naturalization procedure for the marriage provision, and in-stead called for a longer period before which the foreign spouse could declare for French citizenship.[26] However, it retained a voluntarist revision of Article 44, the lengthy list of convictions in Article 79, and the formal condition of assimilation. On November 12, the Council of Ministers finalized the draft, and the "Chirac-Chalandon" reform or the "proposition of Law 444" was formally deposited at the National Assembly (Chirac and Chalandon 1986).

The state reform processes shaped the configurations of the Right's politics of citizenship in two ways. First, the statist and highly bureacratic institutional configuration certainly limited the possibilities for a grand, politicized reform as laid out by the political Right. Administrative practices led state agents to refuse to wholly eliminate the territorial principle of citizenship. As with previous reform processes, state officials strove to define revisions under their domain of control. When different parts of the state pursued distinctive agendas, varied assertions of state autonomy, universalistic aspirations, and administrative priorities came to the fore. Second, the dissension within the state aided the mobilization against the reform and increased the possibility for further dedifferentiation, that is for in-corporating nonstate agents into the reform process. The conflicts among the dif-ferent Ministries, Councils, and governmental members echoed similar splits within the political Right, and insured that those splits resonated even deeper. The conflicts contributed to the organization of protests among the Left and other opponents to the reform by providing an institutional nexus for cross coalitions.

The Reform and the Political Process, October 1986–May 1987

Despite the dissent in the state and growing opposition to the reform by a myriad of groups, the passage of a reform still appeared inevitable in the Fall of 1986. The government "seemed persuaded that the reform would pass like mailing a letter" (*Le Monde* 12/11/86). The press concurred that "if (there were) no gathering of forces enough to protest it, (the reform) will be adopted without too many prob-lems by the parliament" (*Le Témoignage Chrétien* 10/13–19/86; *Le Matin* 11/13/86). Why did the government's restrictive reform fail? Or, in other words, why did the opposition to the reform succeed? Political process models have iden-tified three sets of factors that shape the emergence of successful protest: the level of organization in the insurgent groups, the "structure of political opportunities" in the larger political environment, and the collective assessment of the prospects for successful protest (McAdam 1982:40; also see McAdam, McCarthy, and Zald 1996). Examining the interaction and confluence of these factors in the reform process can explain the success of the protests against the reform and the concurrent retreat of the government.[27]

The opposition to the reform was composed of many broadly based and disparate groups, including immigrant groups, human rights groups, clergy, the left parties, and unions. Since the mid-eighties, immigrant groups had established links with the political parties, and social support networks. Opposition to the reform was partly situated in the existing infrastructure of immigrant activist associations, immigrant support groups, and human rights or antiracist organizations. It also was based on some new linkages, especially among the clergy, immigrant associations, and human rights groups, such as the League of Human Rights (LDH).

The efforts to oppose the code reform strengthened the developing organizational linkages. When Socialist party representatives met with France-Plus leaders at the headquarters of the LDH on July 8, 1986, the aim of the meeting was to coordinate efforts to oppose the Right's proposed revisions.[28] A Socialist party document notes how France Plus has contacted "all the parties, associations, (and) petitions have been sent to the churches, Grand-Orient . . . meetings are foreseen with Ministers Chalandon of Justice, Seguin of Social Affairs, and Malhuret of Human Rights." Indeed, the differentiated infrastructure of the immigrant associations had grown enough that the visible rifts between groups affected wider political strategies. By November 1986, the Socialist party had to coordinate separate protest efforts with France-Plus and SOS-Racisme.

The organization of protests against the reform started in the spring and summer of 1986, but forces on the Left were waiting for the formal appearance of the state's proposition. On October 23, the LDH assembled the associations, who had previously protested against other restrictive immigration policies, to draft a petition calling for the retreat of the proposed governmental proposition (*CAIF Infos* November 1986).

> The proposition of law to reform the nationality code, adopted in the council of ministers despite the advice of the Council of State, constitutes a grave regression. In calling into question the right of territory (as basis of citizenship acquisition), it goes back on a very ancient principle in our law, constantly reaffirmed by the republican tradition. Its adoption would return more than hundred years backwards a legislation that has contributed to fashioning the actual face of France. ("Appel Pour Le Retrait du Projet de Réforme du Code de la Nationalité," 1996)

The Council of State's decision provided an important political and philosophical nexus for the opposition, pulling together disparate groups. It helped legitimate and publicize the protest by situating the opposition firmly as the defenders of "the republican tradition." The above petition was eventually signed by more than 200 organizations. It was "no longer a Left-Right combat" (Interview CAIF). The engagement of the clergy was a crucial point for many. In 1984, when the Socialist confronted the clergy over their education reform project, they suffered a bitter loss. Moreover, the church continued to function as a traditional social base of support for the Right. Thus, protesters believed that "Chirac couldn't confront the churches" (Ibid.).[29] The clergy's opposition to the reform became an important element in bolstering the protestors' organizational resources.

Identifying themselves as the defenders of the French humanist, republican tradition, the opposition marshaled three general arguments against the government's reform. First, it linked the code reform to the prior passage by the Chirac government of anti-immigrant legislation, in particular the 1986 harsh "Pasqua laws" on entry and residence (named after Charles Pasqua, Chirac's Interior Minister). The opposition accused the state of "security and national identity preoccupations" (Commission Diocésaine 1986:6). The Council of State's clear rejection of the code reform imbued the link with added drama because it had previously given a negative recommendation on the Pasqua legislation. Together, the two pieces of legislation constituted "a real policy of exclusion toward immigrants" (*Rouge* 10/23–29/86). Second, the Left accused the state of making "a triage between the foreigners that it wants to keep and those it wants to reject" (MRAP 1986b:3). Finally, for the reform's opponents, it was a "law that will fabricate foreigners" (*Libération* 11/13/86, 11/15–16/86). Above all, it was a war against youth, against the second generation immigrants (*Le Matin* 11/13/86, 11/17/86; *Le Monde* 11/14/86; *Lutte Ouvrier* 11/15/86). The organizational strength of the opposition was certainly not enough to ensure its success. Despite heavily organized protests using similar arguments against the restrictive entry and residence legislation, the Pasqua laws passed on September 9, 1986. While that passage proved to the government's opponents that organizational strength was not enough, it also enabled the attention of the various organizations to focus nearly exclusively on the subsequent nationality reform.

What changed in the "structure of political opportunities" in the aftermath of the Council of State's decision and the state's response to it? McAdam has defined the political opportunities structure as "the political alignment of groups within the larger political environment" (1982:40). In normal politics, insurgent groups "face enormous obstacles (to advance their interests) . . . are excluded from routine decision-making processes precisely because their bargaining position, relative to established polity members, is so weak" (Ibid.). In this regard, the type of state is a major factor affecting the mutability of the political environment, and the mobilization of protest in a polity (Birnbaum 1988:30; Skocpol 1985). Scholars have argued that the French state shapes the mobilization of protest by permitting "little/no public space for interest groups pressures," thus leading collective action to be always directed against the state (Birnbaum 1988:8, 188). The structure of opportunities and political alignments, however, are not immutable. Situational changes as well as more long term and underlying processes of political instability, international transformations, and socioeconomic trends can alter the political environment.

During the Fall of 1986, several factors contributed to changing the "structure of political opportunities." One was the negative decision of the Council of State and its aftermath. Other factors were the growing factions in the Rightist parties over the reform and the dramatic changes in the state's responses during this period. Finally, the generalized political instability and social protests against the state in 1986 would enable the opposition to convert their organizational resources and a newly favorable structure of opportunities into successful protests.

The negative decision of the Council of State was a "small bomb" and an embarrassment for the Chirac government (*Le Matin*, 11/4/86). While those in the Right knew that the Council was "hostile" to the reform, "the surprise was created with this attitude so definitive and clear-cut" (*Le Quotidien de Paris* 11/3/86). On a substantive level, The Council's recommendations propelled the state to further limit its revision of the code. The changes belied the government's rhetoric, and confirmed that the reform no longer really affected the Right's original targets, the "Beurs" or second generation North African immigrant population. In this way, the Council also implicated the motivations of the state, tainting the reform with a nativist subtext. On an ideological level, the Council decision signaled the reappropriation of the "republican tradition" by the opponents of the reform. Earlier, both sides drew interpretations of French traditions in their revisions of citizenship. Both sides used the optic of the "republican" heritage to elaborate very different visions of national membership, citizenship and national identity. The Council buttressed the opposition's claims to French republican traditions and seemingly limited the malleability of republicanist arguments. Likewise, it contributed to a recentering of the debate, from a voluntarist or automaticity dichotomy to an exclusionary and inclusive one. The visibility of the exclusionary and nativist aspects of the Right's restrictive revisions put the state on the defensive, forcing it to recast its own rhetoric from restrictionist to more inclusive.

The aftermath of the Council's decision helped expose the electoralist and nativist dimensions of the Right's politics of citizenship. It heightened conflicts among the Right parties between those who advocated a strongly restrictive reform, and those who were already protesting its nativist aspects. RPR-UDF parliamentary leaders declared that the government did not have to follow the advice of the Council, calling the Council's decision "partisan and political." Others in the Right argued the need to modify the code for "tactical reasons," in order to undercut the appeal of Le Pen, and the extreme Right. At the same time, centrist politicians took the opportunity to voice their own reservations about the text (*Libération* 11/4/86; *Le Monde* 11/6/86).[30] The increased dissension in the Right further al-

tered the political terrain of the combat over the code. It turned from a struggle—
to borrow the language of political process models—between "members of the
polity" and "challengers" to a struggle between "established polity members"
(Rule and Tilly 1975:55–56; McAdam 1982).

By limiting the restrictive revision of the code, the state undercut the voluntarist, communitarian, and nativist arguments propelling the reform. By November,
the visible targets of the state's reform proposition were only the 17,500 or so youths
a year who informally acquired French citizenship through Article 44. The removal
of the oath and the naturalization process for foreign spouses undermined the thrust
of the Right's complaints about the commodification and desacralization of citizenship, complaints that had helped mask the reform's nativist subtext. Changes in
the government's rhetoric confirmed the recasting of earlier arguments. According
to a government official, the "proposition is not one of exclusion but of the manifestation of the governmental desire to organize the best integration of candidates
into the national community" (cited in *Le Figaro* 11/7/86). From an effort to profoundly modify the code, the Right's revisions withered into an effort that did not,
according to Minister of Justice Chalandon, substantively change French nationality law. Not surprisingly, the significance of the Chirac-Chalandon proposition was
contested within the Right. The conservative newspaper, *Le Figaro*, defended the
government's text, as permitting "the state to best exercise its normal power of admission of future citizens" (*Le Figaro*, 11/7/86). *Le Quotidien de Paris* characterized
the modified reform as "relaxed . . . without having lost the essential" elements of
the reform (11/10/86). Others, like Le Pen, denounced the government's reform
proposal as being "largely emptied of its content" (cited in Brubaker 1992).

Political process models argue that the structure of political opportunities
and the developing organizational resources and linkages offer the structural potential for successful collective action. But they are necessary and not sufficient
conditions. Crucial to successful insurgency is the nature of the collective assessment of the participants in the struggle. "Mediating between opportunity and action are people and the subjective meanings they attach to their situations"
(McAdam 1982:48; see also Edelman 1971). The last major factor altering the
French political environment also transformed the assessments of both the opponents and proponents about the nationality code reform.

In 1986, social protests and strikes were sweeping across France.[31] In November, the unrest was brought dramatically to the fore by student protests against
another of the Chirac government reforms, a reform of the university system. The
protests drew students not only in universities but also in high schools across
France. These protests expanded into sympathy strikes and solidarities with
unions and workers, including immigrant workers (Assouline and Zappi 1987).
The polling organization, SOFRES, summarized, "the global judgement was
profoundly marked by the crisis of December 1986–January 1987 (the high
school-university student movement against the Devaquet project, and the strikes

in the public sector), which brought about a clear reversal of opinion," from approval to disapproval of the government (SOFRES 1988:143).

The politics of immigration and education were intertwined from the beginning of the student protests, although immigration and the nationality code were not highly salient issues for most students. Immigrant-origin activists and immigrant association activists (e.g., SOS-Racisme leaders) played major roles in organizing the student protests. A visible proportion of the students protesting were of immigrant origin (Dray 1987). If the immigrant activism of 1983 and 1984 signified the political emergence of the associative movement, the student protests in 1986 signaled for many "the political birth of a new generation," of younger immigrant and antiracist activists entering French partisan politics (*Libération* 6/20–21/87).[32] The protests against the university reform were explicitly linked to the entire package of Chirac's anti-immigrant policies. Student chants included, "I have immigrant pals/students sometimes without papers/equality of rights/this will work for another time . . . ," "French-foreign students, equality," or "Charter for Devaquet (Minister of Education), not for the immigrants" (Assouline and Zuppi 1987:51). The last slogan evoked an expulsion via chartered airline of illegal Malian immigrants orchestrated by Chirac's government earlier in 1986.

The drama continued to build during the student protests. In early December, a young French student of Algerian origin, Malik Oussekine, was shot and killed while protesting. Oussekine quickly became a symbol for both the protests against the university reform and the code reform. In their study of the student protests, Assouline and Zuppi quote student activists who note that "the death of Malik accentuated the turn. Pasqua (Minister of Interior) is the target, through him the entire security and racist policy of the government; one remembers his remarks and his engagement . . . in the expulsions of the Malians by charter. One comes quickly from there to Chalandon, to the reform of the nationality code, to his policy against young drug addicts" (Ibid.:258). Among student protesters, a motion was quickly passed against the Nationality Code reform: "This reform is an encouragement to racism and exclusion . . . we reaffirm our solidarity with all foreign students menaced by expulsion" (cited in Assouline and Zuppi 1987:263). Soon afterward, the state withdrew both the university and the nationality code from the legislative agenda, putting on hold whether the nationality code reform would be debated by the National Assembly in the spring of 1987. The parallels between the two protests and reform processes were striking (*Le Monde* 12/11/86). In both episodes, the Chirac government undertook the reforms with an assertive push, confident of their passage, and was caught by surprise by the amplitude of the protests. In the end, they retreated from both without passing any reform.

Unlike in the student protests, where opposition to the nationality reform played no real role, the student protests did play a critical role for the opposition against the code. It transformed the collective assessment of the participants in the debate. According to participants in the state, the Right, and the reform's opposition, the fiasco of the university reform, and the evocation of the symbol of the murdered Franco-Algerian student were major factors in why the Right's restrictive revision failed. The reform had become too tainted, too risky. In a discussion about the government's proposition that took place in the Commission of Laws in the National Assembly, a Socialist member explicitly drew this link.

> (He) thought that the continuation of this discussion (on the national-ity code reform) constituted a provocation towards the movements of university and high school students, whose spontaneity and magnitude he underlined, and which comes not only from the inquietude that they feel about their future, but also from their attitude vis a vis society. Recalling that last week, there had been a death among the protesters, he observed that this one (Malik) belongs precisely to the generation targeted by the text, and judged that he would be a provocateur to dis-cuss in this context a projet directed against this young man, who has become, for the youth, a symbol of "never again." (Assemblee Na-tionale, Communique a la Press, No. 49, December 11, 1986)[33]

The success of the student protests both contributed to the state's own rea-soning for retreating on the reform, and further empowered the opposition, in particular, the Left and immigrant activists. Its fiasco in handling the university reform, the students, and the protest helped convince the government to retreat on the nationality code reform, to choose the consensual, and not confrontational route. What was once politically profitable was becoming a governing liability.

On January 15, 1987, arguing the need for a "vast national consultation" and a "remodeling of" the reform, the Chirac government retreated from a quick pas-sage of a nationality code reform (*Le Monde* 1/17/87). It was a retreat but not a withdrawal of the reform proposition, as Chirac and Chalandon both periodically reaffirmed their commitment to reform the code. But at every opportunity, the Chirac government chose retreat or consensus, and not confrontation (e.g., *Le Matin* 3/13/87; *L'Humanité* 3/14/87; *Le Figaro* 3/13/87). The government with-drew the reform from consideration by the National Assembly in December 1986. It announced a series of consultations in January 1987. Finally in March 1997, the government assigned the reform to a cross-partisan, independent com-mission (*Le Figaro* 3/14–15/87; *Le Monde* 3/14/87).

There were two central aspects to the Right's retreat. First, the Right signifi-cantly recast its rhetoric in support of the code reform. Second, it sought to dampen the protest by bringing dissenting voices into the state. The Right recast the exclusionary terms of its voluntarist and communitarian arguments into a patently more inclusive rhetoric. Rightist politicians still advanced a nationalist politics of citizenship, but now, many more explicitly rejected any nativist con-notations. Justice Minister Chalandon's new ambition for the nationality code was for it "to be an instrument that enhances the sentiment of belonging to the nation, without giving it any character of an instrument of exclusion against foreigners" (*Le Quotidien de Paris* 1/16/87). Prime Minister Chirac claimed that "France must not be closed upon itself but conquering and open" (*Libération* 5/11/87). As they recast their rhetoric, rightist politicians stressed how voluntarism was an instrument to ensure integration and liberalization, and communitarianism was the basis for enhancing the French national identity.[34] The Minister of Social Affairs Seguin summarized the new defensive stance: "It is not shameful to be French or to become it, and I do not see why foreigners must see themselves be attributed our nationality despite themselves or without knowing it . . . I do not see the interest in complicating or lengthening the procedures when they could be simplified and shortened . . . (this is) a text of integration into French society" (cited in *Le Quotidien de Paris* 3/16/87).

The Right's new envisioning of the reform was not simply a dilution and softening of its prior arguments. Its reversals redefined the actual nature of the project. From a restrictive project, the reform became a seemingly liberalizing effort. In his attempt to undercut the protests in January 1987, Chalandon announced that the existing nationality legislation was "severe, ambiguous, and dangerous" because it "did not offer sufficient guarantees to young foreigners destined to become French." He told the immigrant association, France-Plus that his reform would make the code "more liberal" (*Le Monde* 1/22/87). The Minister of Social Affairs affirmed, "We cannot be suspected of exclusion toward immigrants" (*Libération* 5/11/87). The reform signified above all symbolic change. Chalandon argued that "in reality, this project changes nothing in relation to the existing law except this: the fact that it is necessary to ask the judge to become French instead of coming to ask for a certificate" (Chalandon, on Europe 1 radio, cited in *La Lettre de la Nation*, 3/17/87). The government accused the Left and the reform's opponents of "the most total disinformation" in saying that the code project was exclusionary (*Le Quotidien de Paris* 3/16/87; Perotti 1987).

Yet, the decision of Chirac's government to delay action on the code further empowered the opposition. The delays enabled increased organizing and the retreats increased demands for total retreat of the project. On March 15, 1997, leftist politicians, immigrant groups, clergy, unions, and social support organizations participated in a heavily attended demonstration, demanding full retreat of the code. The murdered Franco-Algerian student, the Pasqua laws, and other immigration policies of the government were all invoked. Among the marchers' chants were "we are millions of Maliks," "Chalandon, Pasqua, Pandraud (Minister of security)/Bermuda triangle/drive without code" (*Le Matin* 3/16/87; *Le Témoignage Chrétien* 3/16–22/87).

The political process reinforced the symbolic tone of the debate. Virtually no attention was paid to Portuguese or other southern European communities, who in terms of numbers were much more affected by the reform project than the North African populations (Cordeiro 1987a, 1987b). For both opponents and proponents, the debate over the reform involved more or less French exclusionary politics toward North African immigrants. More, because it also elicited questions about the nature of French self-identity, the French national community, and definitions of pluralism or the right to difference. Less, because, the debates did not mobilize much attention to the wide array of policies—in housing, school, labor market and so on—which shaped the life experiences of immigrants. The symbolic perceptions of the code clearly informed the government's decision to engage in a "vast national consultation," a decision that would culminate in the referral of the code to a commission in mid-March. Though Justice Minister Chalandon had already spoken with a few organizations, he began in January to officially solicit the opinions of at least fifteen associations, including immigrant associations (SOS-Racisme, France Plus), human rights and antiracist groups (LDH, LICRA), as well as "moral and religious authorities," student representatives, and unions (*Le Monde* 1/22/87; *Le Figaro* 3/13/87).

The results of the national consultation were paradoxical. The aim of the government was to dampen the protest. And in a few cases, it may have done so. France-Plus refused to take part in the large March 15 protest, citing the "conciliatory" stance of the government. However, even the France-Plus decision was understood among the march organizers to be at least partially a product of their strategic infighting with SOS-Racisme. The larger impression of the government's consultation was that of great influence and access afforded to immigrant groups and their effective mobilization of protests. The implications of the consultations were also institutional, and relate to a more general transformation of reform processes in the contemporary French state. The series of consultations certainly aided in incorporating extra-institutional voices into the reform process, in breaking down some of the state's internal barriers. In other words, the consultations contributed to the process of dedifferentiation in the French state (Birnbaum 1988). During winter and spring of 1987, the protests which were fundamentally mobilized against the state were in part brought within the state. In strengthening the protesting groups, the consultations weakened the traditional statist features and autonomy of the French state.

By the end of the consultative period, new strategies emerged. SOS-Racisme, formerly against any kind of reform of the code, changed its position to call for a radical reform of the code that would institute an absolute territorial right to citizenship. The organization's representatives claimed "it is necessary to reform the nationality code but in opposition to the government projects," in that all persons born in France would automatically be attributed French citizenship (*Le Matin* 6/20–21/87). For his part, Prime Minister Chirac announced the selection of a National Commission on Nationality, a *Commission des Sages*. Chirac lamented that his project, "not exactly understood," always had the intention of retaining the territorial basis of citizenship acquisition. What the governmental proposition actually called for, according to Chirac, was the "necessity of a declaration by which the foreigner manifests the desire to acquire the nationality. This is the heart itself of the reform. It is by this idea of 'voluntary choice' that is expressed the entire conception of the Nation" (Chirac, *Installation de la Commission du Code de la Nationalité, Lundi 22 Juin 1987*, Nationality Commission Archives).

Conclusion

The failure of the restrictive politics of citizenship can be largely explained by institutional and political process constraints that effectively limited the Right's attempt to revise the nationality code. The state played a dialectical role in the reform process. The state's administrative priorities and autonomy straightforwardly limited some aspects of the reform. The internal agendas of different ministries and councils meant that the reform process became an opportunity to pursue distinctive institutional goals and a terrain for intrabureaucratic battles. The product of the state's doubled pursuit of the general interest and particular administrative interests were the narrow parameters of the Right's reform text in the fall of 1986 (see also Verbunt, Bovenkerk, and Miles 1988; Miles 1987).

The institutional implications of the reform process for the state can also be understood in dialectical terms. The ways in which different parts of the state stood in tension with each other strengthened the reform's opponents in the Left as well as Right. The tensions further limited the resources of the Chirac government and its possibility of enacting a restrictive version of the reform. The Chirac government's response was to bring the protesters into the state. Such a response undermined the state's own autonomy and still again limited the possibilities for any restrictive reform passage. These constraints and their ramifications would inform the rest of the reform process. Factors in the political process played a decisive role in the government's eventual retreat from its restrictive reform as well. Most dramatic of all were the conjunctural effects of the student protests, which were converted by the protestors of the code revision into part of their own successful opposition. The burgeoning organizational resources of the opposition and the changing structure of political opportunities too shaped the configurations of the reform process.

I have not provided a political cultural explanation of why the Right's restrictive politics of citizenship failed in this chapter. Culturalist explanations and the national models they rely on largely attribute the failure of the Right's revisions to seemingly nonideological and nonstrategic use of national traditions. For example, Rogers Brubaker identified the "prevailing idiom of nationhood" in France as the critical obstacle to a restrictive revision. He argued that the way of understanding the nation in France as a "product and project of the state . . . in this statist and assimilationist tradition . . . (means) it is the civic exclusion of immigrants, not their civic incorporation that demands special justification . . . (The) restrictionists were arguing against a distinctive and deeply rooted tradition . . . (this) raised the political costs of the reform, and thereby made the government less likely to push it through" (Brubaker 1992). Such an interpretation resonated well with French views that saw the debate over the code as essentially a "Franco-Francophone" debate, pitting the conservative nationalists against the republican humanists (Perotti 1986, 1987). Culturalist interpretations argue citizenship conflicts are embedded in specific national models of historical, ideological, and institutional traditions. While specificity is a strength of cultural explanations, it is also part of their weakness in that understandings of citizenship appear so embedded in the national model as to be static and fixed.

Unquestionably, the French republican tradition and universalist, assimilationist goals of the French state were the core of the "vocabulary of motives" predominant in the reform process (Mills 1984:22).[35] What is not clear, however, is the extent to which the Right, apart from the articulation of certain nativist arguments, was arguing against these traditions and the associated national model. In the reform context, French political-cultural interpretations became a political ploy to delegitimate one's opponents (Pinto 1984). As an analytical tool, the French national model became an uncritical receptacle and accepting framework of some set of national membership notions. Assuming a culturalist perspective actually leads one to draw the distinction between the opponents and proponents of the reform too sharply.

The arguments of many of the proponents and opponents of the code reform drew on and were shaped by the ambiguities in French nationalism and the French assimilationist tradition. That in itself may not be striking. What was striking in the reform process was the more explicit usage by the political elite, press, and state agents of a common nationalist — or at the very least nation-oriented — vocabulary of motives in defending their disparate visions of citizenship. In effect, the struggles over the nationality code exposed how in the modern nation-state there is usually a "general acceptance of common membership so that nationalism has become internalized and implicit" (Apter 1964). In the struggle to reconstruct the French tradition of citizenship, all were becoming traditionalists and nationalists (Geertz 1973).

CHAPTER 6

Reconstructing Citizenship

The Nationality Commission

The failure of the Right's restrictive revision of the code did not translate into a failure of a nationalist politics of citizenship. To the contrary, the next phase of the reform process transformed an untenable revision into an admirable reform. This chapter provides an extensive examination of the Chirac-appointed National Commission on Nationality (also called the Commission des Sages), from its initial constitution to its final report. I argue that, despite the defeat of the legislative effort in 1987, the work of the Nationality Commission effectively built on the debates of the previous years and laid the framework for a reconstructed French citizenship.

Most interpretations underestimate or dismiss the significance of the Nationality Commission and, ultimately of the entire reform process. They argue that the reform process ended with a return to the status quo, or at least, with a lack of substantive changes. The Commission "buried" or "postponed" the real debates about immigration and the integration of the Maghrebi, Muslim population (Leveau 1990:42; Costa-Lascoux 1989c). The work of the Commission was indicative of how "the battle of the code has become . . . essentially symbolic," even if it did "put the finger on the essential, that is, on the integration of the children of foreigners" (*Le Monde* 9/8/87). The Commission's major significance was "pedagogic," "cathartic"; it proved to be a calming influence on a passionate subject (*L'Express* 10/23/87). It was "a sociological interrogation of the French identity" (Krulic 1988b:31), expressive of French society's "doubts" about "its capacity to assimilate" the new immigrants (Perotti 1988; Verbunt 1988b). The reform process constituted a deadlock in both ideological terms—left only with the inescapable alternative of "to be or not to be French" (Balibar 1988a)—and in policy terms, given that neither side had the resources or aims to push through their preferences (Weil 1988c; Costa-Lascoux 1987a).

101

These interpretations of the Commission, while describing aspects of the final reform process, display a crucial misunderstanding of the political process itself. They situate the Commission in terms of its physical product, which featured a book-length compilation of their hearings and recommendations. But it did not produce an immediate nationality reform. The interpretations define the political process primarily in attenuated terms of outcomes, decision-making results, and allocations of resources. They imply a definition of the interpretative aspects of the political process as "curtains that obscure the real politics, or artifacts of an effort to make decisions" (March and Olsen 1989:48). In contrast, my analysis situates the Commission and its work as part of the process shaping and constituting citizenship conflict.

The central contention here is that the National Commission on Nationality constituted a critical phase in the new citizenship politics. Why? The Right's recasting of its rhetoric in late 1986 and early 1987 had highlighted the existing substantive commonalities between the Left and Right. But it did not create a political opening for a new orientation in the politics of citizenship. The political opening was instead created by the National Commission on Nationality in 1987 and 1988 through their public hearings and recommendations. The Commission gradually provided the keys for a specifically nationalist reconstruction of citizenship. Their understanding of citizenship incorporated four kinds of claims: the fusion of national and pluralist identity, the necessity of a national integration of immigrants, the appropriateness of a voluntarist citizenship, and finally, the reaffirmation of a statist perspective on citizenship. Via this reconstruction of citizenship, an effective consensus formed across the political spectrum. The consensus rejected pluralist arguments for a "right to difference" and defined the Maghrebi, Muslim immigration as a challenge to be managed through national statist integration.

Certainly, these developments were not a rupture from the previous phases of the new politics of citizenship in France. Rather, they represented a turning point. As has been argued throughout this book, the processes of creating, defining, legitimizing, and managing interpretations are as constitutive of the political process as political conflict and institutional outcomes. The significance of the Commission lay in how it effectively reconstructed citizenship and managed the discourse of citizenship and integration. "As history constantly teaches us, discourse is not simply that which translates struggles or systems of domination, but is the thing for which, and by which there is a struggle, discourse is the power which is to be seized" (Foucault 1984:110).

During previous phrases of the reform process, the growing commonalities between the Left and Right—including their overlapping stress on voluntarism and communitarianism, preoccupations with the national identity, and redefinitions of pluralism—either were left unexplained or defined as problematic. The commonalities appeared to be in tension with the general polarized divisions of

French immigration politics. In contrast, the Commission redefined such commonalities as seemingly natural and commonsensical developments. I believe a focus on process can clarify how the Commission became the crucial part in the ideological struggle over "mak(ing) things mean," to borrow a phrase from Stuart Hall (1988:188). As Hall goes on to explain, (w)hat matters is which frameworks are in play, which definitions fill out and articulate the 'common sense' of a conjuncture, which have become so naturalized and consensual that they are identical with common sense, with the taken-for-granted, and represent the point of origin from which all political calculation begins" (1988:188).

The Commission formulated their specific understandings of citizenship as "the common sense" basis or framework for the new French citizenship politics. Why was this National Commission on Nationality able to do so? It may be helpful to look at the Commission, its work and its series of public hearings as a kind of "political spectacle" in French politics. Michael Rogin has argued that political spectacles—events or certain dramatic moments in politics—are "a form of power and not just window dressing" (1990:100).[1] According to Rogin, what makes an event a spectacle is when it can become an "instrument for the operation of political amnesia," that is when it can enable the articulation of myths, pleasures or desires which "the culture can no longer unproblematically embrace." Political spectacles can "seize control of the interpretations," and "preserve a false center by burying the actual past" (Rogin 1990:107, 117).

Rogin specifies that political spectacles operate through a process of "displaying" and "forgetting"; they display the "enabling myths," but at the same time, allow the audience to distance itself from the problematic context of those images. In the following analysis, I suggest that the Commission effectively employed "politically repudiated but socially potent" French myths of assimilationism and nationalism to serve a new "common-sense" framework for citizenship politics. It reconstituted the institutionalized meanings that defined citizenship in France, while maintaining a distance from its problematic history. This reform phase more than any other phase formulated and legitimated a new "vocabulary of motives" (Mills 1984:13) or set of justifications for citizenship politics in France.[2]

The Fusion of National Identity and Pluralism

On June 22, 1987, Jacques Chirac installed the Nationality Commission, or as it quickly became known, the commission of experts ("commission des sages"). It was a nonpartisan, "perfectly independent" commission that "must not be submitted to influences of any sort" (*Le Quotidien de Paris* 6/23/87). Headed by the highest functionary of the French state (Marceau Long, Vice-President of the Council of State), the Commission was composed of two other state functionaries

(P. P. Kaltenbach and J. J. de Bresson), five law professors and one lawyer (B. Gold-man, P. Catala, Y. Loussouarn, J. Rivaro, and J. M. Varaut), three historians (P. Chaunu, H. Carrère d'Encausse, and E. B. Le Roy Ladurie), two sociologists (A. Touraine and D. Schnapper), two doctors (S. Kacet and L. Boutbien), and one filmmaker (H. Verneuil).[3] Four members were not French at birth.[4] While a majority came from the moderate Right, the members represented a wide range of the French political class. Chaunu (who just signed a petition for a restrictive reform), and Catala, were representative of the conservative Right, and Touraine and Schnapper, of the Left and center, respectively.[5]

During the summer of 1987, the newly formed Commission met almost weekly to learn about the code, discuss their opinions, and engage in extensive consultations with each of the ministries involved in nationality issues. In September and October, the Commission then held televised public hearings, the first of its kind in France, over the course of which they heard over fifty testimonies from a diversity of sources. The Commission continued to meet through November and December, discussing their recommendations, consulting with various ministries, and taking "field trips" to local bureaus and police stations which dealt with nationality requests. Finally, in early January 1988, the Commission delivered a two-volume report detailing their work, hearings, and recommendations to Prime Minister Chirac.

The Commission and its work highlighted many of the key paradoxes evident during the reform process. Substantive commonalities underlay polarized conflict. Bifurcated politics masked convergence. On the one hand, the Socialist party spokesman commented, "There cannot be possible convergences between those that rest in the straight line of our tradition and those that want to restrict access to French nationality. A consensus then must not be envisaged" (*Le Quotidien de Paris* 9/10/87). On the other hand, Chirac, in his installation speech, stressed the recast interpretation of the Right's voluntarist and communitarian priorities. He advised the commission to "avoid all systematic and brutal exclusion, and to the contrary, search for ways and means for a successful insertion in the French community," defined the "idea of 'voluntary choice' (as expressive of) the entire conception of nation," and rejected any nativist connotation of his government's proposals; "it was never a question . . . to have adopted dispositions depriving the nationality of notably the French Muslims of the second generation, those that one sometimes calls the 'Beurs' . . . or *even less* to exclude someone from the national community" (underlining in the original).[6]

Commonalities between the Right and Left were exposed quickly in the Commission. By September, the Commissioners expressed agreement on a wide array of issues: "We have already arrived at very similar conclusions," said one member. "Alain Touraine and me," proclaimed Chaunu, "represent the extremes, but let us say for 95 percent we are in accord." "There is not, between us," confirmed another member of the Commission, "ideological differences, our differences are only technical" (*L'Express* 9/17/87). Commission members envisioned their function less in terms of policy recommendations, and more in terms of their symbolic import. In a July meeting, Touraine claimed the "essential of this commission was not so much in submitting a report as in opening a debate before the country."[7] Or, given how the Commission would later frame the issues, closing a debate.

Since the debates redefining pluralism in the early 1980s, the Right and Left increasingly invoked competing definitions of nation and national identity. The commission set up its discussions of the code reform in terms of this preoccupation.[8] "What is most at issue in the current debates," writes Touraine in the fall of 1987, "is our image of the nation."[9] Already in July 1987, Touraine, who had previously commented on the loss of French national identity, focused on the need to strengthen the national identity.

> The immigrants of today are caught between an identity of departure and an identity of arrival: They must choose between them . . . let us not oppose the overture of the French society at any cost with the maintenance of its identity. It is false and dangerous to speak of mixture, even less the dissolution of nationality, a notion that would be out-of-date . . . the overture to newcomers must to the contrary enrich and reinforce our identity. (*Le Nouvel Observateur* 7/3–9/87)

"National identity is a bit of a myth," affirmed Marceau Long, "but in politics, myths count, they count a lot, more than reality" (Interview 1988). The Commission members—as evident in their internal discussions, public hearings, report, and subsequent interviews—interchanged two versions of the nation. The first recalled communitarian arguments, and the second the voluntarist arguments, which initially propelled the reform movement.[10]

The first version stressed a cultural understanding of the nation, and evoked a national communitarianism perspective. Elaborating the contours of the national identity meant a definition of the French nation in terms of its "history, values, and culture" which were determinant of that identity (Interview 1988, Long). Commissioner Goldman defined the national identity as "the language, the culture . . . to which one refers principally . . . fundamentally." To act and choose to be French implied a fundamental attachment to the national community, and the necessity for the citizenry to foster some degree of homogeneity. "This is not the renouncement of the culture of origin," Goldman continued, "but the primordial, even preeminent, reference to the French culture that founds the national identity" (*Plein Droit* 1988:23).[11] The conservative historian Chaunu's stress on "carnal ties" and "love for the land" evoked at times a type of essentialist communitarianism in his definitions of the nation (Interview 1988, Chaunu).[12] The other version stressed "the elective conception of the nation," invoking a positive voluntarism that slipped into assimilationism. The national identity is "the consciousness that our life is associated to the collectivity where we find our-selves," asserted Touraine, and in continuing, he paraphrased Renan, "It is the de-sire to live together" (*Plein Droit* 1988:27). Even as he stressed the cultural aspects of the national identity, Goldman too argued that "the identity is the adhesion to a certain number of values, the fundamental principles of the French society" (Ibid.:23).

In contrast to the bifurcated conflict over the code, what was innovative in the Commission was its ability to create a false center. A key presumption of the Commission was that a strong espousal of a combined communitarian and vol-untarist argument ought to operate as a consensual basis for the Right and Left. Commission members were seemingly unburdened by history, even as they re-called and employed it. Employing the two major arguments underlying the orig-inal impulse to reform the code, the Commission recast them in inclusive and positive terms. Unlike Rightist politicians, the Commission was not burdened with a recent history of restrictive politics. Anchored in its vision of the nation, the Commission privileged the defense of the national identity. Unlike the Left, it was not burdened with a recent history of ambiguities and ambivalence. At the same time, the Commission based its logic on the refashioned pluralism of the eighties shaped by both the Right and Left.

Commission members deliberately situated themselves at counterpoint with earlier differentialist and multicultural visions of French society. Marceau Long explained the Commission's emphasis on the national identity as part of "the cli-mate of the epoch," in which the notion of "multi-cultural society played a cer-tain role" as a destructive influence (Interview 1988, Long). Dominique Schnapper described the Commission's position as symbolizing a dual evolution in French politics: "The Right admitted the massive fact of the definitive presence of Maghrebis, the acculturation of the generation educated in France, and the ne-cessity to do all to integrate them. The Left, it renounced the mirages of multi-culturalism" (1988:61). During the public hearings in 1987, Alain Touraine dismissed both multiculturalism and the idea that "everyone is French, we are all the same, this is the grand melting-pot. This is not serious! As for a purely multi-cultural France, I would say: this is not serious either. No-one desires the liban-ization of France" (Long 1988, vol. 1:408–409). P. P. Kaltenbach encapsulated the historical myth of assimilationist France: All the foreigners were good to take and to assimilate. Because is also a prodigious system of swallowing other cultures. At the interior of the country, the folklores disappeared. One can deplore it, but this is our specificity; this is the free desire that made the French nation, and not the land or blood (*Témoignage Chrétien* 1/18–24/88).

The Commission's vision of the nation privileged sameness over difference, of a pluralism subsumed under the particularistic national identity. Touraine ad-mitted that while "at the moment of the emergence of the Beur movement, I was very sympathetic to the theme of cultural identity . . . I thought it was good to defend first the difference. I must recognize that I was wrong" (*Plein Droit* 1988:27). He claimed that in "a world of transnational cultural assimilation and weak social integration," a strong national identity was necessary (Ibid.). P. Catala explicitly pointed out the implications of the particularistic pluralism espoused by the Commission:

> It is then up to the Commission to affirm that the French nationality law is at the service of the French nation, that its continuity implies a rejection of a multicultural society and the maintenance of a community of culture. Such an affirmation in no way implies the closing of France to exterior contribution . . . it leads simply to control the migratory flux . . . to favor its integration, and to consecrate this by the attribution or acquisition of the nationality.[13]

The Commission members articulated the redefined pluralism which had emerged from the debates over the national identity in the mid-1980s. They also extended it. According to Schnapper, in 1984 and 1985, the "left-wing and centrist Jacobins" still formally subscribed to some form of "multiculturalism," which they defined as a celebration of the existing diversity within the national unity. But Schnapper underscored how the Commission made explicit that "the choice is not between . . . 'multicultural society' and . . . 'the national identity.'" The Commission's perspective insisted on a fusion of the national identity and pluralism to the extent that the national identity could only generate a particularized pluralism and limited universalism. According to Schnapper, "France is historically founded . . . on the synthesis between national identity and the contributions of immigrant populations—on an affirmed will and political unity, and the respect in the private order of particular specificities and loyalties."[14]

National Identity and Concerns About European Integration

Certainly, the overall stress on the national identity and a limited model of pluralism was buttressed by concerns for the need to defend the French national identity in the face of a unifying Europe. In one of the Commission's meetings during the summer, Alain Touraine noted that "European integration renders the conception of the French identity less clear than the past."[15] In his installation of the Commission, Chirac requested that the commission "integrate in your reflection the date of 1992."[16] Catala, who placed particular emphasis on the necessity of a reform in light of the coming European integration, wrote, "France is a country in transit between an Empire that has unraveled and a Europe that is organizing itself . . . in this difficult passage, France must preserve more than ever an identity, of which Europe will have need as much as itself."[17] The Commission's report echoed his concerns, situating French nationality policies on a path between "an Empire that has been effaced and an Europe in construction" (Long 1988, vol. 2:102). During the hearings, one scholar claimed "the French identity seems to me to be much more menaced by the globalization of culture or by Europe than by the 'Beurs,'" though he subsequently situated the Franco-Maghrebis as an important challenge as well (Long 1988, vol. 1:142–143).[18] During an interview, Carrère d'Encause juxtaposed the defense of the national identity with 1992, claiming when "the frontiers will be open . . . all our relations to our identity . . . will be overturned" (*Le Matin* 10/21/87).

Long, as head of the commission, gave the European dimension particular attention.[19] He explicitly linked the reinforcement of French national identity with a European counterpart, calling for a form of "European citizenship" within the European Community (*Libération* 2/17/88). If, in the long term, Long could envision a European citizenship, in which citizenship and nationality were disassociated, in the short term, he situated the idea as an extension of or complement to the French national identity, not as an alternative to French conceptions of national membership. Long's discussion of a European citizenship was limited to encompassing those with the "same religion, mores, fashion of living" as the French, excluding for him non-Europeans, in particular "Muslims" (Interview 1988).

Within the context of these superimposed debates (European integration and the nationality code), the historian and demographer, Hervé Le Bras, argued "the crisis comes neither from the code, nor foreigners, but from the concept of nationality and the transformation of the nation . . . consequently isn't the reform of the code a deception to dissimulate (this) crisis . . . a way out to not have to deal with the real question: what will remain of the nation, of the nations, in a multicultural Europe?" (*Libération* 9/30/87).[20] But Long's presentation of a European citizenship as an extension of French identity resonated with the majority of French public opinion. In a *Eurobaramètre* poll of March 1987, only 13 percent of the French respondents saw European unity as meaning "the end of national identity," while 72 percent saw European unity as a way of defending the French national identity and interests (*Eurobaramètre* March 1987:10). Other Commission members too rejected that there was a contradiction "between a reinforcement of the French identity and this eventual emergence," that is, of a unified Europe (Goldman in *Plein Droit* 1988:24; Schnapper 1991).

The Commission members believed that the task of defending the national identity meant that their articulation of it must be given "a real form."[21] They translated their priority to reinforce the national identity into a framework that necessitated the national integration of immigrants and valorized a voluntarist citizenship. "We fell very quickly in agreement on the fact that the legislation could only be integrationist," described Schnapper, "it had to rest on the means of consecrating or of encouraging the integration of foreign populations durably installed in France. We were also in agreement to think that this integration must be conscious and voluntary, and there was no opposition but complementarity between a strong [national] identity affirmation and a generous overture" (1988:59; cf. Chaunu in *Le Figaro* 2/17/88).

Reinforcing National Identity and National Integration

In drafting it final report, the Commission placed the injunction that "nationality policy can and must play a decisive role in the process of integration" as one of their guiding principles. Importantly, the integration referred to was understood to be a national integration (Long 1988, vol. 2:85–87).[22] The term, *national integration*, has historically referred to the process of "ethnicization of the polity," which involved "the construction and transmission of a strong sense of the common identity . . . the spread of common cultural forms" (Grillo 1980:7–8). Even as it rejected the traditional French "assimilationist" model and myth, the Commission recalled the power of that imagery:[23] France, "inheritor of a secular, cultural and political centralization . . . was occupied by instinct to transform [its] foreigners into French citizens, speaking *the same language,* sharing the *same* cultural and patriotic *values,* participating in the national life like the others, *even if they retain in the private order their religious and cultural loyalties*" (underlining in the original).[24]

The logic for a national integration of immigrants was constructed from three, interrelated arguments. National integration of immigrants was an integral part of the defense of the national identity, both because it was product of the French tradition of nationhood, and because of the weakened and limited French capacity for integration. National integration was the mode by which to manage the Maghrebi, Muslim immigration, which was constituted as a challenge. Finally, it was the emergent, commonsensical route being taken by the immigrants themselves. The logic behind these arguments differed along political commitments. Their articulations variously expressed the underlying voluntarist, communitarian, and nativist arguments of the nationality code debates.

Above all, the defense of the national identity framed the need for a national integration of immigrants. Privileging the nation meant to "pose as a central principle that the integration of immigrants will be that much easier as the awareness (conscience) of the identity of the French nation will be reinforced . . . the integration of immigrants must be constantly associated with the affirmation of the national identity," Touraine wrote to his colleagues.[25] In the first public hearing held by the Commission, Touraine summarized the testimony of a representative from the Ministry of Social Affairs as a confirmation that "a fundamental objective for our country is to reinforce its identity in reinforcing and accelerating the integration of a great number of foreigners" (Long 1988, vol. 1:69). The equation — stronger national identity equals easier integration of immigrants — became the leitmotif of the Commission, and its report. According to Commission members, the idea of stronger national identity presupposed a voluntarist and communitarian model of the nation, which enforced the general will and homogenized (to some extent) the citizenry. Commissioner Goldman argued "the integration supposes a power of absorption. It supposes that that which integrates has the possibility of transmitting its moral, cultural values, etc." (*Plein Droit* 1988:23). In drafting their final report, the Commission underscored that "national identity and integration must be correlated . . . It (integration) must not be nourished by a weakening of the national identity. The French 'creuset' can only play its role if the French identity exercises a strong attraction, and for that, it is still necessary that it be firm (ferme)."[26]

These arguments for a national integration relied partly on interpretations of the French model and traditions of nationhood. "What one is in the process of showing" claimed Commissioner Varaut, "is that the French model—at once a desire to live common values and an universalist overture—is the one which can realize the integration [of immigrants] without reducing it to the idea of territory or of blood" (*Le Quotidien de Paris* 10/23/87). The Commission's report asserted that legislation on nationality constituted "one of the means to at once encourage and consecrate this necessary process of francization" (Long 1988, vol. 1:25). These views were supported by the representatives of the state at the public hearings. The representative from the Ministry of Social Affairs opened his presentation by declaring that the nationality code had two objectives: "The first is to ensure the integration of foreigners who desire it and who merit it into French nationality. The second is to ensure the radiance and grandeur of France and contribute to this radiance" (Long 1988, vol. 1:60).

These interpretations insisted on an integration based on a model of cultural membership.[27] The published introduction of the Commission's report emphasizes that in the France, "national unity rests on cultural unity" (Long 1988, vol. 1:24). "It is necessary to be able to say to the immigrants: here is what you must accept, here is what you can remain yourselves," asserted Schnapper (*Plein Droit* 1988:25). The insistence on a national integration exposed how both the Left and Right used the republicanist and Jacobin ideologies, while referring to a doubled sided *volonté* (individual and national will). Thus, the conservative Commissioner Catala could second his fellow Commissioner Alain Touraine's equation of national identity and integration, saying simply "his demonstration is convincing, I have nothing to add there."[28] Other Commission members argued that the French model assumed the necessity for a certain amount of "assimilation" by the immigrant populations, and a rejection of any sort of public manifestation of difference.[29]

> An integration implies a minimum assimilation, and preparing, at medium or long term, for a definitive assimilation, that does not exclude the maintenance, in the background of particularism linked to

culture of origin, no more than the maintenance, throughout history, of the particularisms of the provinces, the Gascons, the Burgundians or Bretons compromised their insertion into the French ensemble. (Commissioner Rivaro)[30]

The insistence on national integration set itself off and indeed partly defined itself by a rejection of another type of integration, one based on an American model, or an ethnic politics style. As a sociologist, Alain Touraine would made sweeping generalizations about immigrant integration. "National integration is in effect one thing and social integration is another thing . . . and so in the United States, integration is accomplished by the society, in Europe integration is accomplished by the state" (Touraine in *Plein Droit* 1988:27). Elsewhere, Touraine contrasted those who would adopt a "laissez-faire" attitude toward the integration of immigrants, and those who "think it is necessary to organize in a conscious manner the transit from one membership, more national than cultural, to another national membership."[31] This distinction between social and national integration was buttressed by arguments that the French capacity for integration was weakened.[32] In identifying himself with the latter "conscious" approach, Touraine argued that France's integrationist institutions ("school," "church," "unions," etc.) "have largely lost their capacity for integration," and that the "laissez-faire" attitude would only "provoke serious social crises," leading to "American"-style ethnic strife and racial violence.[33] At the public hearings, the Commissioners looked on approvingly when one historian claimed the fundamental question was, "Do we still have enough interior institutions, the will to be French, to stay French, to transmit a certain number of values on which we are in agreement." The "principal problem . . . is in our capacity to be French" (Long 1988, vol. 1:78).

It is here that Touraine's equation that stronger national identity will translate into an easier integration of immigrants can be set more fully in context. Taking the perspective of a weakened national identity, assimilationist tradition of nationhood, and limited French integrationist capacity, the Commissioners formulated a comprehensively national, and not just social, integration of the immigrants as a necessity. Likewise, they could consider the religious and cultural particularities of the immigrants as menacing the integration process, just as in the past "all particularism . . . appeared as a menace to the national unity" (Long 1988, vol. 1:24). Indeed, the Commission's report argued that "this weakening of institutions and universalist values around which is elaborated the national tradition, and which permitted the integration of foreign populations over the course of the last two centuries constitutes a real danger to the national future." Even if nationality law cannot "refurnish the capacity for integration," the least it could do, the report seemed to imply, is to stress and insist on a national integration (Long 1988, vol. 1:28; vol. 2:44–46).[34]

Arguments about national identity and national integration then operated to legitimate and confirm that the integration of the Maghrebi, Muslim immigrants was a challenge best managed by national integration. On the whole, the Commission simultaneously re-enacted the immigrant challenge as inevitable, and national integration as the just solution. Commission members identified features of the contemporary immigration that were creating "new difficulties of integration." The role of Islam in France was a highly visible issue. Or, in so far as it was an increasingly non-European population, the contemporary immigrants were seen as "an immigration less sensitive to European influence" (Long 1988, vol. 2:43–50). The Commission called attention to "problems" of Islamic practices, including polygamy, and the lack of public-private division. They claimed, as Touraine put it, that these problems are to be addressed by referring "to the general principle . . . the integration of immigrants must be constantly associated with the affirmation of the French identity." For example, given that "monogamy (is) one of the elements of this identity, it is appropriate to oppose very firmly the extension of the collective effect (Article 84) to the ensemble of children of a naturalized polygamist."[35] Certainly, such concerns retained a nativist cast in some Commissioner's discourses. The "grand question," according to Commissioner LeRoy Ladurie, was "Is the African immigration, in the large sense, assimilable?" (*Le Matin* 10/21/87).

In important ways, the commission's stress on national integration benefited from the changing structure of political opportunities of the mid-eighties that led to the move from differentialist to integrationist themes. At the public hearings, most of the representatives of immigrant associations, and their social support network emphasized integrationist goals. These associations situated their appeals within French traditions of nationhood. Their representatives made sure to invoke Renan's definition of the nation, and reject a differentialist approach. Though the integrationist orientation did not fully represent the Maghrebi or "Beur" movement, it did reflect the growing predominance of the integrationist oriented associations in French politics. An antiracist pro–equal rights march organized by SOS-Racisme in November 1987 affirmed this evolution. The march's central theme was integration: "Our choice is the integration as the essential value of the communal life" (*Le Monde* 9/24/87; *Le Matin de Paris*, 10/20/87; *Libération*, 10/21/87).[36]

The nationality code debates further strengthened the position of the integrationists. Certainly, most of the immigrant activists and associations selected to testify before the Commission were visibly integrationist. Immigrant associations pursuing other more differentialist agendas were not active participants in the process. Discussing "where the Beur movement went," *IM'media* editor, Mognis Abdallah argued "the Beur associations are paying the consequences of their playing the ostrich vis-à-vis the debate on the nationality code . . . under the pretext that it is an affair 'Franco-French'" (*IM'media* 1987:9). Even when advocating a reform of the code so that automatic attribution at birth of French citizenship applies to all those born in the territory ("absolute *jus soli*"), as France-Plus and SOS-Racisme did, the associations testifying before the commission embraced a form of national integration. Harlem Desir of SOS-Racisme defined integration as

> the refusal of this perversion of the right to difference that institutes different laws for people of different origins . . . the Republic is just the possibility for men and women of different origins, different cultures to live according to common values, to adhere to principles of common laws, to be submitted to the same responsibilities with, in counterpart, the same rights. (Long 1988, vol. 1:558–559)

Arezki Dahmani, the president of France-Plus, argued that France does not need a "code of nationality" but rather "a code of integration . . .

> what we call for today is the right to resemblance. This right to resemblance poses the problem of identity, What is for us the identity? Is it the beret and the baguette? Is it a manner of eating? No. Our values, these are the values of the French revolution. Our values are the values of secularity. Our values are the values of democracy. We adhere to that totally. It is that for us. We adhere to a system of values that is by the way a universal system, that is no longer today only that of France, since many people were inspired by this movement . . . the movement we develop today is a movement that adheres totally to the values of the French revolution, to republican values. (Long 1988, vol. 1:473–474).

The public hearings revealed the extent to which France-Plus and SOS-Racisme "disputed the same topics, applied the same recipes for a strangely similar discourse on integration and republican values" (*IM'media* 1987:9). Other immigrant associations argued as well that the process of national integration was already well underway.[37] As part of a group representing the Jeunes Arabs de Lyon (JALB), the clergyman, Delorme alluded to Renan's definition in declaring that "the belonging to the nation is the ratification of every day, and I believe that the youth issued from immigration practice this ratification like all the others" (Long 1988, vol. 1:407).

The integrationist appeals played a crucial role in naturalizing the Commission's priority of national integration, making it seem as part of the common sense of the times. I use the term *naturalizing* to refer to the way in which integrationist themes were recalled by the Commission so that they could interpret national integration as a part of a natural process in which to practice citizenship in France. Despite the fact that integration was clearly articulated as a priority in the Commission from their first meetings in the summer, Commission members denied that the focus on integration came from within. Instead, the Commission stressed how the priority of integration was imposed by the immigrants and minorities themselves:

> The word and idea of integration appeared progressively and was imposed upon us as the hearings advanced. But this integration must translate into a voluntary adhesion in the sense that Renan defined the nation. I note that it was M. Adj Sari of the Mosque of Paris who cited Renan: "the nation is a soul, a spiritual principle, the desire clearly expressed to continue the common life." (Varaut in *Le Quotidien de Paris* 10/21/91)

> It is necessary certainly to defend difference, but I realized during the *l'Heure de Vérité* of Harlem Desire [TV interview show on which Desire spoke] that it was correct to privilege the theme of integration, and this for reasons associated with the Le Pen phenomena. (Touraine in *Plein Droit* 1988:27)

> I was on the defensive, I didn't believe in the immigrants' desire for assimilation. But, I heard sincere men who convinced me. (Chaunu in *L'Express* 10/23/87)

During the hearings, the Commission consistently synthesized the testimonies referring to integration. Already, in the second day of hearings held by the Commission on September 18, Carrère d'Encausse remarked, "It seems to me that one is observing all the same more a search for the right to integration than of the right to difference" (Long 1988, vol. 1:138). Commissioners Verneuil and Kaltenbach declared that the hearings reinforced their conviction of "assimilation at all costs" (*L'Express* 10/23/87). A draft of the Commission's final report stated bluntly, "to note, in particular, that the word 'integration' is used unanimously today. At right, there is no longer the question of assimilation. At left, one no longer extols the 'right to difference.' "[38] The press too reported the consensus on integration as a "novelty," a new trend emerging from the hearings: "The accent is put henceforth on integration of immigrants and their children. It appears more and more that a nationality code can only have this as its first objective" (*Le Monde* 10/17/87). "The work of the commission will have shown that nationality—by blood or territory—is only part of the problem. Integration is the indispensable corollary of citizenship" (*L'Express* 10/23/87).

The processes by and through which the Commission accomplished its work certainly played a critical role in shaping the reconstruction of citizenship. To return to the language of spectacles, I would argue that two episodes in particular within the larger spectacle of the Commission's public hearings enabled the Commission to effectively "seize control of the interpretations" (Rogin 1990:107) of immigration and citizenship, and recast them in terms of a national integration. The first episode can be entitled, "Chaunu's tears," and the second, the "spontaneous consensus." "Chaunu's tears" took place when Pierre Chaunu dissolved into tears while listening to a tale of love and woe told during the public hearings by a "harki" (Harkis refers to those Algerians who fought for France during the 1962 war, and were then repatriated to France). It was a tale of love and desire for France through endured suffering and discrimination at the hands of France.

Chaunu's tears permitted the covert display of French enabling myths of paternalistic universalism, and assimilationist nationalism.[39] His tears displayed an "imperialist nostalgia" for French colonialist history, to use Renato Rosaldo's term (1989).[40] Yet Chaunu's own interpretation of his experience as the turning point in his decision to wholeheartedly support a nonrestrictive, inclusive, voluntarist acquisition permitted a "forgetting" of these desires (Interview 1988). In other words, a conservative paternalism and communitarianism were articulated as a liberal, modernizing politics of citizenship.

The "spontaneous consensus" took place on the last day of the hearings. This last day was nontelevised, and featured, finally, representatives of the Portuguese communities, the population actually most affected by a revision of Article 44. In reaction to Roger Errera, an official of the Council of State, the Commission members "spontaneously" resolved the problem of a voluntarist acquisition of citizenship for the youth of Article 44. Their solution was to institute a system by which these youth would "ask" for French citizenship between the ages of sixteen to eighteen, no restrictions being placed on this request; conversely, parents would no longer be able to request French citizenship for their minor children, and after eighteen years, the restrictions of Article 79 and so on would again apply.[41] Errera (the State) played the "straight man," while the conservative Pierre Chaunu, and the centrist Helen Carrère d'Encausse who became French through Article 44 enacted the innovators "against the State," in classic French tradition. Pierre-Patrick Kaltenbach (a higher state functionary than Errera) played the facilitator, while Salem Kacet, the naturalized French Algerian, assumed the role of interpreter:

CARRÈRE D'ENCAUSSE: What do you think of a system where to sixteen to eighteen year olds, one would pose the question "do you want to be French?" . . .

P. P. KALTENBACH: Rather than "do you want to be French?," one could put "I do not refuse to be it". . . .

CHAUNU: It would suffice, for example, a form with two columns with the formula "delete where applicable."

KACET: One is living an extraordinary moment. One proposes nothing less than to liberalize Article 44.

ROGER ERRERA: This system proposed in collaboration between Helen Carrère d'Encausse and Pierre Chaunu . . .

KACET: It is rather a co-production.

KALTENBACH (totally hilarious): A monstrous coupling!

ERRERA: This is not a very dignified way to become French.

CHAUNU (indignant): This is a very good system. One says, "yes, I want to become," and it is definitive. (*Libération* 10/22/87; *Le Quotidien de Paris* 10/22/87)

Even as one part of the state vaguely protested (Ererra), the other part (Kaltenbach) assisted with the "birth" of a liberalizing politics of citizenship, as conceived by the conservative and naturalized French, and approved by the immigrant.

To use Rogin's terminology of political spectacles, this scene at once displayed the "enabling" myths of the French assimilationist model, and "buried" the problematic of assimilationist voluntarism (Rogin 1990). Elusively present in this exchange was Carrere d'Encausse's own description, presented earlier in the hearings, of her history of becoming French through Article 44: "I am very attached to France, at times one even reproaches me for my outdated nationalism" (Long 1988, vol. 1). By the end of the day, assimilationist imperatives were articulated as a liberalizing politics of citizenship.

Stripped down, the convergence on integration exposed the already increasing commonalities in rhetorical logic and themes between the Right and the Left, even if their intentions were dissimilar and political immigration agendas divergent. "I felt totally in accord with his basic analysis of immigration," commented the conservative director and editorialist for *Le Figaro*, L. Pauwels about Harlem Desir's interview on *L'Heure de la Vérité*, "Simply I do not understand how one passes without transition from the call for a multicultural France to the principle of assimilation. In any case, if it is sincere, I rejoice in this evolution." Then Pauwels continued, raising explicitly his understanding of how the priority of national integration implicated a particularized and limited definition of pluralism:

> The grand debate remains nonetheless that of assimilation. I say to Harlem Desir that there exists a European culture and specificity, that if one does not want to become another American peninsula, if one has for Europe another dream than to make it an immense New York, one must take care. The assimilation has been, in the past, a great French quality. This must not become the instrument of a melting pot. (*L'Express* 10/2/87)

The argument that national integration implied some form of assimilation and adherence to French particularities resonated with the Commission's perspective. It too assumed a process by which immigrants agreed to integrate, agreed to enter within French nationality, at which point their ability to appeal to difference was sharply limited. Consider one of Touraine's interventions during the hearings that took place just a few days after Pauwels' comments were published. Questioning the degree to which an immigrant activist from JALB actually was endorsing integration or voicing a more differentialist politics, Touraine rejected the idea of a "purely multicultural France" or France as a "grand melting pot," and then explained his position:

> I would say that it seems to me shocking enough to appeal to a Portuguese, Turk, Algerian, Moroccan identity or what have you, and at the same time to call for automaticity [of citizenship acquisition] . . . in this particular case, within French nationality, since this has not been posed, but it could be posed outside of French nationality. I think it is essential to realize that we are not living in an American illusion of the nineteenth century where the people come from nowhere, and go towards the land of the New World. (Long 1988, vol. 1:409)

Touraine's remarks capture the premise of the nationalist defense of citizenship formulated by the commission. The premise was that the space "within French nationality" needed to be defended and delimited in terms of a French particularized identity. Accompanying the premise was an underlying aura of challenge or menace. If French citizenship was not reconstructed in this manner, the French would lose their identity, they would fall into the trap of an "American illusion." The premise formed the basis of the Commission's formulation of a national identity fused with a particularistic pluralism and a strong national integration, a formulation articulated in voluntarist and communitarian terms. This framework enabled the transformation of the commonalities between the Right and Left from the paradoxical components of a polarized politics to becoming part of commonsensical understandings of French citizenship and pluralism.

Elective Conception of the Nation and a Voluntarist Citizenship

The fusion of national identity and pluralism followed by the assumption of national integration laid the groundwork for the third component of the Commission's recommendations: voluntarist citizenship. The Commission's endorsement of a voluntarist acquisition of citizenship for youth born in France of noncitizen parents (Article 44) was constructed on the basis of four arguments. A voluntarist citizenship conformed best to French republicanist and Jacobinist traditions of nationhood, and thus to French understandings of citizenship and national identity. It encouraged the national integration of immigrants. It addressed the concerns of the modern trend privileging human and individual rights. Finally, a voluntarist citizenship complemented a mitigated statism. As with the defense of the national identity and the calls for a national integration of immigrants, the appeal for a voluntarist citizenship exposed the existing commonalities between Left and Right, and extended them.

The question of voluntarism was always central in the commission. Whereas the reform's opponents had attempted to recenter the reform around the question of exclusion/inclusion, the Commission rejected that approach, and situated the reform around the question of voluntarism. They considered the choice of enforcing or not a voluntarist citizenship as the "fundamental" component of the debates.[42] Despite disagreements within the Commission over questions of dual nationality, Article 79 (list of convictions preventing the acquisition of citizenship), and fraud (paper marriages), there was agreement by the end of the summer — before the public hearings — to modify Article 44. "The members of the commission thought it desirable," summarized a September 9 Commission report, "to increase the part of individual choice (desire) in the determination of nationality, and to avoid cases of automatic acquisition and loss of nationality . . . a trend is clearly manifest in favor of a positive choice clearly expressing the desire to become French."[43]

The Commission claimed that a voluntarist citizenship best conformed to French republicanist, political-cultural traditions of nationhood (Long 1988, vol. 2:89–90). In contrast, to earlier interpretations of the French "tradition" employed to reject a reform, the Commission's draft report claimed that "the inherited tradition . . . of Renan, according to which a *nation is constituted by the desire and free consent of individual . . .* implies that one demands of individuals a *clear adhesion to the values* of the French society and to the rules of laws that it entails"; at the same time, the "host society" must take into account "the expressed desire and render possible integration by an active policy of accompaniment leaving place for a tolerance with respect to certain cultural differences" (underlining in original).[44]

During the hearings, the participants from the Right and Left overlapped in their support of a voluntarist citizenship. Each side recalled arguments voiced in the initial phases of the code conflict about French traditions, adherence to a double-sided desire or will (*volonté*) the need to revalorize national belonging, and the problem of a commodified citizenship. The Left-identified philosopher Alain Finkielkraut argued strongly that a voluntarist citizenship was grounded in the French "elective" tradition of nationhood, which he opposed to ethnic conceptions of the nation: "In reversing the automatic acquisition to a voluntarist act, one would be faithful to the elective tradition that made of the nation a pact, a secular association" (Long 1988, vol. 1:595–596; *Libération* 10/17–18/87). Adding that the state should not have discretionary power over this positive act, Finkielkraut argued a reversal of positions had taken place, given that Left traditionally supported voluntarist understandings of citizenship.[45] His testimony elicited the ambiguous and ambivalent positions that those on the Left held about voluntarist citizenship. Some expressed support for a "positive voluntarism," while others rejected the need for it. Some critiqued the "passeiste" reading of the nation, others voiced a republican communitarianism. (*Libération* 10/20/87). Many, including the Commission members, applauded Finkielkraut's interpretations. The Commission's report singled out his testimony as informing their thinking, and organized their arguments for a voluntarist citizenship around his claims (Long 1988, vol. 2:89–90; cf. *L'Express* 10/23/87).[46]

The Commissioners consistently referred to both the collective will and individualist logic of *volonté*. "There is less difference than one says between Renan [i.e., political-cultural conception of nation] and the German thinkers [i.e., ethnocultural ones]," asserted Touraine, "both conceptions of nation are two different forms of the same general principle of (*volonté*)."[47] Touraine, like others on the commission, insistently invoked this principle during the public hearings, asking, for example, "Aren't we headed for a new conception of nationality around voluntarism?" (Long 1988, vol. 1:122–123). He linked defense of national identity to an affirmation of a voluntarist citizenship, so that "we advance toward a more positive conception of our nationality" (*Le Nouvel Observateur* 7/3–9/87).

The blurred divisions between the proponents and opponents of the earlier code reform were often pronounced during the hearings. Pierre-Bloch, president of the antiracist organization, LICRA, firmly upheld the idea of a revalorized citizenship, evoking as well the dual imagery of individual voluntarism and collective will.

> It is an honor to be French and it is not a dishonor to ask to become it ... we think that the nationality code must be rethought, revised, and if a certain number of youth actually want to be French it is necessary to facilitate for them the thing, this is incontestable, but inversely, it is necessary, in order to become French, to prove one wants to become French, that one is assimilated and one really wants to become French. (Long 1988, vol. 1:394, 396)[48]

Following Pierre-Bloch, representatives from the conservative Club 89 also cited Renan as they declared in remarkably similar arguments that it is

> necessary that (the youth born in France of foreign parents) opt for our nationality; it is for them to decide that they are linked to our country. It is not a matter of closing the doors, but it is a matter of opening the doors to those who want it, who manifest clearly for it, and who merit it." (Long 1988, vol. 1:418–419)

Commenting on the juxtaposition of testimonies, the newspaper *Libération* noted that "it was only a few years ago that the propositions of this club [Club 89] seemed close to the theses of the extreme right. Today, they nearly seem accepted as postulates" (10/7/87). Chaunu epitomized a form of this convergence, arguing that adhesion to the nation must be translated by a "positive act, but without conditions of exclusion . . . all this must be done with precaution and finally a lot of love" (*Le Matin* 10/21/8).

Support for the national integration of immigrants buttressed the call for a positive acquisition of citizenship. Many argued that a positive step, particularly one with no restrictions placed on it, was opportune as a means to help ensure integration. When Marceau Long asked a French historian "if the voluntary choice in your opinion is a factor of exclusion or of insertion facilitating integration," the reply was "I am more favorable to a rite of voluntary passage" (Long 1988, vol. 1:82–83). The report confirmed "that, on this point, the representative associations . . . notably those of youth issued from immigration, have manifested their accord with clarity" (Long 1988, vol. 2:90). Subsidiary arguments that voluntarism conformed with the progressive conception of nationality and human rights also reinforced support for a positive step. That logic shifted the emphasis from a collective national interest to the individual interest, drawing on human rights discourse. "To assure that the acquisition of nationality corresponds with an expressed desire is a progress in the way of human rights," asserted LICRA president, Pierre-Bloch. The Commission consistently pointed to this logic of a voluntarist citizenship: "To chose and not submit to nationality, this is a human right," affirmed Varaut (*Le Matin* 10/21/87).[49]

Most dissenting views of the construction of this voluntarist conception of citizenship—all views that questioned the extent it conformed to French traditions of nationhood, actually was beneficial to immigrant populations, or expressive of human rights concerns—were shunted aside during the hearings.[50] Danielle Lochak, the president of the immigrant legal aid association, Groupe d'information et de soutien des travailleurs immigrés (GISTI), forcefully denounced the logic of the voluntarist conception of citizenship: "One hears since a while ago talk of free choice, voluntary adhesion. To choose is more modern, this is the ideology of human rights. But, this is the very type of a false just idea" (Long 1988, vol. 1). On the Commission, Goldman was the most articulate dissenter of the need for a positive demand for citizenship, refuting in his internal memoranda to the Commission that the idea that a human rights outlook supported the idea of a positive step. Goldman preferred a "negative" step, that is, permitting these youth to decline French nationality, which addressed the same concerns just as well.[51] But, by the end of the Commission, Goldman too actively supported a voluntarist citizenship, referring to both logics—that of national integration and individualism.

The individualist logic played a dual function in the Commission's report. Certainly, the support for the principle of individualism helped to buttress support for a voluntarist citizenship. Beyond that, the Commissioners also used the logic of individualism to situate their report as a critique of blind statism and a call for mitigated statism. This position found broad appeal with those in the Left and center, who may have espoused a statist Jacobin model of national membership, but simultaneously sought to limit the state's "triage" capacity to choose among immigrants. The Commission claimed that privileging individual choice would mean a diminishment of previous state power. "For a long time, liberty was exercised by procuration: the state chose for its citizens, the husband, for the wife, the parents for the adolescents. This time is over, obliging the state to release more personal liberty. From the time the existence of a choice is acknowledged, it is necessary to permit the individual to exercise it" (Long 1988, vol. 2:98). In January, amidst the initial reactions to the Commission, Touraine stated, "The governing idea of the Commission is that the 'volonté' of the person . . . must be substituted in place of the demographic and military interests of the state" (*Le Nouvel Observateur* 1/8–14/88). The Commission expanded their critique of French statism by calling for more "transparency" in administrative procedures. Its recommendations suggested some decentralization in handling nationality requests and cases, and in general, noted the need for less arbitrariness and discretionary power in the state's decision-making process (Long 1988, vol. 2:98–101, 146–154).

It is useful to note that despite the growing convergence within the political class, public opinion defined the issues of the code reform and voluntarism along partisan lines. Public opinion polls in the fall of 1987 indicated that support for a reform had somewhat declined, as there was not a clear majority of French who thought that "one accords French nationality too easily"; in a *Paris Match*–BVA poll taken in September, 48 percent of the respondents agreed with the statement. This division was significantly skewed when partisan affiliation was taken into account, with 64 percent of the right electorate believing French nationality was accorded too easily, and 67 percent supportive of the government's reform project, while only 39 percent of the left electorate believe the current system was too easy, and only 24 percent supportive of the government's project. As important, regardless of the saliency of the nationality code for the political class, a significant proportion of the respondents in the poll, 32 percent, had never heard of the reform project (*Paris-Match* 10/8/87).

Reaffirming and Resituating the Statist Perspective

Despite its critique of state practices, the Commission clearly reaffirmed the necessity for a statist perspective on nationality. It did so through a series of arguments and propositions. On a general level, the Commission's constant stress on the national identity and national integration defined these processes as framed by the state, and not society. As noted earlier, commission members contrasted an American societal generated social integration with the French model of state-directed integration. They contrasted ethnic definitions of the nation with the French model of the nation organized around the state (cf. Leca 1985). They privileged the particularized French pluralism, while rejecting other approaches to pluralism, including ethnic, transnational, or multicultural forms of pluralism as not reliant on the state or "nation." On specific issues, their statist perspective translated into propositions calling for the renegotiation of the Algerian-French military service accord, the limiting of voting rights by dual nationals, the retention of Article 79, and the firm rejection of a form of "absolute" territorial right to citizenship (Long 1988, vol. 2:157–185).

Not surprisingly, the Commission also resituated the statist perspective; its recommendations expressed different priorities from those articulated by the earlier reform project of the Ministry of Justice. The commission expressed must succinctly the views and specific priorities of the Council of State. Though the Commission urged, in contrast to the Council of State's decision in 1986, the reform of the nationality code, its most significant innovation from the previous proposals was its formulation of an inclusive and integrationist idiom anchored in the national terrain. The emphasis on such an idiom clearly complemented the Council of State's perspective. The linkages between the Commission and the Council of State were great. Besides being directed by Long, the Vice-President of the Council of State, the Commission used, as its chief staff the staff and lawyers of the Council of State (Interviews, staff of the Nationality Commission). Its report demonstrated concern for a "national interest," the goal to "francisize" the immigrants. The provisions elaborating on changes in administrative procedure reflected a willingness to displace some authority from the Ministries of Justice and Interior, perhaps indicative in certain respects of the ongoing disputes between these parts of the state.[52] Officials at the Ministries of Justice and Foreign Relations, in particular, expressed disagreement with several of the Commission's provisions, including their recommendations to renegotiate the French-Algerian military service accord and limit voting rights for dual nationals (Interviews, Ministries of Justice, Foreign Relations).[53]

In the end, the National Commission on Nationality, or Commission des Sages as the press called it, presented a reconstructed French citizenship on the basis of their defense of the national identity, insistence on a national integration of immigrants, valorization of a voluntarist citizenship, and reaffirmation of a statist perspective. Given their recommendations, it was unclear to what extent the Commission, in fact, rejected much of the driving motivation of the earlier restrictive revision attempts.[54] Despite their inclusionary idiom, the Commission proposed revising the acquisition of citizenship to make it more voluntaristic, similar to other previous proposals. It too subscribed to the logic of strengthening the national identity. It too fashioned voluntarist and communitarian arguments within the limits of a particular French pluralism.

On January 7, 1988, Marceau Long, accompanied by the other members of the Commission, handed a two-volume report (which included a transcription of the hearings and their own recommendations for a code reform) to Prime Minister Chirac. The report set forth the Commission's three guiding principles: nationality legislation can and must play a positive role in the integration process; national identity and integration must be correlated because the integration of immigrants will be much easier when the consciousness of the French national identity is stronger; and the French conception of the nation privileges a voluntarist citizenship (Long 1988, vol. 2:82–90). To the great surprise of many, the commission had reached a unanimous consensus on its recommendations.

Reactions to the Commission's Report

The immediate reaction to the Commission's report and recommendations on January 7 was general acclaim across the political spectrum. Those in the Right, Left, immigrant association movement, and their support network greeted the Commission's conclusions favorably. In a sense, the reactions echoed the unexpected consensus "found" by the Commission. The most visible exceptions were labeled "extremes" in the press. The National Front on the one hand, and SOS-Racisme on the other, both issued statements rejecting the Commission's conclusions (*Le Figaro* 1/9–10/88; *Le Monde* 1/11/88). The Communist party and certain of the antiracist organizations expressed even harsher reservations about the Commission.

The focal point of reaction was the consensus. "A sort of miracle: who would have said this only a few months ago that such an explosive subject would have given place to as large a consensus" (*Libération* 1/8/88; see also *Le Monde* 1/11/88; *Réforme* 1/16/88; *Démocratie Moderne* 1/14/88; *Le Figaro* 1/9/88). Indeed, the consensus marked a turning point in the interpretations of French citizenship politics. Previously the focus centered on the polarization of the Right and Left. Now, the consensus provided the French public and political class with the space to recognize the commonalities and convergences that had begun emerging years earlier with the debates over refashioning pluralism and privileging the national identity. The consensus is "result of convergent evolutions," summarized the moderate Right politician, Michel Hannoun in *Le Figaro* (2/12/88). The Socialists' support of the commission's report was interpreted as a confirmation of both the Left's rupture with the differentialist pluralism of the early eighties, and its emergent preoccupation with the national identity. "The left has abandoned the idea of a multi-cultural France which was dangerous," claimed Touraine (*Libération* 1/8/88). An editorial in the *Libération*, agreed that the Left "already has done without the hasty concept of 'multiculture' and, habituated by the internationalist tradition to relativize national belonging, it had to accept to revalorize the idea of nationality" (Ibid.). The Right's (RPR and UDF) support of the Commission's report was interpreted as a confirmation of their recognition that immigrants were in France to stay, and of the need to "adapt and modernize" the code to meet the new realities (*Libération* 1/8/88).

The consensus of January 1988 crystallized the commonalities between the Right and Left. These commonalities revolved around a refashioned pluralism, a redeveloped voluntarism and communitarian republicanism. Beyond recognizing the rejection of multiculturalism and the necessity of national integration, commentators in the Left and Right synthesized these commonalities as constitutive of a new framework for immigration and citizenship politics. This new perspective seemed both naturalist and nationalist.

> The sign that the consensus is not synonymous with the absence of conviction, but rather with the existence of a real exchange giving rise to a communal vision . . . since several years, the mentalities have evolved, the exacerbation of differences is no longer the recipe, no more than the idea of a multicultural nation. Integration is the way of reason and of the future . . . the acquisition of French nationality finally offers a perspective: from the point of view of the individual it is the adhesion to a collective identity. The partisans of the right for an absolute territorial right to citizenship and abstract universalism have come to an impasse on the national sentiment . . . beyond individual boundaries one participates in a community of destiny. (Hannoun in *Le Figaro* 2/17/88)

The question remains why did both the opponents and proponents of the government's code reform accept the Commission's propositions in January? Certainly, their reactions were nuanced, each side disagreeing over specific propositions, and claiming that the recommendations actually complemented their past stances. But the reactions signified more than semantic shifts. More important, the confluence of a changing structure of political opportunities, the upcoming presidential elections, the internal orientation of the immigrant associations, and the specific point of departure provided by the Commission's framework enabled the consummation of the period in which the Commission operated as a critical moment for French citizenship politics.

While the Left argued that "the projects had nothing to do with each other," the Right claimed there was not much difference between its 1986 project and the commission's proposals. Congratulating the Commission for clarifying and calming the debate, Michel Hannoun declared that its report helped dissipate

> a double misunderstanding on the sense and import of the reform. The adaption of the nationality code must not derive from a desire of exclusion. To insist upon the necessary strengthening of the French identity is not to reject those who are not French, but to favor the real adhesion of foreigners durably established on our territory to the values that incarnate French citizenship. In taking clearly a position in favor of the principle of voluntary acquisition of nationality, the commission has re-

called the evidence which must no longer be contested. (*Le Quotidien de Paris* 1/9–10/88)

In January, on the eve of the presidential campaigns, Chirac both reaffirmed his support for his government's own project and affirmed his agreement with the commission's recommendations: "My own position is inscribed in the governmental project deposited a year ago and in the project of the Sages" (*Libération* 1/12/88; cf. *Le Monde* 1/10–11/88). Although he brought up the possibility of a national referendum, Chirac postponed all discussion of nationality reform till after the presidential election of Spring 1988 (*Agence Républicaine d'Information* 1/28/88).[55]

The Commission's report enabled the Right to embrace its recast position. The report's stress on voluntarism, a necessarily limited pluralism, and the national identity justified the Right's ongoing voluntarist and communitarian arguments. Its stress on an inclusive and integrative idiom framed the Right's recast position of 1987. "A simple idea, of common sense has been imposed with force on all," affirmed Bernard Stasi writing in the centrist journal, *Démocratie Moderne*, "youth will stay here, their integration is good for themselves, and also for the 'national community'," national integration, inclusiveness, and a positive adhesion being the guiding principles (1/14/88). Chaunu, who revised his position from a staunch defender of a restrictive reform to a supporter of the inclusive idiom, defended his role on the Commission to the conservative right as the upholder of French assimilationist and integrationist traditions, tracing them back to the ancien regime (*Le Quotidien de Paris* 1/14/88; *Le Figaro* 2/17/88; *Libération* 1/8/88). A conservative editorial mused, "The questions that are posed will prove to be fundamental for the future of our country: who must be French and to do what?" Accept all foreigners "or those who believe in France and adhere to its mores, customs, and ideals . . . must we prepare for a multiracial and pluricultural society or continue to assure a certain unity to this country?" (*Le Figaro* 1/9–10/88). In short, the Commission's positions permitted the rightist politicians to elaborate a nationalist framework, situated in a particularlist voluntarism and communitarianism, while using a more inclusive discourse.

The extreme Right's denouncement of the Commission seemed to reflect more its displeasure at the clear rejection of the nativist impulse originally behind the reform, than at the voluntarist and communitarian implications of the Commission's report. In arguing that the RPR-UDF "had changed a 180 degrees in relation to their promises of 1986," Le Pen framed his remarks using a nativist argument: The French will have to say "if they are for a French France or a foreign France" (*Libération* 1/8/88; see also *Le Spectacle du Monde* February 1988; *Aspects de la France* 1/14/88; *Le Rivarol* 2/12/88). While denouncing the rejection of an oath of allegiance by the commission, Y. Briant of the National Front, couched his arguments in terms not unlike the Commission's: "It is imperative that foreigners acquiring French nationality manifest their desire of attachment to the national community. It is not a matter of forbidding to become French those who want it but precisely to acknowledge as French those who have the conscience and desire to be it, because this desire is the best possible guarantee of their integration" (*Le Figaro* 2/17/88).

The Socialists sought to claim the Commission's voluntarism and communitarianism as expressive of their own evolving arguments. They argued that the Commission's report was a "repudiation" of the government's project (*Le Monde* 1/10–11/88). Though the Socialists emitted reservations about certain propositions in the reform, the Socialist party spokesman saluted it as a "text of common sense," approving its stress on an activist integrationist approach (*Le Figaro* 1/9–10/88). If they remained divided, as they were in 1985 and 1986, over the need for an actual positive step, the Socialists recognized that the report supported their rejection of an absolute territorial right to citizenship, a revision called for by SOS-Racisme and others. (*Libération* 1/12/88).[56] Like the Right, the Socialists too saw the strategic need, given the upcoming elections and Le Pen's presence, to distance themselves from an actual reform of the code, even though many seemed to agree with the Commission that the code needed revisions.

Importantly, the Commission legitimized the refashioning of pluralism and privileging of national identity undertaken by the Left during the eighties. It defined a French republican communitarianism that celebrated a pluralism necessarily confined to upholding the national unity. *Libération* saluted the "gentle France" fashioned by Commission's stance. During the presidential campaign in 1988, Mitterrand voiced themes that resonated with those formulated by the Commission, including the call for a "valorized" (but not voluntarist) citizenship (Mitterrand 1988:41–44). While Mitterrand rejected the need to reform the nationality code, the Socialist party characterized Mitterrand's candidacy as "a defense without the conservatism," the "reestablishment of a real contractual politics," "the reinforcement of social cohesion," and the ways to "lead to a unified France."

For the most part, the reservations expressed by those on the Left, including many immigrant associations, antiracist organizations, and human rights groups, as well as by the clergy and the unions, were limited to specific propositions, while being supportive of the commission's general orientations (e.g., *Témoignage Chrétien* 1/18–24/88; *Libération* 1/8/88, 1/12/88; *Le Monde* 1/11/88; *L'Evénement du Jeudi* 1/21–27/88).[58] Dahmani, president of France-Plus, was representative of this current of opinion. He quoted approvingly from the Commission's definition of national identity ("the republican model, the values of the Revolution . . . they propose to reinvigorate the Francophone space") and stress on national integration. He argued it was a "real repudiation" of the previous project, though he too critiqued the Commission on specific issues (*Libération* 1/9–19/88; *L'Evénement du Jeudi* 1/21–27/88).

In contrast, SOS-Racisme criticized both the orientation and contents of the Commission's report (SOS-Racisme 1988). But, SOS-Racisme's rejection actually focused specifically the Commission's call for a positive step in the acquisition of French citizenship. SOS-Racisme called for an absolute territorial right to citizenship, and argued that the report called into question the principle of *jus soli*, making it so "access to the nationality is no longer a right," and leading to "the marginalization" of the youth (*Le Figaro* 1/9–10/88; see *Libération* 1/12/88). Just as Le Pen's denouncement did not fully extend to the voluntarist and communitarian implications of the Commission's report, SOS-Racisme's denouncement did not seem to extend to the Commission's emphasis on national identity and national integration.

There were some global critiques of the Commission and the consensus. The legal rights group, GISTI devoted an issue of their journal Plein Droit to the Commission's report. The issue criticized the Commission's principal orientations, challenged its identification of a "nation," and questioned its arguments that the national identity must be strengthened and its pursuit for a "national integration" of immigrants. "Perhaps it would be more reasonable to accept to banish once and for all from our vocabulary the words 'nation' or 'national belonging,' to replace the term 'nationality,' source of such confusion, if not even slippages, by that of 'staticity' (étaticité)" (*Plein Droit* 1988:15). On the far Left, the PCF too rejected the commission's report and consensus, citing a "colonialist nostalgia" and exclusionary logic implicit in the report, and faulting the "strange convergences" of the Left and Right (*L'Humanité* 1/7, 8, 9/88; see also *Rouge* 1/14–20/88, 3/10–16/88). The PCF's stance was partly indicative of its changing strategies toward immigrant associations, from a strategy of neglect to one devoted to defense against their marginalization (*IM'media* 1988).

Overall, the position of the immigrant association movement, or at least of the most visible organizations in the movement, reflected the changed structure of political opportunities. The trend toward fashioning an identity politics of difference had shifted to an identity politics of resemblance or sameness. In fact, the Commission's reconstruction of citizenship and the associations' favorable reactions exposed some of the difficulties with the shift from identity to sameness politics. Stuart Clarke has written that the "the major weaknesses of identity politics are its potential for coaptation and fragmentation. These potentials are realized when new cultural actors emerge, but new political modalities do not develop and new political scripts are not written. When agents are all dressed up in new social clothes but have no place to go but the same old political homes. These new social energies are articulated through old political modalities in ways that buttress old concentrations of power. This is an identity as sameness politics" (1991).

Though the immigrant associations during the hearings tried to force the issue of new forms of citizenship and national identity, they firmly anchored themselves in the "old political modalities," the system of French republicanism, national integration, secularity, and limited universalism (cf. *L'Express* 10/23/87; *IM'media* 1987 and 1988). The Commission's modification of the voluntarist and communitarian arguments into a new "common-sense" framework undermined further the association movement's attempts to formulate an identity politics of citizenship that would be in some way "counterhegemonic." In assuming "the simplest opposition between the right to resemblance and the right to difference" (*L'Express* 10/23/87), the immigrant associations exposed a major weakness of identity politics.

In the end, the Commission constructed not a new citizenship but reconstructed the predominant "institutionalized structure of meanings" of French citizenship. At times, immigrant activists strove to define the televised hearings as a new political modality—this "semi-direct democracy"—because television was a forum identified as belonging to their generation. According to one activist who testified before the commission, "the television, this is our culture. When one thinks that it was hardly any years ago, that it was taboo to talk of immigration on the TV. That said, if the hearings had not been transmitted directly, I wouldn't have gone [and testified]" (*Libération* 10/23/88). But, these activists, "all dressed up in new social clothes," only buttressed old concentrations of power. The Commission did not provide an innovative forum for "new political modalities," but rather, an effective "spectacle" for the dominant political agents. Through the final contributions of the Nationality Commission, the new citizenship politics in France emerged firmly reconstructed around the triple priorities of national identity, national integration, and a valorized, noncommodified citizenship.

CHAPTER 7

Who's Wearing the Veil?

Ethnic Politics and the New Citizenship

What were the implications of the new citizenship politics in France? Until the 1993 reform of the Nationality Code, attention to citizenship politics and processes receded into the background of the larger immigration context. The recommendations brought forth by the National Commission on Nationality lay untouched by the Socialist government, now back in complete control of the government after Mitterrand's successful defense of his presidency and a new Socialist majority in the National Assembly. Yet, the absence of legislative reform should not obscure the effects of the citizenship reform processes on the wider context of immigration, immigrants, and membership in France. This chapter tells the story of one incident in the politics of immigrant incorporation—the "Foulard or headscarf affair"—which took place in France in the Fall of 1989. My aim here is to show how this incident, which soon became a national crisis, illustrates the effects of the shifting processes of citizenship as well as of the recast notions of pluralism.

In September 1989, three schoolgirls of North African origin insisted on wearing Muslim veils or scarves to their school in the commune of Creil. In response, their principal moved to expel them. By mid-October, the affair of "foulards islamiques," or Muslim headscarves, had swept French politics into a divisive national crisis. Debates raged between "pure and hard" (*pur et dur*) secularists and more tolerant ones, between those condemning the headscarves as "aggressive religious particularisms" and those defending the girls'—and more broadly, immigrant communities'—"right to difference." Once again, a major stake in the affair was the integration of the Muslim, North African immigrant and immigrant-origin populations into the "national community." One of the questions arising from the incident and its aftermath was that concerning the changing possibilities for ethnic politics in France. Were the girls' actions and the subsequent support for them indicative of the emergence of ethnic politics in France? Were "Franco-Maghrebis" a critical challenge to the "French model" of immigrant integration?

The practice of ethnic politics has long been considered antithetical to French republicanist ideology and to the statist, Jacobin system. Since the middle of the 1980s, the emergence of the nationalist citizenship politics certainly reinforced the model of "no ethnic politics." Indeed, French public opinion on the foulard affair strongly rejected the "Anglo-Saxon" model of ethnic politics in favor of the French model of assimilation.[1] But at the same time, the contemporary French state and political system have appeared to be moving from a refusal to recognize differences to a pragmatic management of the religious and cultural particularities of its immigrant groups. French studies suggested that the Beurs or Franco-Maghrebis were in fact engaging in a type of ethnic or "communitarian" politics, in which Islam serves as an "identity marker" and mobilizing mechanism (Leveau 1989–90; Leveau and de Wenden 1988a; 1988b). To be sure, immigrant activist organizations such as France-Plus, JALB, and TEXTURE emerged in the 1980s as pressure groups in French politics with specific demands for expanding their political and cultural rights.

In this chapter, I argue that ethnic politics in France has been shaped by a series of constraints. The major constraints include existing French ideologies and institutional arrangements that refused to acknowledge ethnic differences and the emergent nationalist politics of citizenship that discouraged ethnic identities. I also suggest that the changing strategic orientations of the immigrant associations, which came about during the conflicts over citizenship and national identity, deflated what could have been a growing challenge. The combination of such factors has limited the configuration of ethnic politics in France. Overall, these constraints and their effects can be discerned in the ways in which the foulard affair was created, defined, and managed.

Immigrants to Ethnics: Constraints on Ethnic Citizenship and Difference

The student population at the school the girls attended, the College Gabriel Havez, numbered 876, of which at least 500 were of Muslim origin, and a majority of these from North Africa (*Libération* 10/10/89).[2] To recall the proportions of the North African or Maghrebi immigrant communities in France, immigrants originating from Algeria, Tunisia, and Morocco constituted approximately 40 percent or over a million and half of the foreign resident population in the late eighties (Voisard and Ducastelle 1988; Lebon 1988). To those numbers were added the growing population who are of North African origin but also of French nationality. It was estimated that there were over 1.5 million Franco-Maghrebis (Leveau and de Wenden 1988). In all, the second-generation youth or Beurs themselves accounted for over 40 percent of the Maghrebi populations in France (Gonzalez-Quinjano 1988). These populations made up the majority of the 2.5–3 million Muslims estimated to live in France (*Le Monde* 11/30/89; Voisard and Ducastelle 1988).

Throughout the eighties, the emergent Beur activist associations and other immigrant organizations were increasingly demanding recognition of their collective, cultural, ethnic, and religious identities. During the specific conflicts over citizenship and immigration, these groups also advocated political engagement, through marches, protests, participation in the reform process, and the establishment of new associations (Jazouli 1987). In fact, after 1987, some organizations such as France-Plus engaged in explicit electoral negotiations with the major political parties regarding party tickets and candidates. As with the earlier debates over diverse regional identities and the meaning of pluralism in the French model, the demands of the immigrant activists for acknowledgment of their differences are considered to challenge French understandings of national membership, political participation, integration, and equality. The classic statement by Comte de Clermont-Tonnerre in the nineteenth century, "It is necessary to refuse all to the Jews as nation, and accord all to the Jews as individuals" (cited in Phillipe 1981), encapsulated the official stance toward difference and equality. The "universalizing individualism of citizenship" emanating from the Revolution was defined partly as the emancipation from the "status of minorities as collectivities or communities" (Gallisot 1989:27; cf. Kates 1986).

Thus, the refusal to recognize differences, or in other words, the absence of ethnic group politics in France can be traced to the French revolution, to republicanism, and Jacobin institutionalist practices, along with the accompanying state and political system (e.g., Safran 1985; Krulic 1988b; Hollifield 1989). According to scholars, republicanist thought fuses the political and cultural communities so that political membership implies acceptance of French cultural values and bases (Schnapper 1987; Weber 1976; Safran 1990). At the same time, the centralized, unitary Jacobin system insists on an individualist relation between the state and people so that no intermediary bodies ought to represent particular groups within society (Lochak 1989b).[3] The general principles of "egalité," "homogénéité," and "unité" have historically been the central ideological components governing against the recognition of differences and for the assertion of an individualist citizenship (Lochak 1989b). As legal scholar Daniele Lochak explains, equality in France traditionally has been understood on an individualist basis. French society was presumed to be homogeneous, which meant the exclusion of "intermediary bodies or partial solidarities." The society was presumed to be unitary, which meant the exclusion of local or regional particularities. The revolutionary ideologies "proscribed, even denied" the concept of difference, "because it contradicted the foundations of the new society, in which individuals, equal by essence, must be treated in an identical fashion" (Ibid.:113). The immigrant groups' demands and their emergent religious and cultural particularities, therefore, clash with the limited universality of these French principles.

The refusal to accept internal differentiated communities like ethnic groups into the national political community should not be considered solely an ideological refusal. It has had institutional implications. The concept of minority group is absent in French legal and legislative texts. According to Danielle Lochak, this has translated into the "impossibility" for policy makers, legislators, and jurists to think about the notion of a minority (Lochak 1989b). In French immigration politics, for example, most state policies do not recognize or take into account the ethnic specificities of the different immigrant groups (Soysal 1994; Kastoryano 1989, 1996). The French institutional model has implied an individualist, assimilationist mode of integration (Leca 1985; Pinto 1988). In France, the classic integrationist institutions for immigrants have been the public ("republican") school system, the army, and unions, and not intermediary organizations articulating immigrant interests (Noiriel 1988).[4] Within this framework, the "immigre" in France was either marginalized under the bias of state immigration policies, where the specific differences of immigrants are externalized, or assimilated, and so ethnically invisible, or at least, silent (cf. Sayad 1984, 1987). The "ethnic citizen" does not exist.

Overall, the citizenship conflicts and reform processes of the 1980s reinforced these kinds of ideologies and integration priorities. Within the context of the new citizenship politics, many on the Left and Right rejected arguments to separate nationality from citizenship as certain immigrant activists advocated. They upheld the divisions between the public status of membership in the national community and the private status of religion and culture (Safran 1990). The consensus that greeted the National Commission on Nationality's recommendations regarding the acquisition of French citizenship followed a similar logic. The priority of making citizenship acquisition a voluntaristic process was linked to the need to strengthen and reaffirm the French national identity and its specific republicanist features (Long 1988). Certainly, on an ideological level, the debates over the Nationality code signified the reaffirmation of the assimilationist model of national integration, and a rejection of any notion of a right to difference in the public sphere (*Plein Droit* 1988).

Likewise, the citizenship reform conflicts and their aftermath signaled an undeniable break from the previous Socialist commitments to a pluralist approach and ethnic accommodation (Safran 1985; de Wenden 1988b). The reconstructed nationalist citizenship laid out by the Nationality Commission repudiated the earlier trend toward recognizing distinct ethnic identities and substantive differences.[5] It discouraged the idea and practice of ethnic politics. Regardless of the strategic decision not to move on a nationality reform, the Socialists did continue to institutionalize a narrowed pluralist logic when they returned to power in 1988 (Lochak 1989a). In one of his first speeches touching on the topic of immigration politics, Prime Minister Rocard rejected any need for a minister of immigration. He argued that the immigrant communities in France did not have any specific differences from the rest of those on their same social-economic level, and so, he rejected the need to recognize or manage any substantive differences of Franco-Maghrebis (*Le Monde Hebdomaire* 2/9–15/89).

Contemporary Challenges

In recent decades there have been important challenges to the dominant French ideologies and institutional arrangements that refuse the notion and practice of ethnic politics. Some have arisen out of general trends of changing societal developments, demands by French groups for equality, and the necessity for the state to manage and not ignore differences (Lochak 1989b). Others have been more directly tied to the flow and settlement of contemporary immigrants in France. The most important ones have been those involving changes in institutional practices as the state has been confronted with managing differences, and changes in the political process, as the immigrant association movement and activities of the younger immigrant and dual national generations emerged in the 1980s.

In the postwar period, the French state has attempted to manage the growing differences in society and demands for equality by increasingly negotiating with minority groups. For example, though the state imposes the principle of secularity, and refuses to recognize religious particularities, it has negotiated with Christian and Jewish groups to take into account their religious needs. Thus, even before the Muslim scarf affair ignited a furor over the issue of secularity, the principle was being ignored and undermined in various ways by the state and other groups (Lochak 1989b). These negotiations between the state and minority groups eroded traditional Jacobin and republican principles, and modify existing institutional arrangements. Though this management was largely ad hoc, pragmatic, case by case, and not based on a coherent policy, it created opportunities for group politics. Lochak has argued that the public authorities have moved from simple "tolerance" of differences to "official recognition" of them, and even to the "management" and "institutionalization" of differences (1989b).

It should be noted, however, that changes in state practices did not necessarily encourage the practice of differentialist politics in all spheres. When the Socialists actively engaged in policies of "ethno-cultural accommodation" (Safran 1985), their recognition of differences was at times double edged. In part, it signified an institutionalization of differences, which could then contribute to the emergence of new forms of pluralism. In part, the policies arguably also led to a form of marginalization for those of immigrant origin. The Socialist commitment to the right to difference and ethnocultural accommodation in education, for example, did not succeed in redefining pluralism in the schools. Rather, the management of differences was externalized outside of the general French educational structure. While Maghrebi students were taught Arab language and culture classes in the school, the programs were conducted by the countries of origin, not the school, and the policy instruments used were those created in the seventies specifically for foreign immigrants (Berque 1985; *Le Monde* 12/1/89). However, even when the rhetoric has been explicitly anti-ethnic in French immigration and citizenship, proposed changes in institutional arrangements can implicitly recognize and legitimize substantive differences. During the debates on the Nationality code, for example, the Commission on Nationality recommended a long list of changes in the state agencies and policy stances even as its overriding approach was assimilationist. Their recommended changes in institutional arrangements implicitly took into account the group identities of the immigrants (Pinto 1988).

More than any other phenomena, the emergence of immigrants into politics, and the growth and efficacy of the association movement led scholars to speculate that the possibilities for ethnic politics are opening up in France today. Scholars argued that the immigrant association movement has encouraged an American-style approach to politics, that is, an ethnic politics style, or at least a more pluralistic, communitarian style. They cited the incidence of the "Beur" vote, their electoral organizing, their demands for Mosques, their collective mode of participation, and their visibility as a specific group in French politics (Leveau and de Wenden, 1988a; 1988b; Pinto 1988; Kastoryano 1989b).

Scholars argued that the immigrant activist movement challenged the French model of integration on several levels: as a form of "identity politics," a generator of political intermediaries, and a forum for ethnic lobbies (de Wenden 1988b; Catani and Pallida 1987; Jazouli 1986). During the immigration and citizenship conflicts, the diverse associations grouped under this movement did organize themselves around shared Arab or Beur identities. Other groups such as the highly publicized SOS-Racisme politicized issues that were previously relegated to the private sphere—issues such as "sexuality, interpersonal relations, lifestyle and culture" (Kaufman 1990). These associations also emerged as sites for the promotion of young immigrant women and the incorporation of gender issues in immigrant communities. For the 1989 local electoral campaigns, France-Plus created a voting promotion poster, which featured a play on the words, mother–mayor (mère–maire) and that explicitly paid tribute to such women candidates: The poster displayed a sketch of a young woman candidate with the caption "In nine months I will be mayor." France-Plus, FASTI, Texture, JALB, and as well as many other immigrant-related centers and groups generated an array of elites or intermediaries migrant associations, which when coupled with changes in state policy and decentralization of power to the local levels in the 1980s, increased the strategic efficacy of ethnic demands. Through their organizations, the new elites negotiated with the state, social institutions, and political groups at local and national levels (de Wenden 1988b).

As shown in previous chapters, by the late 1980s, the original thrust of many of the associations' demands of proclaiming a "right to difference" were discredited by the rise of the extreme Right, which distorted the theme for its own goals, and by the changing ideological stances in the mainstream Left and Right. From their strong advocacy of a right to difference, these groups changed their priorities to insist on integration into the "national community" and republican values. At the same time, they extended themselves into deliberate "ethnic lobbies" and ethnic-style politics. The groups began to use their culture, their national origin, and their religion to mobilize their constituencies for political stakes.

The move from "beur" to "Franco-Maghrebi," which by the late 1980s was often considered the more accurate appellation for the diverse North African immigrant population, seemed to parallel the move from an absolute demand for cultural difference and a refusal to enter French politics to a deepening engagement with French political parties and institutions (Gonzalez-Quijano 1988). It accentuated the evolving image of these communities as building American-style ethnic lobbies. It emphasized a functional interpretation of their Maghrebi origin, and seemed to discourage promoting a cultural interpretation of some understanding of "maghrebinité" (Césari 1989–1990). In organizing themselves on an ethnic basis in French politics, "Franco-Maghrebis" have centered their identity around the Muslim, Maghrebi culture (Leveau and Zghal 1989). But many activists did not see any contradiction between an attachment to the Moslem culture and adherence to French political and secular values (Gonzalez-Quijano 1987; Césari 1989–1990; *Le Monde* 11/30/89). When the association, "Génération Beur" was created in 1988, it insisted on its Muslim character even as it situated itself firmly on the terrain of republican, secular values. While almost all members of this population seemed to define themselves as Muslim, only around half were actually practicing Muslims. Membership in this Muslim Maghrebi community served as a functional entry into the sphere of French politics (Leveau and de Wenden 1988a).

France-Plus, composed largely of those of Maghrebi origin and dual nationality, and actively engaged in electoral politics, has exemplified the form of emergent ethnic politics evident in France. During the 1988 presidential elections, they organized drives to register the million or more "Franco-Maghrebis," and in the 1989 municipal elections, they organized both their own candidate lists and negotiated with parties on both the left and mainstream right for other spaces.[6] Alongside its identification with the Muslim, Maghrebi culture, the organization has been insistently secular and integrationist. France-Plus clearly uses the tools of ethnic politics, and at the same time has sought to incorporate the ideological bases of the French secular integrationist model (Leveau and de Wenden 1988b; see Leveau 1989–1990).

But do the strategic aims of the immigrant organizations render an ethnic politics incompatible with the French political process? In fact, despite its appearance as a possible challenge to the "no ethnic politics" model, the Franco-Maghrebi association movement was limited by its own internal constraints. Their strategies to make integrationist themes a top priority limited the impact of their challenge. Their efforts to mobilize their constituencies on an ethnic basis were shaped by their overall strategies regarding the extent to which they aimed to conform to a model of national integration. From this perspective, the Foulard affair well reflected the state of ethnic and membership politics in France. To what extent should the affair be understood in terms of ethnic politics? Was the act of wearing the veil an act of ethnic affirmation, cultural identification, or religious obligation? Was the affair defined as a conflict of competing principles or group interests? Did the resolution of the affair take into account or help institutionalize, differences in the public sphere in France? An examination of the drama shows the extent to which challenges to the predominant French membership and integration patterns have emerged and the ways in which such challenges have been constrained.

The Muslim head scarf affair did not erupt into a national crisis simply because of the conflict between the three girls and their principal. It revived existing controversies, played on French fears of a fundamentalist Islam, and dramatized anew continuing concerns about the future of immigrant communities in France. There were four major dimensions to the affair, each of which touched on questions of difference, ethnic politics, and national membership. The first was the conflict over the definition of secularity and freedom of religion in the country's public school system. This debate was not new; in 1984, Socialist efforts to reform the school system provoked an intense battle over secularity. This time, however, traditional battle lines between secularists and their opponents blurred with the addition of the three other dimensions (*Le Monde* 10/21/89). One was the issue of women's equality. This conflict pitted those denouncing the headscarf as a symbol of women's subordination against those defending the "right to difference" and who pronounced the headscarf a symbol of religious and cultural expression. The specter of a fundamentalist, aggressive Islam proselytizing France was another image heavily emphasized by the press. Finally, the affair revived the always charged debates over the integration of the non-European, especially North African, immigrant communities.

L'Affaire du Foulard: Creating the Affair

In early November, during the height of the crisis, the newspaper, *Libération*, noted that this was the first time that a national debate on immigration was provoked neither by the Right nor extreme Right initiatives, but rather by a "cultural manifestation" from the "Maghrebi community" itself (*Libération* 11/6/89). Several aspects in the creation of the affair suggested the growing possibilities for ethnic politics in France: the use of Islamic religion and culture to mobilize a community, the arguments that differences and different treatment were legitimate in the public sphere, the sense of a collective Maghrebi interest and view, and the important role of Islamic, Maghrebi and other immigrant-support organizations in the development of the affair.

Though the three girls in Creil spoke only of their religious obligation and their need to serve Allah, other participants and commentators connected the headscarves to a larger strategy of cultural identification and community mobilization. According to the French scholar, Remy Leveau, the religious demands combined affective ties with group interests. On one level, the affirmation of religious identity signified "a desire to affirm the legitimacy of their [the protagonists'] right to stay without renouncing their true selves" (Leveau 1989–1990:25). On another level, it translated into French politics a "collective pressure" for "recognition of a social reality of a communitarian type" (Ibid.:28, 31).

The Foulard affair confirms the use of Islam in organizing immigrant-origin communities and their political goals. Beyond the narrow desire of the individual students, the creation of the affair was compatible with a broader strategy of Maghrebi and immigrant "group elites" in French society. It served as "a response to the insufficiency of social insertion" (Jouffa in *Le Monde* 11/9/89). The "religious factor" constituted "the easiest mobilizing element available for the group and the most provocative one for French society" (Leveau 1989–1990:28).

An IFOP poll published in *Le Monde* substantiates this sense of a collective Maghrebi perspective and interests. The poll, conducted in November during the height of the affair, showed a substantial gap between the so-called "French" population and those of "Muslim origin"; though it should be noted that the latter category included 26 percent who held French nationality. On a range of issues relating to the practice of Islam in the public sphere—the construction of mosques, serving food to meet Muslim dietary restrictions in school cafeterias, official holidays for Islamic holy days, wearing Islamic headscarves in the school or on the street—the Muslim origin population were favorable to public affirmations and specialized treatment. In contrast, the French population was significantly opposed to visible affirmations of difference or special treatment (*Le Monde* 11/30/89).

Previous erosions of the secularity principle certainly contributed to the tensions that created the affair. Some of the most vocal supporters of the scarf demands were Jewish and Christian religious authorities. They argued that the headscarves were cultural as well as religious symbols and, more important, a new definition of secularity was needed to take into account differences and different treatment (*Le Monde* 10/21/89; *Libération* 10/16/89). For these groups, the demands illustrated the "aging of the laws on secularity" (*Le Monde* 10/24, 25/89).

The collective activism of Franco-Maghrebi and immigrant support groups was another key factor in the development of the affair. From the outset of the conflict in Creil in September, Islamic organizations were important negotiation partners for the school. After the girls were expelled from school on September 18, the president of the "cultural association of Tunisians in Creil" mediated between the families and schools to reach a compromise so that the girls returned to school on October 9 (*Libération* 10/10/89). Later, another group, the "National Federation of Muslims in France" took part in the negotiations (*Le Monde* 10/21/89). Besides Islamic groups, other immigrant support associations influenced the development of the scarf conflict into a national crisis. SOS-Racisme and MRAP argued that the Creil expulsion was a case of anti-Maghrebi discrimination (*Le Monde* 11/7/89; *Le Nouvel Observateur* 11/9–15/89). In their defenses of the headscarves, all these groups situated the conflict in terms of group interests and well as principles (*Libération* 10/16/89). The creation of the Muslim scarf affair included many of the characteristics of ethnic politics: the religious affirmations as an identity marker and community mobilizer, the focus on group interests, the role of community and ethnic organizations as mediators, the calls for the recognition and specific treatment of differences in the public sphere, and the accompanying self-definition of members of the Maghrebi Muslim community reinforced by the attitudes and definitions of the majority community. These characteristics can easily be traced to the challenges to the traditional French model discussed in the previous section. But most of the participants and commentators in the affair resisted defining the conflict as a clash of ethnic or group interests. Indeed, if the creation of the scarf demands seemed to suggest the possibilities for ethnic politics in France, then the dominant response to the demands was explicit opposition to such an emergence of ethnic politics.

Defining the Drama

For the most part, the press, politicians, and other participants and commentators in the affair situated the conflict on two successive levels: as an attack on secularity, and as a threat to the French model of national integration (e.g., *Libération* 10/10/89; *Le Nouvel Observateur* 10/12–18/89; *Le Monde* 10/21/89). Situating the conflict on these levels effectively removed it from the terrain of ethnic politics. This definition of the headscarf demands conceived of ethnicity in primarily negative terms and through anti-ethnic references. It meant that the affair could not be a legitimate conflict of cultural or group interests; the affirmation of differences in the public sphere being essentially illegitimate. These understandings of the affair were rooted in the ideological, institutional and political constraints on ethnic politics in France.

Early in the drama, the press portrayed the scarves as a symbol of Islamic fundamentalism; *Le Nouvel Observateur*, for example, labeled the demands an attack by "aggressive religious particularisms" (10/12–18/89; 11/9–15/89). The specter of Islam cast over the headscarf demands an immediate veil of incompatibility with secular, egalitarian, and democratic (i.e., "western") values.[7] Simultaneously, the press and participants recalled the French-specific history of secularity, especially the conflict over its definition in the schools (*Le Monde* 11/7, 9/89).

Basic to the traditional integrationist role of the "republican," public school system in France has been the inculcation of secular values. A primary function of the schools was to mold the students into the "homogeneous," "unitary," national community, and in doing so, reinforce the predominating national identity.[8] The decision to exclude the three girls from classes if they wore the scarves pitted "pur et dur" secularists against more tolerant ones. The former—which included those on the Right and Left—argued that absolute neutrality must reign in the public school; all differences must be left at the door. The latter—which included the Education Minister Lionel Jospin and the Prime Minister of the Socialist government—argued that exclusion would only further isolate the students from republican teaching (*Le Monde* 11/7/89). France-Plus actively protested against the scarves, proclaiming they violated the principles of secularity and equality. Having always maintained a secularist discourse, France-Plus was not inconsistent in its actions. Nevertheless, their position highlights the internal constraints of the ethnic politics promoted by Franco-Maghrebis. The group evaded the ethnic dimension of the scarf demands throughout the affair.

Public opinion supported the strict interpretation of the secularity principle. In a SOFRES poll taken during the affair and published in *Le Nouvel Observateur*, 83 percent of the respondents thought it was "not normal" that the Muslim students wear Islamic scarves to school (11/23–29/89). When the Education Minister Lionel Jospin pronounced himself against the exclusion of the girls from class, surveys showed between 47 percent to 66 percent of those polled disapproving of his position (*Libération* 11/7/89; *Le Nouvel Observateur* 11/23–29/89). The limited scope of the secularity debate itself was a reflection of the ideological constraints on affirmations of difference in the public sphere in France. Though the application of the secularity standard was at issue, the basic premise of the principle was never really challenged. Many of the girls' defenders argued on the basis that the act of wearing the headscarf was not a "menace" to the principle. Those who declared that a new definition of secularity was in order argued on the basis that a secular school meant a tolerant school.

By mid-October 1989, the parties on the Right began to take the opportunity to call for a general debate in the National Assembly on immigration, to criticize the general immigration policies of the socialist government, and to revive proposals to reform in a restrictive manner French nationality legislation (*Le Monde* 11/9/89). The affair enlarged from the more narrow issues of secularity and Islam to those of immigration and integration. The focus became "the place of Islam in France and the future of millions of immigrants who will never return to their countries" (*Le Monde* 10/24/89). As the stakes of the affair became more explic-itly centered on the integration of the Muslim, North African origin communi-ties, there was again disagreement on the ways to achieve integration. But there was a general consensus on the necessity of a "French" model of integration. At this point, the headscarves symbolized a threat of ethnic affirmations, "ghettoiza-tion," the "Anglo-Saxon" model of ethnic relations (*Libération* 11/6/89).

Some commentators characterized the crisis as the first significant time that the lines between the Left and Right in France blurred on issues regarding the in-tegration of immigrants in France. They argued that the affair was a critical point for a resurgence of Jacobinist and republican sentiments, and a rejection of the right to difference (Beriss 1990; Vichniac 1990). The reactions by those on the Left and Right, however, were not unexpected. Since the emergence of the focus on national identity in the mid-eighties, lines between the Right and Left on is-sues of integration have blurred. By the end of the debates on the Nationality Code in 1987, there was a consensus on the need to reinforce the French national identity as a means for integrating immigrants (*Plein Droit* 1988; Verbunt 1988b). Thus, the political responses to the Foulard affair followed the renewed con-straints imposed on ethnic politics by the trends in French citizenship politics.

The Foulard affair did present a more explicit rejection of pluralist politics and the right to difference than the previous debates over nationality and citizen-ship had. In an interview, Ernest Cherniere, the principal of the college in Creil, described how Muslim and Jewish students "self-segregate" themselves in his school, and agreed that he managed "more a series of ghettos than a real collec-tivity" (*Le Nouvel Observateur* 10/12–18/89). The former Socialist Minister of ed-ucation, J.-P. Chevenement, asserted that to support the "right to difference" along the "American" model was to prepare France for "a Lebanon very simply" (*Le Monde* 11/9/89). It was widely argued that the affair presented the choice be-tween a superior, French, assimilationist model of integration and a threatening Anglo-Saxon model of "ghettos," "segregation," and ethnic conflict (e.g., *Libéra-tion* 11/6, 7/89; *Le Nouvel Observateur* 10/12–18/89 and 11/23–29/89). A scholar on the Muslim communities in France, Gilles Kepel asserted that integration in France "supposes that the communitarian logic be broken" (*Le Monde* 11/30/89). The anti-ethnic rhetoric surrounding the affair, though present from the begin-ning disputes over secularity, gained most of its momentum within this context of the integration of Muslim, North African, immigrant communities.

Changes in public opinion from 1985 to 1989 substantiate this rejection of the right to difference and the endorsement of an assimilationist integration. The SOFRES poll published in *Le Nouvel Observateur* and taken in early November showed that the majority of public opinion thought that the "customs" and "reli-gion" of immigrants made their "cohabitation" with the French more difficult. These findings contrast sharply with a similar SOFRES poll taken in 1985: whereas 57 percent thought religion was an obstacle in 1989, only 23 percent thought so in 1985; for customs, 58 percent in 1989 and 49 percent in 1985 thought it was an obstacle. While only 15 percent in 1989 thought such characteristics (including language and race) were not obstacles to integration, 27 percent in 1985 thought so.

The conclusions drawn from this survey have been that if previously the "right to difference" was still seen as a viable alternative to the French model, today "a majority of French" of all persuasions "pronounce themselves, without false honesty, without complex, in favor of the French identity . . . (that) foreigners must adopt our customs, our values" (*Le Nouvel Observateur* 11/23–29/89). While the rhetoric surrounding the drama was predominantly anti-ethnic, the management of the foulard affair reflected the more paradoxical reality of ethnic politics in France.

Managing the Affair

Managing the affair and its aftermath progressed from attempts at local mediation and pressures on the national government to resolve the crisis to a legal ruling on wearing scarves by the Council d'Etat and the government's revised immigration stances. While changes in state practices to take into account differences in the public sphere seemed to belie the anti–"ethnic politics" discourse, the resolution of the affair confirmed the ways in which constraints are shaping the emergence of ethnic politics in France.

Until the Foulard affair, local compromises were worked out in many schools confronting similar religion-based conflicts. As noted earlier, these type of compromises have been handled case by case, with the state taking a pragmatic approach. In the Foulard affair, compromises broke down in mid-October. One reason for this is that Muslim groups have great difficulties in engaging in exactly these kinds of negotiations. In contrast to the Christian and Jewish communities, the Muslim communities lacked national, representative institutions that could operate as partners with the state. During the affair, Muslim group leaders, state officials, and others strongly bemoaned the absence of such representatives (*Le Monde* 10/21, 24/89). Publicizing the conflict revealed how the trend of local compromises eroded the traditional French models of absolute secularity in the schools and no ethnic politics. It also revealed the lack of coherent state policy regulating ethnic-related conflicts.

Under pressure from the political community to resolve the crisis, the Socialist government was forced to take a position and assume responsibility for managing the conflict. In mid-October, Lionel Jospin stated that the "secularity of the school" must be respected, but "the school is made for receiving children and not for excluding them" (*Libération* 10/10/89). By the end of October, Jospin as Education Minister issued a more complete statement along the same lines (*Le*

Monde 10/26/89). Jospin argued that while schools should try to discourage their students from wearing headscarves, they ought not expel them for that reason. His position provoked an uproar among politicians on the Right and Left. Jospin's position in the Foulard affair reflected the trend of the state to use a pragmatic approach in dealing with differences (Lochak 1989b). Prime Minister Rocard, supported Jospin's statements: "This concrete and pragmatic approach to reconcile at once our values (secularity) and our principles (refusal of exclusions) is that which Lionel Jospin expressed in the name of the government. Here is the firm, realist, responsible direction I have chosen to follow" (*Libération* 11/6/89). To deflect attention and pressure, Jospin then assigned the Conseil d'Etat (Council of State) to review the case and issue a legal ruling on the wearing of the scarves.

Through its decisions in the past, the Council has remained one of the state institutions advancing the legitimacy of substantive differences in the public sphere (Lochak 1989b). The advances have come not through any sweeping, direct challenge to French principles but through individual cases and limited recognition of differences. In commenting on the foulard case, for example, a judge on the Council noted "There is no line of clear separation" of when secularity imposes absolute neutrality, rather "it is case by case" (*Libération* 11/6/89). On November 27, the Council issued its ruling. While the case institutionalized the treatment of differences further, the way it was articulated actually limited the practice of ethnic group politics. On the one hand, the Council essentially reinforced the case-by-case, negotiation approach even as it recommended that the government formulate a set of guidelines for the schools to use (*Le Monde* 11/29/89). On the other hand, the circular released by the Ministry of Education on December 6 set limits to the wearing of religious symbols though it too emphasized the need for dialogue and compromise (*Le Monde* 12/8/89). One result has been that local compromises are threatened by this new attempt by the state to institutionalize a policy regulating differences (cf. the article "Mercredi ou Samedi?" *Le Monde* 12/9/89).

Government efforts to resolve the Foulard affair were also determined by the constraints on ethnic politics imposed by immigration politics. Before the affair, the Socialist government's stance in 1988 was to refuse any special or differential treatment for the immigrant or immigrant-origin populations. The "very word itself (immigrant) became taboo" (*Le Monde* 10/24/89). This policy approach contributed to the government's problem in dealing with the conflict (*Le Monde* 11/7/89). Not only did the affair involve the recognition and management of difference, but it was situated within a context of difference — the Franco-Maghrebi communities — that the government refused to acknowledge.

At the end of November, speaking before the executive committee of the Socialist party, the Socialist Prime Minister, Michel Rocard, explicitly rejected an ethnic-politics approach to problems like the Foulard affair: France cannot be "a juxtaposition of communities," it cannot follow the Anglo-Saxon models that allowed ethnic groups to live in geographic and cultural "ghettos," and resulted in "soft forms of apartheid." Rocard rebuffed demands from SOS-Racisme and others to appoint a special "Minister of Integration" or a Franco-Maghrebi minister for such issues. He called instead for implementing integration "a la Française" (*Le Monde* 12/1/89). A French-style integration, according to Rocard, was neither strict assimilation nor ethnic coexistence, but rather the "recognition of mutual obligations" and the treatment of immigrants as if they were citizens (*Le Monde* 12/7/89).

The Foulard affair forced the Socialists to refashion their immigration policies and stances regarding the Franco-Maghrebi communities. Rocard pledged to set up both a permanent interministerial committee to oversee integration and another special committee of "sages," and issued forty-eight practical recommendations. The new strategy implicitly recognized those of immigrant origin as a population with differences specific to its membership, although the accompanying political discourse, which was clearly anti-ethnic, did not (*Le Monde* 12/1,7/89). Even as the management of the Foulard affair contributed to the institutionalization of differences, it also illustrated how the configuration of ethnic politics in France has been limited. Rocard's proposals are indicative of how an "immigre" perspective masks the "ethnic" and "ethnic citizen" in France. In the Foulard affair, the state addressed the crisis and its own relations with Franco-Maghrebis solely within the framework of immigration and according to the imperatives of integration. The recognition of ethnic differences under the categories of immigration and integration obfuscated the fact that the differences are a permanent part of French society.

The phenomenon in which the "immigré" masks the "ethnic" is the key to understanding the ethnic politics paradox that exists in France. As seen in the Foulard affair, the ethnicity of Franco-Maghrebis has been externalized, hidden behind the "immigre" perspective. Despite their seeming challenge to the classic model, Franco-Maghrebis have not been acknowledged as ethnic citizens.[9] As noted earlier, changes in state practices and strategy and in the political process do not necessarily encourage the practice of ethnic politics. For example, the categorization of Arab language classes in the early eighties as part of the new policies of ethno-cultural accommodation obscured in part the "immigre" perspective within which these policies operated. That marginalization in the schools has been recalled to explain in part why the state had "no clear discourse on the 'management' of differences" in 1989 (*Le Monde* 12/1/89).

The Foulard affair was indeed indicative that some limited configuration of ethnic politics is emerging in France. In this regard, an analysis of the affair points to the need to rethink our conceptions of ethnic politics. Some scholars, however, argue that the changes in state practices, in the political participation of Franco-Maghrebi groups, and in the evolving discourse on national identity are translating into more openings for the emergence of an "Anglo-Saxon" style ethnic politics in France. But as I have argued here, there is a series of constraints limiting the emergence and configuration of an Anglo-Saxon or American-style ethnic politics in France. The constraints can be traced to predominant French ideologies and institutional arrangements, including the long-standing "immigre" perspective of the state and political system. But the ideologies and institutional regime by themselves do not explain the intensity and specific direction of the contemporary politics. As important, the new discourse on pluralism, national identity, citizenship, and national integration, the new politics around citizenship, and the integrationist strategies of the immigrant groups, especially Franco-Maghrebi associations, are now shaping the specific character of ethnic politics in France.

Conclusion

Beyond the specific focus on ethnic politics, what the Foulard affair uncovered were some of the ramifications of the new nationalist citizenship in France. By the end of the reform process in 1988, and despite the lack of an actual restrictive reform, the discourse and public practices of the new nationalist citizenship were already shaping French politics. The discourse had institutional ramifications. In 1990, a "High Council for Integration" was established by the French government, whose purpose was to clarify the needs and conditions of the integration of immigrants in France. The Council was chaired by none other than Marceau Long, the previous chair of the National Commission on Nationality. Established amid the political furor of the headscarves affair, the Council maintained a clear preoccupation with the "integration" of immigrants and a specific "French model of integration." The High Commission's first annual report was entitled, "For a French Model of Integration"; its subsequent reports were updates on "immigration and integration."[10]

In each report, the Council outlined definitions and principles of integration, and provided recommendations for integration policies and other measures. The Council understood the integration of immigrants as a challenge to be met. It specified that the "French conception of integration must obey a *logic of equality and not a logic of minorities*" (Haut Conseil à l'Intégration 1991, p. 19, italics in the original). The logic and priorities of the High Council of Integration clearly followed the work laid out by the National Commission on Nationality. The implications of the new nationalist politics have been, in important ways exclusionary. Despite a stress on inclusiveness, the strong defense of the national identity urged by the commission, and continued later in such settings as the Foulard affair, has been situated as a defense against menacing challenges, both within and without the national community. The articulation of this defense by the Commission, High Council, the state, political parties, and even immigrant support groups, has relied partly on the ambiguities separating patriotism and nationalism, and partly on rejection of any sort of cosmopolitan perspective.[11] Despite the calls for tolerance, the refashioned pluralism articulated by the Nationality Commission and later, the High Commission for Integration, implied an intolerance for a diversity of particularisms and minority politics. Indeed, even though the opportunities for an ethnic politics were increasing in France, due in part to changed patterns of incorporation of immigrants, the new nationalist logic of citizenship and integration contributed to constraining those opportunities.

CHAPTER 8

Nationality Reform in the 1990s

No legislative reform of the French nationality code passed in the 1980s. Despite the absence of actual nationality revisions, I have sought to show that the conflicts over membership, identity, immigration, and integration resulted in a reconstructed French citizenship. The central features of the new citizenship politics were an apparently commonsensical consensus constructed around national identity, a self-conscious valorization of a French cultural citizenship, and a widespread belief that the national integration of immigrants through citizenship was needed to manage the immigrant "challenge." This consensus was refined and given public approbation by the 1987 National Commission on Nationality, which articulated the priorities around their specific recommendations for revising the French nationality code. Later, French politicians, state officials, immigrant activists, and others engaged in discourse and public practices that reflected and extended those priorities, as evidenced in the scarves affair and its aftermath.

But actual nationality reform does take place in France in the 1990s, not only once but twice, relatively swiftly and consecutively. The first time was in 1993, when a newly elected conservative government realized a restrictive revision of the French nationality code. The second time was in 1997, when a newly elected Socialist government led by Lionel Jospin began a new legislative reform process to rescind parts of the earlier law, with the reform passing in March 1998. In neither period does conflict over citizenship reach the levels of the previous debates. Though the revisions attracted strong parliamentary and intragovernmental critique from the opposition, they did not suscitate much visible outcry. Why? In part, both reforms were coupled with the partisan politics of re-election and with more divisive immigration bills, which sustained much of the attention. Yet that explanation is only adequate in situating the opportunities and constraints in the immediate political process. To understand their reception and import, the two successive reforms of the 1990s must be placed in the context of the previous decade. While clearly divergent in some respects, the two reforms featured key components of the ongoing nationalist reconstruction of citizenship, components that I think help explain their appeal and logic.

In this final chapter, I reflect on the nationality reforms of 1993 and 1998. To what extent were they the products or extensions of the emergent nationalist politics of citizenship described in this book? Is it useful to situate the reforms as rejections, revisions, or retrievals of French membership traditions as many of the reform proponents, opponents, and commentators have variously argued? This chapter does not intend to provide an exhaustive account of the two reform efforts. My point here is to highlight the ways in which both reforms were part of continuing citizenship processes in France. The reforms confirm the increasing patterns of divergence and convergence that are visible in France as well as in other European polities. If at times such patterns appear contradictory, they nonetheless are tied to specific political processes. These processes I suggest are shifting the meanings and practices of citizenship in consequential ways.

In 1993, a newly elected conservative government dramatically recaptured control of the government. The legislative elections featured a renewed Center-Right alliance (UDF and RPR), which won more seats and more of an absolute majority than at any point since 1958. While the victory marked the advent of a second period of cohabitation—the President (still François Mitterrand) from one party and the Prime Minister (Edouard Balladur) from another competing one—the conservative government now had the advantage of a strong majority in the National Assembly (Feldblum 1996:134–145). As part of their electoral campaigns against the Socialists and their efforts to counter the appeal of Le Pen, the major rightist parties pledged to reform immigration and nationality policy. Soon after its installation in power, the conservative government passed a set of restrictive immigration measures, known as the Pasqua Law (after Charles Pasqua who was then Minister of the Interior), and a restrictive nationality reform, known as the Méhaignerie Law (after Pierre Méhaignerie who was the Minister of Justice at the time).

The restrictive immigration measures did not cover nationality reform although many commentators and protestors subsumed the Méhaignerie nationality reforms under the general guise of the Pasqua Law. Indeed, the conflation of the two laws may help explain the lack of specialized focus on the nationality reforms. On the one hand, it was clearly the case that the immigration provisions provoked considerably more protest from a wide array of groups as well as segments of the state. In fact, the French Constitutional Council ruled that several provisions in the Pasqua Law violated the rights of foreigners as individuals. Writing of the decision, a lead article in *Le Monde* stated that the Council had ruled that "foreigners are not French but they are people (*Le Monde* 8/16/93, p. 1).[1] The nationality reform, on the other hand, incorporated many of the recommendations issued in 1988 by the National Commission on Nationality, which had been approved by those on the Left and Right. Indeed, according to the government and other proponents of the reform, the law simply translated the recommendations of the Nationality Commission. The 1993 nationality reform, introduced three major modifications to the French Nationality code, two of which affected those of immigrant origin who acquired French nationality under Article 44, and another which affected those of immigrant origin who were attributed French nationality under Article 23 and its extensions. Recall that Article 44 constituted the major mode of nationality acquisition for second-generation immigrants, covering those born and raised in France of foreign parents themselves born elsewhere. The reform required that those born in France of foreign parents would henceforth have to file formal requests to become French. In the words of the law, youth of immigrant origin would have to "manifest their wish" for French citizenship between the ages of sixteen and twenty-one (*Journal Officiel* 12/31/93; Philippe Bernard, "Nationalité Française, nouveau mode d'emploi," *Le Monde* 1/1/94). As with the prior regulation of Article 44, there was a list of conditions with which eligible youth had to comply, including the demonstration of residence for the previous five consecutive years in France. Failure to complete the procedure during the period allowed, whether through neglect or ignorance, would result in the loss of eligibility to become French under Article 44, while leaving open the possibility for naturalization.

A second prong of the 1993 revision dealt a further modification to Article 44. The law removed the possibility for parents to obtain the French nationality for their minor children born in France. Previously, immigrant parents could anticipate their children's right to French nationality at the age of their majority by filing a claim while their children were minors (de la Pradelle 1994).[2] For example, over 20,000 foreign minors acquired French nationality in 1994 as a result of applications filed by their parents before the new law went into effect on January 1, 1994 (*Le Monde* 1/26–27/97:22).[3] Now, the territorial rights to citizenship in France — Articles 44 and 23 — were based on the presumption of inevitable (and required) socialization by immigrants in France. From the perspective of the 1889 law that refined the territorial right of the automatic acquisition of citizenship at the age of majority for children born in France of immigrant parents, such children had a vocation to become French.

Up until 1993, children born in France to immigrant parents not born in France arguably were defined — if only in principle — less by their nationality status at birth (i.e., foreigner) than by their birthright (i.e., the absolute right to be French). The 1993 reform inverted this logic. "The weakening of the territorial right," argued French scholar Géraud de la Pradelle, "indirectly reinforces the preeminence of the lineage (blood) right" (1993–1994:29). Children born in France of immigrant parents were to be defined by their birth status — as foreigners — until they achieved their birthright. They were to be foreign until they could prove themselves French.

The insertion of a voluntaristic step by immigrant youth was of course an implementation of one of the recommendations of the Commission on Nationality.

It was a recommendation that had been greeted in 1988 with widespread support. In this respect, the modified Article 44 was not simply a rightist solution, but reflected the general changed political commitments to citizenship. From 1988 onward, the leading parties in France had supported a new commitment to integrationist voluntarism in citizenship or at least in national membership. In other words, politicians on both the Right and Left as well as numerous immigrant activist groups called for a commitment to national ("French-style") integration by immigrants. In 1988, the President of France-Plus approvingly claimed of the Nationality Commission that its recommendations upheld "the republican model, the values of the Revolution . . . they propose to reinvigorate the Francophone space" (interview in *Libération* 1/1/88).

According to the government, the impetus for the second modification of Article 44 once again came from the Nationality Commission, which had stressed the need for awareness and acceptance in becoming French. The slogans of no "French against their will" and no "French without their will/desire" were traced to the Nationality Commission's recommendations. Of course, these slogans have other lineages as well. In the mid-eighties, Le Pen and the National Front used these slogans to target Franco-Algerians in France and call for a radical deletion of all territorial rights in the French Nationality Code. In 1983, reflecting postcolonial politics and the politics of the right to difference, the Socialist minister Gaston Deferre also invoked the slogan of no more French against their will in his call to reform the application of *double jus soli* for children of Algerian immigrants. But those antecedents were blurred in favor of the Nationality Commission, which had effectively diminished the taint of Le Pen from a restrictive citizenship reform, removed the problematic memories of the colonial and postcolonial past, and reduced the possibility for differentialist reasoning.

At the same time, government officials also defined the decision to remove from parents the right to claim French citizenship for their minor children as an antifraud measure. According to the government, foreign parents claimed French nationality for their French-born children in order to avoid or at least diminish the possibility of deportation. Once again, these concerns certainly reflected the influence of the Bureau of Nationality and the Ministry of Interior. Likewise, another antifraud measure of the reform was the provision that greatly extended the waiting period for nationality eligibility for foreign spouses of French nationals. Henceforth foreign spouses would have to wait two years before becoming eligible for French citizenship, up from six months.

The final major revision of the 1993 reform sharply curtailed the privileged lien—in terms of *double jus soli*—of former French colonial populations. The Méhaignerie Law rescinded the 1973 reform that had extended Article 23—the provision granting the right of *double jus soli*—to certain of France's former colonies and overseas territories. Besides rescinding the 1973 extension of Article 23, the 1993 reform also modified its application of *double jus soli* as it concerned

Algeria. Recall that the children of many immigrants from Algeria were covered under the original Article 23 of the nationality code because Algeria had been considered akin to a French department prior to its independence. The government established new conditions of prolonged legal residence in France for the parents in order for *double jus soli* to apply to their children born in France (*Le Monde* 1/1/94). Overall, the 1993 reform entailed a series of exclusions for traditional Francophone citizens. In this manner, the 1993 revision conformed best to the priorities and needs of the Nationality Bureau. As the Nationality Bureau had discussed during the earlier efforts, modification of Article 23 was aimed exclusively at its applications with regard to Algeria and other former French colonies.

It is important to note what the 1993 reform did not do. It did not abolish the territorial rights to citizenship. The reform did not abolish outright Article 44 or 23. Rather, the reform formally reconstructed the rights and criteria underlying French citizenship, a reconstruction that I have argued occurred in substance earlier. While the Left protested specific provisions of these revisions and more aggressively the Pasqua Law on immigration, their own changed discourse on citizenship complemented rather than contradicted the major thrust of 1993 nationality reform. Without question, the political impetus of the 1993 reform was most immediately a product of French partisan and electoral politics. Yet its substantive components were not simply products of rightist politics. To the contrary, the reform's core features entailed the active consent and national integration of immigrants and laid down constricted parameters of French membership, features that were part of the new nationalist consensus over citizenship priorities.

Opponents of the 1993 revisions feared that immigrant youth would not file the formal requests to become French due to neglect, ignorance, or protest. However, those fears were, for the most part, not realized. Although the new law went into effect January 1, 1994, the numbers of nationality acquisitions registered in 1994 incorporated those who became French under the new regulations as well as the completion of processes begun under the old regulations. Most likely in anticipation of the new law's effects and concerned about future revisions, the number of citizenship acquisitions, declarations, and naturalizations registered in France for 1994 rose dramatically. While approximately 23,000 foreign youth usually became French each year through Article 44, over 33,000 foreign youth filed formal declarations in 1994. Naturalizations rose 21 percent, with over 49,000 persons being naturalized in 1994. Likewise, nationality acquisitions by foreign spouses of French nationals and by foreign minors were also higher. Overall, 126,337 persons became French in 1994 in contrast to previous years where the number of nationality acquisitions was approximately 100,000. By 1995, the number of persons becoming French dropped to 92,410. The numbers of immigrant youth requesting French nationality declined somewhat but most commentators interpreted the decrease as a reflection of the changing immigrant base (*Le Monde* 1/26–27/97:22).

In 1997, the newly reinstalled Socialist government sought to introduce both immigration and nationality reforms to follow up on its campaign slogans to roll back the rightist immigration and citizenship policies of the previous years, including the 1993 Pasqua and Mehaignerie restrictive revisions. What were the central flaws of the 1993 reform according to the Socialists? The Socialists sought to symbolically reconstruct the republican tradition of membership and integration appropriated in years past by the restrictionist Right. The government's rhetoric on nationality reform was articulated less in terms of specific concerns with the 1993 law than in general terms of retrieving and reestablishing the French tradition of citizenship. Though the 1993 reform did not abolish territorial rights to citizenship, that did not prevent Lionel Jospin and the Socialists in 1997 from defining their charge against the rightist policies as an effort to "reestablish" the territorial right to French citizenship.[4] The Socialists argued that their revision would reaffirm the French "republican tradition" of membership.

French political scientist Patrick Weil's report on the history and current conditions of nationality and immigration policy in France—commissioned by Prime Minister Jospin on July 1, 1997, and submitted as an official document at the end of that month—formed the foundation of the Socialists' rhetoric and legislative proposal (Weil 1997). Weil framed his entire analysis of French nationality history and the recent reforms along the lines of automaticity and voluntarism. Voluntarism, he argued, was not an integral part of the French nationality traditions. According to Weil, from the perspective of the republican tradition, the 1993 reform's introduction of a required "manifestion of desire" appeared as its " most contestable" point (Weil 1997, chapter 3). Weil nonetheless endorsed the revalorization of French citizenship constructed during the previous decade. He argued that immigrants must not become French without their knowledge or against their will. Indeed, Weil allowed that much of the 1993 nationality provisions conformed with the "logic" of the Republican tradition. Following Weil's report, the Socialists called for the rescinding of the requirement for an actual declaration step and a few other restrictions, while they agreed to keep other key components of the 1993 law.

Beyond the symbolism of another citizenship reform, Weil's report also focused on the pragmatic needs for citizenship and immigration reform. Here too, his report formed the basis for the government's legislation. Weil argued, for example, that the problems with the 1993 reform stemmed from certain of the conditions attached to the procedure, from administrative confusion or disparities, from ignorance on the part of some immigrant youth, and finally from incoherency within the legislation's applications (1997). As pointed out by the Nationality Bureau in the earlier reform discussions of 1987, second-generation immigrant youth, who drop out of school and are unemployed, encountered great difficulty in obtaining the necessary proof of residence. Administration statistics showed that lack of residency proof was listed as the reason for 42 percent of all citizenship rejections in 1996. Moreover, a survey of administrations across France demonstrated substantial regional disparities in rejection rates. The national rejection rate in France was 2.6 percent, but some localities appeared more lenient while others were clearly more strict or arbitrary.[5] The distinctive nature of local administrative processes also informed how the 1993 reform was carried out. Certain localities within France appeared to make of an effort to get the information out to youth than others. Some local administrative institutions appeared to provide inadequate information, while others seemed themselves confused about the procedures. Finally, it was evident that some immigrant youth did not complete the step because they thought they were already French. Such confusion was not new. In the 1990 census, 130,000 foreigners wrongly declared themselves French nationals (Haut Conseil à l'Intégration 1993, p. 26).

Despite these inconsistencies, Weil disputed the notion that French immigrant youth were boycotting the procedures to request French nationality (1997).[6] Analyzing the results of the law from January 1, 1994, to the end of December 1996, Weil contended that many eligible youth were filing formal requests for citizenship acquisition. Among second-generation youth, Moroccans (37%), Portuguese (28.6%), Tunisians (12.3%), and Turks (10.2%) accounted for over 70 percent of the requests. In fact, the number of sixteen-year-old youths filing requests increased with each year; in 1996, 46 percent of eligible sixteen-year-olds filed the demand for citizenship, up from 32 percent in 1994. Of course, the increase most likely reflected less an endorsement of the new procedures than a strategic realization of possible problems.[7]

The Guigou bill (named after Elisabeth Guigou, the Socialist Minister of Justice) entailed several revisions to the existing law. Most important for many, the bill reintroduced the quasi-automatic acquisition of citizenship for immigrant youth (those covered under Article 44) at the age of majority: At eighteen, youth born in France of immigrant parents would acquire French nationality on the condition of having resided regularly in France, "during a period continuous or discontinuous of at least five years since the age of eleven." In order to ensure that these youth did not become French against their wishes—a preoccupation of the proponents of the 1993 reform and a continuing concern for the Right and some on the Left—the bill included a provision that would allow them to decline French nationality acquisition in the six months preceding the age of majority or in the year following that anniversary. The bill also restored the complete rights of *double jus soli* (as laid out in Article 23 of the French nationality code) for children of Algerians, thus lifting the restrictions placed on their rights by the 1993 reform. The Socialist proposal however did not restore the extended application of *double jus soli* for certain former French colonies, which had been laid out in the 1973 French Nationality Code reform and abolished by the 1993 reform.

Several months of debate and compromise, both within the Socialist's ruling coalition of leftist parties and among the Parliamentary opposition, the National

Assembly ensued over the Socialist government's legislative project, lasting through the end of November 1997 (Philippe Bernard, "Les Dispositions adoptees en premiere lecture," *Le Monde* 11/30/97). Certain provisions of the new reform proposal suscitated much debate. If central to the Socialists' rhetoric was the reform's reestablishment of the automatic acqusition of citizenship, several of the provisions seemed to highlight inconsistencies in their logic. Under the new law, immigrant youth eligible for French nationality under Article 44 could anticipate the acquisition of nationality by simple declaration without the accord of their parents at the age of sixteen (given they meet the same conditions of residence). The Socialist project also stated that parents could only anticipate their minor children's claim on French nationality when the child was thirteen or older, and only under under the conditions of having received the "personal consent" of the latter and if the child lived habitually in France since the age of eight (*Le Monde* 11/27/97). To recall, from 1889 until 1993, it was easy for parents to obtain French nationality for their children from birth onward. In other words, prior to the 1993 reform, such parents enjoyed full rights to anticipate their minor children's claim on French citizenship. The 1993 reform abolished that provision, and the government refused to reestablish it in the 1997 bill.[8] The 1997 bill only restored such rights for children old enough (i.e., 13 or older) to give some kind of consent.

The rhetoric of voluntarism and consent-based citizenship, while eschewed for youth at the age of majority, was brought back full force in the case of minor children. For the Gaullist politician Pierre Mazeaud, the Socialist reform was "illogical" insofar as it defended the need for consent before the age of majority and the need for automaticity afterwards.[9] For critics on the Left, the 1997 bill only partially restored the right of foreign parents to claim French nationality for their minor children born in France.

Throughout the process of parliamentary negotiations and political debates, the Socialist's nationality project drew protests as much from the Left as from the Right.[10] Interestingly, both the Right and Left drew on arguments ranging from French national traditions to human rights considerations and European concerns. As President of the High Council for Integration, the former conservative minister Simone Veil, noted that the Council had approved the Socialist reform proposals unanimously "except for that which concerns the automaticity of nationality acquisition." Veil defended the provision requiring a thirteen year old's consent as in compliance with the human rights stress on children's rights. She concluded by observing that the reform proposal, which was substantively similar in many ways to the 1993 law, "raised stronger objections from the Left than in the opposition."[11] Some Socialist and Green politicians as well as the immigrant activist organization, SOS-Racisme, contended that human rights considerations and French republican ideals called for "integral" or full territorial rights for children born in France of immigrant parents. In the end, the majority of Communist deputies as well as the Green politicians decided to abstain from the vote (*Le Monde* 11/27/97). Meanwhile, the one National Front deputy in the National Assembly condemned the "agreement" between the Left and Right leading to the "destruction of France," and protested against a "Europe submerged" by African immigration.[12] In fact, the National Front in the 1990s often drew on the wider parameters of the European Union or conflated European and French cultural identities to define their "national preference" in membership matters.[13]

The motivations behind different parts of the bill were contested. On the one hand, despite concerns by conservatives over the incidence of "paper marriages," the new legislation liberalized the provisions for foreign spouses that had been lengthened by 1993 reform. Instead of waiting two years before being eligible for nationality acquisition (as laid out in the 1993 reform), the 1998 legislation entailed that the foreign spouse of a French national would acquire French nationality by simple declaration after a delay of only a year after marriage. On the other hand, part of the Socialists' reluctance to fully restore the rights of parents to claim French nationality for their children involved their desire to combat what the government and others saw as potential opportunities for fraud by immigrants. Moreover, certain new provisions may have unintended consequences. Although the Socialists did not intend to reinforce rhetoric that immigrant origin children were foreign until their request to become or shown to be (via schooling and socialization) French, that stress was arguably formalized in another way by the 1997 bill.[14] In order to facilitate proof of French nationality—a long-standing concern of the Nationality Bureau—the legislation included a provision to require that an infant's nationality be marked on the recording of the birth (*Le Monde* 11/30/97).[15]

Regardless of their stated claim of returning to and reestablishing the republican tradition of citizenship, the Socialists' reform of 1998 certainly did not return to the legal status quo that existed prior to the 1993 revisions. In his analysis of the legislation in the French newspaper, *Le Monde*, Philippe Bernard argued that the bill advanced by the Socialists was "hardly more liberal" than the 1993 reform: "Contrary to the promises, it does not fully reestablish the situation of before 1993" (*Le Monde* 11/29/97). Bernard cites Minister of Justice Guigou's contention that "it is not possible to return to a system that creates French without their desiring it." At the same time, Bernard notes the contradiction of the Socialists' abandonment of the expression of desire for eighteen-year-old youth and continued demand for the expression of independent desire/will for minor children. Bernard concluded that the Minister of Justice Guigou's reasoning "is identical to that employed by her conservative predecessor" (*Le Monde* 11/29/97).

Like the proponents of the new reform, the reform's opponents appealed as well to the French republican tradition. Former Nationality Commission member Dominique Schnapper sharply criticized the Socialists for introducing another nationality reform, given that the 1993 reform had already adopted the

Nationality Commission's recommendations. In contrast to the Socialists who argued that to restore automatic acquisition of nationality meant a return to republican traditions, Schnapper contended that removing the new declarative step was "to renounce the symbolism of the Republic," which lay in stating the desire to be French.[16] Calling the French nation "a living community and not a community of automatic belonging," UDF Deputy François Bayrou too defended the principle of manifesting the desire to be French as part of French membership traditions (*Le Monde* 11/27/97). At one point during the final night of negotiations in the National Assembly, several deputies, including the Gaullist Pierre Mazeaud (RPR) and the former SOS-Racisme organizer Julien Dray (PS), sought to pass an amendment calling for a "republican ceremony" to be held each July 14 for all youth acceding to French citizenship. While that amendment did not pass, the Socialists did incorporate the creation of a "republican identity card" for immigrant youth to reassure their critics (*Le Monde* 11/30/97:6).

Overall, the political commitment by the various parties of the Left to roll back the previous immigration and nationality policies and the Socialist predominance in the legislative process ensured the passage of the nationality project in the National Assembly on December 1, 1997, not withstanding the abstention of the Communist and Green deputies and the opposition by parts of the Right. The battle over French nationality reform, however, did not end with the passage of bill in the French National Assembly. The French Senate, dominated by a RPR-UDF majority, continued to fight the legislative reform on other levels. While there was disagreement among the opposition about the desirability of calling for a national referendum on nationality reform, in mid-December, the Senate passed a motion demanding that President Jacques Chirac organize such a referendum.[17] The disarray and disagreement among the various parties, along with the competing focus on immigration policy, meant that opposition to the new nationality reform never became heavily publicized or politicized. In March 1998, the new nationality legislation was passed.[18]

Citizenship Reform, Membership Traditions, and the Political Process

To what extent were these two consecutive reforms of the 1990s expressions of French membership traditions? The reform processes in the 1990s affirms once again the political use and the analytical abuse of political culture arguments. Certainly, in both 1993 and 1997–1998 the reformers situated their revisions and re-envisioning of French citizenship in self-consciously referential terms to French historical and ideological traditions. Specifically, each set of reformers argued that their revision embodied the true articulation of republican membership ideals, enabled the best reinforcement of French national identity, and complied with the contemporary consensus that understood citizenship as a means to manage the challenges of immigration. What differed from 1993 to 1998 were the framing of the debate and the political opportunities of the reform. Whereas the 1993 reform was framed by its stress on voluntarism and cultural closures, the 1998 reform was in response framed by its stress on automaticity and pragmatic enclosures. The 1993 conservative reform was set in a context of domestic disarray among the Left and ambiguities about membership parameters and immigration within the larger European context. In contrast, the 1998 Socialist reform benefited from losses among the rightist parties in the domestic sphere and monetary preoccupations within the larger European context.

Proponents of the Méhaignerie Law argued that the 1993 reform simply implemented the Nationality Commission's recommendations, which had themselves been presented and represented as the republican solution. The National Commission on Nationality had strongly recommended—throughout its report as well as in specific propositions—that the quasi-automatic acquisition of French nationality by youth of immigrant origin be revised to incorporate a required voluntary step (e.g., Long 1988, vol. 2:214–218). Defending the 1993 reform in the face of the Socialist efforts in 1997, the moderate-right politician Simone Veil, who had been Minister of Cities and Integration in the previous Rightist government, asserted that the reform simply followed the spirit of the Commission by introducing a required step to ask for French nationality so to "confer on the acquisition of nationality the value of engagement" (*Le Monde* 10/16/97). The conservatives focused on the central importance of voluntarism to justify their restrictive revisions for the acquisition of French nationality in 1993.

Likewise, the 1987 Nationality Commission had consistently stressed the need to affirm anew the parameters of the French national identity and community. Their reasons included transformations due to decolonialization, continuing changes in Europe, and prospective economic and demographic shifts along North-South lines (Long 1988, vol. 2:168–184, 234–236). Thus, the conservatives were able to focus simultaneously on the need to reinforce French national identity and their right to enforce restrictive closures against former colonial populations and other prospective migrants and citizens. The constrictive Pasqua Law on immigration and accompanying conservative rhetoric of zero immigration was of a piece with the citizenship reform, its stress on closure, and its exclusionary implications.

The 1992 Maastricht Treaty of the European Union, which established a new category of European Union citizenship, reinforced French public opinion about the need to defend French national identity. While not a central factor in the passage of the immigration and citizenship reforms, the continuing integration of the European Union acted as a counterpart to the variegated nationalist politics of citizenship within France. For some opponents of European integration on the Right and Left, a revised and re-envisioned French citizenship was part of the elaboration and defense of the French national identity. For other proponents of European integration, the promotion of a culturalist Europe complemented the promotion of a culturalist French citizenship and a supplemental European citizenship.

The new citizenship trends and politics that had enabled the 1993 reform did not drop out in 1997. Consensus remained about the need to reinforce the French national identity and the necessity for a republican nationality solution to immigration. Indeed, these linkages, which had been newly stressed and forged during the 1980s, contributed to the logic and appeal of the 1998 reform. Consider the contrast between the 1973 Nationality reform and the reforms of the 1990s. The last major nationality reform of 1973 had presumed the assimilationist impulse. "It is contrary to (France's) tradition, as to her role in the world, to restrain the possibilities offered to foreigners to become one of ours," declaimed Pierre Mazeaud, the Gaullist politician who would later become a major supporter for more restrictive nationality reforms, "it is contrary to our profoundly liberal ideas to deceive the hopes of those who, working in France, search for the best possible assimilation."[19] By the 1990s the relationship between immigrants and French citizenship had become problematized by those across the political spectrum. In contrast to the 1973 reform, the management of citizenship was intricately tied to the management of immigrant and immigration policy. It is no surprise that while in 1984, the French legislature was able to produce consensus on residency legislation for immigrants apart from citizenship policy, by the early 1990s immigration policy and citizenship policy were of a piece.[20]

In requesting Patrick Weil to submit legislative proposals for both immigration and nationality reform, the Socialist Prime Minister Lionel Jospin underscored the intertwined character of the two policy domains. "France is an old country of immigration and republican integration," opens Jospin's letter. The need to define a "firm and dignified immigration policy . . . a determined and generous policy of republican integration," implicated simultaneously revising immigration regulations and citizenship-access criteria.[21] Recalling the same republican traditions and membership ideologies referenced by the National Commission on Nationality and the 1993 reformers, Patrick Weil and the Socialists inversed the voluntarist argument. They contended that the French political cultural framework insisted on the automatic acquisition of citizenship for at least certain groups of citizens. They stressed a series of pragmatic citizenship enclosures in order to manage immigration in the face of both external and domestic pressures.

Domestic Political Processes and Changes in Citizenship

What are the implications of changes in French citizenship? Are there coherent or clear directions in citizenship trends? For over a decade from the 1980s to the 1990s, changes in the politics and policy of French citizenship and nationality pointed in exclusionary and restrictive directions. In fact, the reform of 1998 did not rescind all those changes. The nationalist reconstruction of French citizenship that emerged through the eighties continued to inform both Conservative and Socialist reforms of nationality in the nineties. What explains French restrictive politics? The nationalist character of French citizenship politics, while informed by the parameters of historical traditions and institutional patterns, was constructed through the series of political conflicts, debates, and reform processes portrayed in this book. Understanding the historical and institutional membership traditions could not suffice nor substitute for an analysis of citizenship changes.

The implications of French citizenship politics points to the need to bring back in the political process, and especially domestic political processes, in our analyses of citizenship.[22] This book has focused on how domestic political processes contributed to the reconstruction of citizenship meanings and to the emergence of a largely restrictive politics of citizenship in France. This is not to argue, however, that domestic political processes inevitably or necessarily shape citizenship outcomes in exclusionary directions. The series of citizenship conflicts and reforms from the early 1980s to the late 1990s underscore the causal importance of the domestic political processes in shaping both restrictive and expansive politics and policies. In a similar fashion, I would argue that efforts to understand contemporary German conflicts over membership and the expansive reform efforts there to institute dual nationality regulations and liberalize citizenship acquisition need to turn to the domestic political processes taking place.[23] And I do not mean to suggest that domestic political processes work in isolation of international and transnational forces. The different phases of the French citizenship politics were certainly informed by a variety of such forces, including transnational human rights rhetoric and movements, the actual and prospective changes entailed in European Union migration and citizenship policy, and new levels of governance and intervention.

Domestic political processes are not neutral isolated forums in which activities take place. Rather, the specific dynamics of the political process help shape outcomes. In this study, I have sought to show that attention to the complexities of the political process is critical, change is multicausal, and the specific configuration of determinative factors shift from one phase of the process to another. The interaction of political agency, contingency, institutions, and ideas all shape opportunity, strategy, and change. In the initial phases of French citizenship politics, mobilization of movements and groups and political agents with dissimilar aims were the determinant factors in shaping change. As the reform processes moved on, institutional factors became determinant, as the institutionalized meanings of citizenship, French statism, and French institutional practices, played key roles in shaping the parameters for change. In the later stages, the broadening of the debates, the shift into different terrains, including the Commission and television, and the pactlike style of national consensus that emerged, proved to be key for re-constructing French citizenship along nationalist lines.

The political processes by which the new politics of citizenship were constructed underscores "the diffuse, interactive way in which meaning, intentions, and action are woven together" (March and Olsen 1989:52). In the initial phases, struggles over pluralism and national identity lay the groundwork for an intense contestation over citizenship. By the mid-eighties, a refashioned pluralism, which defined pluralism largely as a defense of national particularisms and the national unity, lay the groundwork for the major components of the Commission's propositions. This direction was reinforced when the Commission, the immigrant associations, politicians, and later the High Council, clearly set themselves off from a differentialist approach, or an "ethnic politics" style of politics. At the same time, the debates and preoccupations with the national identity framed the problematic of citizenship for the Right and Left. Reformulating citizenship and immigrants into a problematic enabled the perspective that constituted the Muslim, Maghrebi populations as a critical challenge to French conceptions and practices of citizenship, a challenge to be managed by nationality reform. These processes formed the basis on which actual nationality revisions were carried out in the 1990s.

Throughout this book, I have insisted on the malleability of nationhood traditions, the importance of political agency and contingency, and the pressures of institutional and ideological constraints. As the contestation over citizenship progressed through the eighties and nineties, republican ideologies were used in a variety of ways by diverse agents to justify contradictory aims. As divergent political agents strove to reconstruct and reinvent French citizenship traditions, ideas of political culture became part and product of the political processes. At the same time, the political processes were shaped by the array of institutional parameters and factors. The state, French ideologies, and the institutionalized regime of citizenship meanings all provided resources and pressures, while imposing constraints and limits on the political processes. By interweaving all the different dimensions of the political process, we can begin to understand the transformations taking place in citizenship today.

APPENDIX A

State Agencies, Political Parties, Social Organizations, and Immigrant Associations at Which Interviews Were Conducted

State Agencies

Conseil de l'Etat.
Ministère des Affaires Etrangères. Bureau de la Nationalité; Français de l'Etranger et des Etrangers de France.
Ministère des Affaires Sociales et de la Solidarité Nationale. Direction de la Population et des Migrations.
Ministère de l'Intérieur. Libertés Publiques et des Affaires Juridiques.
Ministère de la Justice. Bureau de la Nationalitè à la Direction des Affaires Civiles.

State Commission

National Commission on Nationality (also called the Nationality Commission and the Commission des Sages)

Political Parties

Front National (FN). Paris.
Parti Socialiste (PS). Paris.
Parti Communiste Français (PCF). Paris.
Union pour La Démocratie Française (UDF). Paris.
Rassemblement Pour la République (RPR). Paris.

Solidarity and Antiracist Organizations

Centre d'Information et d'Etudes sur les Migrations Internationales (CIEMI).
    Paris.
Fédération des Associations de Solidarité avec des Travailleurs Immigrés
    (FASTI). Paris.
Groupe d'Information et de Soutien des Travailleurs Immigrés (GISTI). Paris.
Ligue de Droits de l'Homme (LDH). Paris.
Mouvement Contre le Racisme et Pour l'Amitié entre des Peuples (MRAP). Paris.

Immigrant Associations

Conseil des Associations Immigrées en France (CAIF). Paris.
Collectif d'Etudes et Dynamisation de l'Immigration Portugaise (CEDEP). Paris.
France-Plus. Paris.
Memoire Fertile.
SOS-Racisme. Paris.
TEXTURE. Lille.

Appendix B

Legislative Propositions to Reform the French Nationality Code, 1979–1987

Bas, P. 1979. "Proposition de Loi Tendant à Modifier les Conditions d'Acquisition de la Nationalité Française." Assemblée Nationale. No. 1096. May 16. Paris.

Chirac, J., and A. Chalandon. 1986. "Projet de Loi Portant Réforme du Code de la Nationalité Française." Assemblée Nationale. No. 444. November 12. Paris.

Mayoud, A. 1986. "Proposition de Loi Modifiant les Conditions d'Acquisition de la Nationalité Française à raison de la Naissance et de la Résidence en rance." Assemblée Nationale. No. 70. April 23. Paris.

Mayoud, A. 1988. "Proposition de Loi Relative à l'Acquisition de la Nationalité Française et au Retour dans le Pays d'Origine." Assemblée Nationale. No. 181. July 21. Paris.

Mazeaud, P. et al. 1986. "Proposition de Loi Tendant à Réformer le Code de la Nationalité." Assemblée Nationale. No. 183. June 4. Paris.

Le Pen, J.-M. et al. 1986. "Proposition de Loi Tendant à Modifier le code de la Nationalité Française." Assemblée Nationale. No. 82. April 21. Paris.

Roatta, J. et al. 1987. "Proposition de Loi Tendant à Rendre Incompatible la Citoyenneté Française et l'Accomplissement d'un Service Militaire dans une Armée Etrangère." Assemblée Nationale. No. 957. October 2. Paris.

Notes

1. Studying Citizenship

1. For studies on the expanded rights of noncitizens in postwar Europe, see Soysal (1994), Layton-Henry (1990), and Hammar (1990).

2. There is a burgeoning literature on nationalist thought of the Right across Europe, as well as some analyses of Left nationalism.

3. Global trends, such as those toward regionalization and subnational identities and those toward transnationalization and supranational identities, are changing citizenship practices and the organization of membership in the nation-state system (Soysal 1994). For example, anticipation of a unifying Europe played a role in the debates over the nationality code (see chapter 6).

4. Since the early 1990s, the extension of European Union competency into numerous policy areas has led to more concerted efforts to harmonize the immigration, citizenship, and immigrant incorporation policies of European Union member states. These efforts have not been very successful. There has been more harmonization on policies governing the access of foreigners to European Union member states than on policies governing domestic citizenship or incorporation legislation.

5. Political process, in the sense that political scientists such as Bentley or Easton used the term, was defined as "the activities of people in various groups as they struggle for—and use—power to achieve personal and group purposes." According to this framework, "the world is seen as an ongoing stream of events in time, as becoming rather than merely being . . . single causation is impossible. Multiple causation and multiple effects are inevitable." As an agent-centered approach, most political process analyses were "elite-focused," but they also acknowledged that "there is rarely a single dividing line between major and minor actors" (Gross 1968).

6. This revised political process approach was developed in some early work by Charles Tilly and others (Tilly, Tilly, and Tilly [1975]; Tilly [1978]; also see McAdam 1982:36–60). These analyses, for the most part applied the framework to one spectrum of politics. They primarily focused on political process in the contentious politics involving social movements or revolutionary change. Tilly's work on revolutionary change and McAdam's work on the rise of a social movement, for example, focused on the role of political agency, the "interplay of both environment factors (and) factors internal to" the group(s) studied, and the changing "structure of political opportunities" (McAdam, 1982, pp. 6–60). Such models stressed the political "factors shaping institutionalized political processes." More recently, social movement scholars have refined their process-oriented analyses to incorporate a focus on "political opportunities, mobilizing structures, and cultural framings" as determinants shaping movement development and contentious politics (McAdam, McCarthy, and Zald, eds., 1996; McAdam, Tarrow, and Tilly, 1996).

7. For a recent exposition of the political process approach that still limits its application to studies of social movements and revolutionary change, see McAdam, Tarrow, and Tilly (1996). Even where scholars have attempted to bring the political process framework into new areas of analysis, such as governance in the European Union, they nonetheless focus their work on the influence of social movement activity. See, Gary Marks and Doug McAdam (1996). Also see Marks's exposition of his "actor-centered approach," which is similar to political process approaches but not focused on social movements (1996).

8. For comparative studies, see, e.g., Martin Baldwin-Edwards and Martin Schain, eds. (1994); Tomas Hammar (1990); W. R. Brubaker, ed., (1989); Zig Layton-Henry, ed. (1990); also see Barbara Schmitter Heisler (1992). For studies on France, see Patrick Weil (1991); Jacqueline Costa-Lascoux (1990); and Catherine Wihtol de Wenden (1988b).

9. For a sampling of the reflections on citizenship that have appeared in the eighties, see Leca (1985); Balibar (1984, 1988); Le Gallou (1987); *Après-Demain* (1986); and de Wenden (1988a). There have been numerous articles and special journal issues on specific episodes of the new politics of citizenship, such as civic rights or the attempted revision of the nationality code. For a sampling, see *Hommes & Libertés* (1985, 1987); *Hommes & Migrations* (1987b, 1990); *IM'media Magazine* (1988); Costa-Lascoux (1987); *Plein Droit* (1988); *IRIS* (1987); Verbunt (1988); Brubaker (1990). For a sampling of the commentary on questions of national identity and citizenship, see Krulic (1988a, b), and Safran (1990). For an overview of the issues and political context, see de Wenden (1985, 1988a, b, c). Finally, for analyses of the political logic underlying the new politics, see Sayad (1982), Lochak (1987), Brubaker (1990). For recent collections offering a broader comparative view of the new politics of citizenship in Western Europe, see Cesarani and Fulbrook (1996); Hansen and Weil (1999).

10. Nationalism signals the "re-casting and re-formation of communities and of political boundaries where the old basis of the polity has been radically undermined" (Kamenka 1973:15). It is articulated as a process where there is "the desire to preserve or enhance a people's national or cultural identity when that identity is threatened," or is popularly understood as threatened (Plamenatz 1973:24). Ernest Gellner noted that the imperative for homogeneity "appears on the surface in the form of nationalism," the principle being "the convergence of political and cultural units" (1983:1, 39).

11. The literature focusing on the constructedness of nations and national identity is burgeoning, perhaps, partly in response to the numerous new states and re-articulated nations of Eastern Europe. In his book, *Nationalism Reframed*, Rogers Brubaker (1996) moves away from the reified national models of his earlier work to emphatically support the notion of nations as constitutive of contingent, constructed, and dynamic processes.

12. The usage of these arguments to define and defend conceptions of citizenship are not French-specific. See Smith (1988, 1997), who analyzes American conceptions of citizenship and national identity along three perspectives, liberal, republican, and Americanist. For a comparison of American and French republicanism, see Higonnet (1988).

13. The contemporary phenomena regarding citizenship has generated a large and diverse array of scholarship and commentary, but the discussion here is confined to works specifically on citizenship and immigration.

14. For studies on French citizenship that rely on a "national model" approach, see for example, Weil (1991); Hollifield (1994); Brubaker (1992); Schnapper (1991). For comparative studies that rely to a greater or lesser extent on a "national model" approach, see Brubaker (1992); Hollifield (1992). For a critique of the national models approach, see Silverman (1992).

15. Krulic (1988a). For a sampling of those who argue that immigrants pose severe challenges to French model of membership and incorporation, see Costa-Lascoux (1989a), Schnapper (1987, 1991), Le Gallou (1985), and Le Pen (1984). Politicians as diverse as Mitterrand, Chirac, and Le Pen have all stated that contemporary immigrants pose special challenges because of their "cultural distance" and "difference"; though it should be noted that Mitterrand's position substantially changed in the eighties, from a refusal to speak in terms of challenges to an embracing of the terms. Note that this manner of speaking of challenges differs from that of Sayad (1984) who also argues that immigrants pose severe challenges, not because of static qualities, but rather due to the dynamics of their ambiguous status as nationals and nonnationals. Those who argue against the specificity of contemporary immigrants, and stress the need to historicize the construction of the immigrant challenge discourse include Milza (1985), Noiriel (1984, 1985, 1988), and Lochak (1985).

16. For studies that rely on political cultural variables, see for example, Brubaker (1992); Schnapper (1991).

17. The paradigm of racism and racial politics has been increasingly used in studies on immigrants in France. Dubet remarks "One can only be surprised by the place of racism in the description of the immigrant experience, and of the anti-racist arguments in the explanations, compared to the small number of empirical studies concentrated on racism, prejudice and aggression" (1989:123).

18. "Racial" politics has also been used to describe the politics of the PCF during the seventies and early eighties. See Schain (1985), and Cuches (1982) on racism and the expression "seuill de tolerance" or "threshold of tolerance" (1990).

19. On British politics, see Dummont and Nicol (1990); Layton-Henry (1993); and Miles (1993). On France and racial politics, see Silverman (1992).

20. The group of "new institutionalists" is actually quite diverse, and includes scholars whose work examines historical legacies that are combined with the ongoing interactive processes taking place between agents and institutions, those whose work provides new analytical outlooks on the impact of institutional processes and pathways, and those whose work is on the development of institutional norms and state and global institutional frameworks (Skocpol, 1992; Steinmo, Thelen, and Longstreth 1992; Hall, 1993; North 1990; Kato 1996; Soysal 1994; Scott et al. 1994; Finnemore 1996).

21. For a discussion of the need to incorporate more process-oriented factors in the new institutionalist framework, see Fitzgerald (1996:54–95).

22. For example, using a process-oriented approach, Karl illuminated the role that specific kinds of transition processes—the distinctive mode and scope of each transitional phase—in democratization can have in shaping the new regime. See Karl (1991:163–191).

23. Attention to the influence of interpretations and interpretative contexts, or what some scholars have labeled "cultural framings," has become part of the conceptual framework of political process studies. See McAdam, McCarthy, and Zald (1996). Zald defines "cultural framings" as the "cultural construction of repertoires of contention and frames," which are "strategically produced" (1996:261).

24. My understanding of interpretative contexts has also been informed by Richard Handler's (1988) study of nationalism in Quebec.

25. By 1992, there were an estimated 18–19 million legal foreign residents in Western Europe. These figures do not take into account undocumented foreigners, estimated by the ILO to number about 2,600,000 in 1991 (Fassmann and Nunz 1994:5; Baldwin-Edwards and Schain 1994:5).

26. Historically, nationality and citizenship have been distinguished along the lines of nation and polity, with nationality referring to the status of belonging to a nation and citizenship to the legal status within a polity. Formally, the rights of nationality—in so far as it delineated membership in a specific nation-state—did not automatically confer on one the full rights of citizenship in French his-

tory. French women, for example, were nationals, yet until they were granted suffrage in 1944, did not have one of the basic rights of citizenship. Foreigners who naturalized were also discriminated against in terms of citizenship rights: Until 1983, a person who acquired French nationality through naturalization was not automatically granted all the rights of citizenship.

27. The Nationality Code is the body of French legislation that governs the acquisition, attribution, and loss of French citizenship. For a compilation of the code and its legislative additions, see *La Nationalité Française. Textes et Documents* (1985).

2. The New Immigrants and Citizenship

1. All census numbers must be qualified. First, different government agencies report different total numbers of foreigners. The census figures are considered to slightly underestimate the total numbers. Second, the numbers of foreigners and nationals are reported through self-identification in the census. Studies after the 1982 census as well as after the 1990 census have shown that the self-reporting results in substantive numbers of wrong declarations. For example, in 1982, approximately 280,000 persons, who were French by attribution at birth, declared themselves to be foreigners. At the same time, approximately 60,000 foreigners wrongly declared themselves French nationals. It has been documented that a large number of Franco-Algerian youth declared themselves foreigners in the 1982 census. In the 1990 census, 130,000 foreigners wrongly declared themselves French nationals, while 131,000 French nationals wrongly declared themselves foreigners. See, the report of the Haut Conseil à l'Intégration (1993:26–34).

2. As Noiriel (1988) notes, the awareness that France is in fact partly constituted by immigration, and interest in that aspect of French history grew substantially in recent decades. An oft-quoted phrase in France is that a third of all French has foreign ancestry.

3. Among policy makers in postwar France, there was a contingent who planned for the permanent settlement of culturally compatible immigrants in France to compensate for the depletion of the population following the World War. But these plans were never really implemented, and when the economic crises arrived, efforts were undertaken to encourage the return of the migrant workers.

4. On the one hand, there was a 31 percent change from 1968 to 1975 in the number of foreigners in France. On the other hand, the proportion of naturalized French remained steady through the sixties and seventies (and eighties), hovering around 2.7 percent. See Tapinos (1988).

5. A Council of Europe—SOPEMI—report noted there was "an approximate zero migration surplus" for the years from 1976 to 1981. This does not address the issue of illegal or so-called "clandestine" immigration.

6. Different sources cite different figures. In contrast to the census results cited in the text, the Department of Interior in France estimated for 1982 a total of 4.2 million foreigners or 7.8 percent of the resident populations. The official demographic institute in France, L'INSEE, considers the census figures to be an underestimation, and the Department of Interior's an overestimation (DPM report 1986).

7. However, the actual census figures do not take into account the number of incorrect self-identifications. After correcting for those figures, the census of 1990 registers, in fact, a slight increase in the number of foreigners in France. See the report published by the Haut Conseil à l'Integration (1993:31).

8. The proportion of French by acquisition was lower than in the eighties; it constituted only .9 percent of the resident population.

9. To explain the conflicts in immigration politics in the eighties, these scholars point to a conjuncture of "crises" affecting France and its integrationist institutions: crises of the postindustrial economic order, cultural model, educational institutions, and so on (cf. Milza 1985).

10. This figure excludes the foreign population from the former Soviet Union. Note, however, that Table 2.1 includes under the category of "European foreign population total" populations from the former Soviet Union.

11. Until the 1981 law permitting the right of association for foreign groups, foreign associations were subject to strict rules. As a result, many organizations were formally set up by the embassies of the countries of origin and other organizations were solidarity organizations, set up by French nationals and including foreigners. For example, the Federation of Associations of Solidarity with Immigrant Workers (FASTI) was established in 1967 (see FASTI 1987). Others include GISTI, a legal-aid group, and CIEMI, a resource organization.

12. At the time, previous flows of immigrants in France were also seen as visibly different from the French native populace. See Schor (1985) on the visibility of immigrant populations in pre–World War II France as perceived by the French popular press and public opinion.

13. See Daniel Carton, "Pierre Mehaignerie et Simone Veil demandant une 'correction' du texte." *Le Monde* (6/22/93).

14. The term *second generation* has suscitated much debate. Another frequently used term is *youth issued from immigration*, a catchall phrase (Marange and Lebon 1982). Partly, the problem has been that many of these people are not technically second generation, but first, third, or even later generations of immigrants. Partly, the problem has been that significant—both in terms of numbers and visibility—proportions of these people are not technically foreigners, but French nationals. See Gonzalez-Quijano (1988); on the Algerian immigration, see Sayad (1977, 1981–1982).

15. These are rough estimates. Y. Gonzalez-Quijano quotes a figure of 785,880 youth of Maghrebi origin in France in 1982: 480,000 Algerians, 216,720 Moroccans, and 89,120 Tunisians. He is only counting those classified as "for-

eigners" in the 1982 census, and not those holding dual nationality. Gonzalez estimated for 1986 that the overall population of youth of Maghrebi origin and Franco-Maghrebis was between 1 and 2 million (1988:71–72). There is a continuing overlap and confusion between these two categories as reported in the French censuses because of youth who declare themselves foreigners when in fact they are also French nationals and the reverse.

16. Article 23 of the CNF reads, "A child, whether legitimate or natural, born in France is French when at least one of the parents is also born there."

17. Article 44 states, "All individuals born in France of foreign parents acquires the French nationality at the age of majority, if at that date, he has in France his residence, and if he had 'during five years' which preceded his habitual residence in France or in the territories or countries for which there is the attribution or acquisition of French nationality, or was during his residence, governed by special dispositions." See *La Nationalité Française* (1985:25). In addition, the government may refuse the acquisition of citizenship for "indignity or for lack of assimilation," as per Article 46 of the code. But such refusals are rare. During the conflicts over Article 44, there was much furor in the press over the exigencies of certain of the requirements, including those dealing with penal violations (Article 79). Immigrant supporters accused the Chirac government of requiring those of immigrant origin to be even better than the French. For its part, the state's Bureau of Nationality was "astounded" at the "countertruths" in the press, given that Article 79 already existed in the code. All the Bureau was doing was "clarifying" and "extending" the provision (Interview, Bureau of Nationality).

18. The major exception to this pattern was the Vichy Regime, which instituted restrictive citizenship legislation, including the retroactive loss of French citizenship. See Brubaker (1992).

19. Children born in France of Algerian parents born in Algeria before the 1963 independence, when Algeria was a French department, are French at birth. This rule led to splits by nationality within families. For example, a sibling of a French national by Article 23 may not be a French national if he or she was either born in Algeria before 1963 (and thus lost French nationality with his or her parents at the time of independence) or after 1963 (when Algeria is no longer considered part of France).

20. The number of these children attributed French citizenship increased from the 1970s to the 1980s, but still remains small in comparison to the Algerian population. In 1975, the figure was estimated at 2,294, in 1982 at 6,091, and in 1985 at 8,033.

21. These youth do have the opportunity to decline French nationality if only one of the parents were also born in France; the number of "répudiations," however, has been very small (Lebon 1987).

22. The total number of estimated acquisitions of French citizenship through Article 44 from 1973 through 1986 was 224,572 (Lebon 1987:5).

Brubaker (1989) cites a figure of "around 250,000" persons acquiring French citizenship via Article 44 since 1972.

23. On its part, the state also has a right to refuse these requests to decline French citizenship. Since 1979 (the first time, figures were available), the number of refusals issued by the state has varied between twenty and sixty.

24. See Mort Rosenblum, "France Views African Immigrants" (AP News Briefs, 8/16/96). Also see "Hunger Strike Divides French Ruling Coalition" (Reuters, 8/20/96), and "Juppe Rejects African Immigrants' Demands" (Reuters 8/22/96).

25. The changes in the parameters of citizenship are not French-specific or even specific to the experiences of modern migration, though their ambiguous status highlights the changes, and in some cases, extends them further (Soysal 1994).

26. The 1977 events were replayed in 1993, when the French government attempted to place greater restrictions on the entry and residency by foreigners, and the Conseil d'Etat ruled against parts of the measures.

27. Pierre Mazeaud was cited in Thierry Bréhier, "La Loi de 1973 avait été votée dans un climat d'unanimité," *Le Monde* 11/26/97.

3. Politicizing Citizenship in French Immigration Politics

1. An extensive survey of the French press, both central and regional journals, was carried out for the 1980s. In 1981–1982, the two primary controversies in citizenship and nationality policy were a possible computerization of national identity cards and the egalitarian changes enacted by the government regarding family name and nationality attribution.

2. In this chapter, I use far and extreme Right interchangeably. The term refers to extreme Right parties, including the National Front (FN) and to extreme right intellectual and political clubs, also known as "the new right" ("la nouvelle droite"), such as the club GRECE. For articles on the rise of the extreme Right movement since the seventies, see Mayer and Perrineau (1989), Charlot (1986), and Taguieff (1984, 1985). It should be noted that the links between the extreme Right and the classic Right ("la droite classique") or majoritarian Right, namely the RPR and UDF, grew closer in the eighties, with clubs and politicians overlapping the two camps. For example, the Club de l'Horloge was an RPR linked club many of whose members and intellectuals then joined the FN; other examples include the RPR politician, A. Gritteray, and the party, CNPI—all served as passageways between the extreme and majoritarian Right.

3. What qualifies as an immigration issue? Immigration policies include those dealing broadly with the regulation of population flows and the incorporation of foreign and immigrant populations within the polity. They include poli-

cies governing entry and residence requirements, as well as housing, education, work, and social welfare policies.

4. See, for example, *Le Monde* 11/24–25/85; *Le Témoignage Chrétien* 10/13–19/86; *La Croix* 12/28/85. These views also surfaced in interviews with politicians and immigrant activists.

5. This analysis does not deal with the rise of ethnic activism in France during the 1960s and 1970s. See Beer (1980), Safran (1984 and 1985); for a broader comparative perspective on ethnic and regionalist movements, see Smith (1979).

6. Identity politics can also be considered as part of an incipient "passage au politique" engaged in by immigrant groups before 1983. The term refers to the movement of issues and styles from the private sphere, from marginal and de-politicized positions into the public sphere (de Wenden 1988b:349–356). Identity politics can be defined as the politicization of issues previously relegated to the private sphere such as "sexuality, interpersonal relations, lifestyle, and culture" (Kaufman 1990). From this perspective, the affirmation of "maghrebinite" and North African culture is an example of identity politics.

7. *Sans Frontière* (No. 80 1983); *Hommes et Migrations (1985:4)*, and Perotti (1983).

8. Other scholars echo the more common public (mis)perception of identifying 1983 as the moment when the extreme Right began to use the logic of a right to difference (see, for example, Vichniac 1991:44).

9. It is not at all clear how much of a shift, in terms of hostility toward immigrants or French estimates to the number of immigrants in France, actually occurred in public opinion in France from the 1970s to the 1980s. See Schain (1987).

10. Schain (1988) does argue that racial politics emerged through the conscious decisions of all the party elites within the context of a changing party system, and not as a result of the National Front's action alone or in response to public hostilities toward immigrants.

11. Interview with G. Bouraz, Rhone-Alps, December 8, 1983, cited in "Les Messieurs de la Famille: Voyage à l'Intérieur du Front National," *Identités et Equalités* (1986:46).

12. For example, in a 1982 interview, a Socialist minister F. Autain declared that "the immigrants are a risk of social explosion" (cited in de Wenden, 1988b:318).

13. In contrast, G. Marchais, the PCF candidate opened the 1981 campaign by declaring that "there was too strong a concentration of immigrants in the population" in France (*Le Matin* 1/10/81, cited in Cuches 1982).

14. The *Figaro Magazine*'s numbers caused a large furor, and extended debate within the press over demographic statistics. It revealed the extent to which statistics and polls were themselves part of the contestation of immigration and

citizenship. The Socialist government was forced to respond quickly to the Right's figures, with officials from the Directorate of Migrant Populations and the INSEE (offical French statistics agency) working nonstop through the weekend following the Friday appearance of the Magazine's dossier. INSEE's and *Figaro Magazine's* figures differed substantially, though the government also admitted that more research needed to be done to obtain better demographic accuracy (Interview, Directorate of Migrant Populations).

15. "Incorporation" does not refer to the subjective processes of "integration" or "assimilation," but to the processes by which immigrants acquire rights and durability in a country. See Soysal (1994) for the important distinction between the terms.

16. Early on, there were a few exceptions. In particular, in 1981, while on a trip to Algeria, one of the Socialist ministers, C. Cheysson issued supportive statements regarding the "right to vote" (de Wenden 1988b).

17. Mitterrand soon prefaced his support for voting rights for immigrants by saying that while the French were not ready for it, he supported it (e.g., Mitterrand 1988).

18. A poll conducted by SOFRES for the magazine *Le Nouvel Observateur* showed even a starker rejection of the right to vote: 74 percent of the respondents were against the right to vote (11/30/84). The question was also put in more dichotomist terms, yes or no, while the MRAP survey qualified the question, in terms of support of the right to vote with conditions, without, and so on.

19. The immediate impetus for the PCF's changed position was most likely the resolution supporting the right to vote passed in the PCF associated organization, MRAP (an antiracist group) earlier in 1985. See MRAP, "Contribution a un debat sur les droits civiques des immigres en France" Mai 1985 (An organizational document received during an interview at MRAP). In interviews with immigrant activists (1988), activists remarked on the new found attention by the PCF, even for those organizations with long ties to the PCF, such as CAIF.

20. For an analysis of a similiar shift in Australian policies, see Castles et al. (1988).

21. Colloquium of CHEAM, "Les Etrangers qui Sont Aussi La France" (The Foreigners Who Are Also France), June 7–8, 1984, cited in de Wenden (1988b:343).

22. There was also renewed emphasis in parts of the Left on a "civic education." During the eighties, there was an increasing consensus on the malfunctioning of these institutions (cf. Leca 1985), though doubt was also cast on the process in which it was assumed to function previously (cf. Noiriel 1988).

23. Other politicians in the center and Right advancing more pluralist conceptions of France included the prominent UDF politician (and presidential aspirant) Raymond Barre, who declared France was already a "multiracial" and "multicultural"; Barre was born in the Reunion Islands, and his remarks were sim-

ilar to those of other politicians who also came from outside metropolitan France. Another moderate politician Simone Veil, who was long active in European politics, advocated in 1985 the right to vote in municipal elections for European Community nationals residing in France.

24. This article also signaled the fierce debates between differentialists, who argued that the contemporary non-European immigration posed unique challenges, and historians, who argued that the contemporary wave of immigrants and French reactions did not differ greatly from past experiences in France. For the latter, it was a case of "old demons" and "new scapegoats." See Milza (1985) and Noiriel (1984, 1985).

25. *Le Figaro* (6/6/85) also quoted the conservative historian, P. Chaunu, who claimed "France was losing itself through extension." Interestingly, both Chaunu and Touraine would serve on the Commission de Sages in 1987, and bring to it their preoccupations with the "nation" and national identity.

26. Handler (1988) discusses how much of social-scientific writing presupposes the existence of the nation, and usually, does not call into question the basis of the images in society and nation. In France, during the eighties, skepticism was sounded, though almost always directed at a competing account of the nation, and not at one's own account, see Noiriel (1984).

27. Hostility toward North Africans, and Algerians in particular, needs to be set in the colonialist and postcolonial context. After a bitter struggle, Algeria gained its independence in 1962. Already in 1968, North Africans were considered by far the immigrant population that was "too numerous"; in 1968, 62 percent of the respondents in SOFRES polls held that view, in 1977, 63 percent, and then in 1984, 66 percent (*Hommes et Migrations* 1/15/85).

28. Though there were some calls for a right to difference for immigrants, they were neither as strong nor as predominant as earlier in the eighties.

29. FASTI is a Paris-based organization that operates as an umbrella for "solidarity associations" with immigrant workers located throughout France. CAIF is also a Paris-based umbrella organization—the Council of Associations of Immigrants in France—which is composed of 17 migrant associations of different nationalities. TEXTURE is an immigrant activist association based in Lyon. Mémoire Fertile is a Paris-based umbrella organization, whose membership overlaps with that of CAIF and FASTI.

30. In interviews, SOS-Racisme activists asserted that nearly their entire discourse was "in function" or in response to Le Pen.

31. Both SOS-Racisme and France-Plus alienated other immigrant activists for their publicization of immigration issues. TEXTURE, a Lyon-based group created in 1984, explicitly opposed both associations, denouncing them for "recuperating the demands of immigrants while emptying them of meaning" (CAIF Info, 1985).

32. Mémoire Fertile. "Synthese de l'Atelier B: les Obstacles a une réelle citoyenneté," 1 p.

33. The concept of a "new citizenship" was not new in France, appearing in the pluralist conceptualizing of the early eighties. For example, the new "cultural citizenship" of Giordan's report, the "workers' citizenship" in the speech to the National Assembly by the Socialist prime minister, P. Mauroy, in 1981, as a "communitarian citizenship," elaborated by A. Cordeiro, and the "new citizenship" advanced by FASTI in 1982. By the mid-eighties, however, this new citizenship assumed a distinctively political interpretation.

34. In the sense that it called for a disassociation of citizenship and nationality, these understandings of citizenship have been labeled differentialist by French scholars (see Krulic 1988a). While calls for the right to vote for immigrants appealed to the concurrent debate over the right to vote for European Community nationals residing in France, the two debates were in many ways separate for the French political class. There was much more willingness to allow EC nationals the right to vote than non-EC nationals. This was indicative of how the idea of a "European citizenship" was not conceived of as an alternative to French citizenship but as an extension of the national citizenship.

35. Boumana, "Citoyenneté j'ecris toujours ton nom," 2 pp., see under Mémoire Fertile (1988).

36. However, in interviews about their own life histories and "work in the field," many of the immigrant activists interviewed for this study articulated more "cosmopolitan" worldviews and practices. This may point to the gap between a continuing discourse about the nation and citizenship and the reorganization of citizenship that has already taken place in postwar Europe. See Soysal (1994).

37. Though this is the predominant trend, many exceptions do exist of course. For example, Danielle Lochak, the president of the immigrant legal aid organization, GISTI, argues against all use of the terms, "nation" and "national identity."

38. According to a table established by the Ministry of Interior for the years 1978–1986, and reprinted in J. Costa-Lascoux (1989a:112); for example, the Ministry cites 13 cases for 1978, 23 cases for 1981, 43 for 1982, 68 for 1983, 53 for 1984, 70 for 1985, and 54 for 1986.

39. Gleason (1981) cited in Bergquist (1986:131).

4. Re-envisioning Citizenship

1. See Lochak (1986). In a different context, there was a legislative proposition in 1979 that proposed the elimination of some the automatic aspects of citizenship attribution on the basis of *jus soli*. See Bas (1979) in Appendix B.

2. Brubaker (1992) analyses the conservative attack on the nationality code along three similar perspectives, as the expression of distinctive voluntarist, statist, and nationalist arguments. Unlike Brubaker, I argue that the arguments are not distinct from nationalist ideology but rather are variants of it.

3. Weber writes of the "great, booming echo of a small, sharp voice" in his study of the spread of nationalist sentiments in pre—World War I France (1959:8). A sampling of books informed by far Right argumentation includes Alain Griotteray (RPR) *Les Immigrés: Le Choc* (1984); Didier Bariani (UDF) *Les Immigrés: Pour ou Contre La France* (1985); Club 89, directed by Michel Aurillac (RPR) *Stratégie Pour Governer La France* (1985); J.-Y. Le Gallou (RPR, then FN) *La Préférence Nationale* (1985).

4. Costa-Lascoux (1987b) commented on the reversal of positions by the Right and Left. For example, in 1979, three propositions of law aimed at revising the nationality code were advanced by conservatives, including solving natality problems by extending French citizenship to descendants of French emigrants abroad, and easing access to naturalization.

5. The information in this section on the internal state discussions is based primarily on two sources: documentation of internal administrative notes, meetings, and proposed revisions of the code from 1973 onward provided to the author by informants in the Bureau of Nationality; and Weil's dissertation and his book based on the dissertation (1988a, 1991). Also see *La Nationality Française* (1985).

6. Most important, this meant eliminating Articles 23 (which enabled Franco-Algerians, among others, to be attributed French at birth) and 44 (which enabled second generation immigrants to acquire French citizenship automatically at the age of majority), 37-1 (acquisition of French nationality by declaration as a spouse of a French national) and 153 (reintegration via declaration).

7. Article 69 of the French Nationality Code reads, "No-one can be naturalized in France if he does not justify his assimilation to the French community, notably by a sufficient knowledge, according to his condition, of the French language" (*La Nationalité Française* 1985).

8. A far-Right journal, *Le Rivarol*, accused Le Gallou of plagarizing the ideas of Le Pen. Le Gallou, a member of RPR, subsequently joined the National Front. See Taguieff (1987:580, ff. 57).

9. Touban was speaking in 1986, defending the government's proposed revisions. While earlier proposals aimed to eliminate both Articles 23 and 44, later ones also suggested eliminating the automatic procedure of Article 44. Thus, government's proposed revision hardly applied to youth of Algerian origin.

10. For example, in 1977 under Giscard, Paul Dijoud, Secretary of State for Migrant Workers, claimed that either the total integration of foreign workers who desire it in the national context must be ensured, normally culminating in the naturalization of the interested party or the retention of sociocultural ties with the country of origin in the perspective of a return of the interested parties to their home countries (see Weil 1991:90–106).

11. Deferre was quoted in *Le Monde* (10/3/81).

12. In understanding the term, negative voluntarism, the definition of negative liberty may be useful. Negative liberty refers to the idea that an individual is

"said to be free to the degree to which no man or body of men interfere with his activity" (Berlin 1974:25).

13. Similar divisions would reappear in the crisis over the wearing the Islamic headscarf in 1989.

14. Some of these alternative revisions were formal, set out in proposals to reform the code, while others were more informal, conveyed as part of the group's position in the debates.

15. The internal MRAP document, dated December 1985, appeared in excerpted form, in *Droit et Liberté*, no. 447, February 1986, with the quotation taken from p. 5. MRAP was the organization closest to the French Communist Party, and was influential in developing some of the party's positions on immigration. For example, according to MRAP officials, their decision to finally support the right to vote for immigrants in municipal elections in 1985 led to the PC changing its position from not supporting the right to vote to a strong support for immigrants' right to vote that same year (Interview, MRAP officials, 1988).

16. For LICRA's statements, see *Le Matin* 11/22–23/86. For France-Plus's position, see Parti Socialist, n.d., 1 p., "propositions de France Plus (le 14 Novembre 1986, par telephone)"; *Libération* 3/13/87.

17. French conservatives have not always situated their communitarianism on the national level. During the French revolution, conservative reactionaries defended the particularisms of the regions contra the national and universalist impulse of the republicanist and Jacobinist ideologies of the Revolution (Gallisot 1989).

18. For a discussion of nationalism and the role of individual choice, see Handler, who argues that nationalism is an ideology of "possessive individualism" (1988:6).

19. For an illuminating analysis on why and how nationalists "consider national identity in terms of choice," see Richard Handler's study of nationalism in Quebec (Handler 1988:34, 6–34).

20. The conservatives were not alone in targeting Franco-Maghrebis' for the functional treatment of French citizenship. The Left- and Right-identified press contained articles illustrating that Franco-Maghrebis held these types of attitudes, for example, obtaining French citizenship for work, vacation, convenience, and so on. Immigrant associations and support organizations also spoke of nationality in utilitarian terms. But it should be noted that such attitudes were neither new nor limited to Franco-Maghrebis. For example, in the sixties, Schreiber (1966) surveyed Polish and Italian immigrant workers on their attitudes toward naturalization: "In all the cases [whether they are favorable, hostile or hesitant], the essential motive is interest: it is useful for oneself and for one's children to be naturalized, or well, it isn't useful for oneself."

21. Darras is addressing the specific case of immigrants, who manifest "socio-cultural divergences" from the French, and making an implicit argument

about the specific national communitarian nature of the French polity. Thus, "there is nothing in common between the experience of a dual national Franco-American of French origin and a Muslim accumulating against his will French and Algerian nationalities" (1986:953).

22. These Franco-Algerians are attributed two nationalities, Algerian because of Algerian law and French. That they were French, however, was neither obvious to nor accepted by many in this population. In the 1975 census, around 200,000 children under the age of eighteen were counted as Algerian, even though they were, in fact, French. Even after much publicity of their situation by immigrant groups in the late seventies, and early eighties, around 220,000 Franco-Algerians were counted as foreigners in the 1982 census. See GISTI (1983).

23. This brings to mind Michael Walzer's analogy that countries are like "national clubs or families" with their own "admissions" processes (1981:13).

24. See Mayoud, Journal Officiel, Débats Parlementaire, Assemblée Nationale, 6/7/85, p. 1492, and see pp. 1491–1533. Also see "La Douloureuse histoire de l'intégration pluri-ethnic" in Le Quotidien de Paris (12/3/85).

25. Contrast this national communitarianism with the discourse on the right to difference, and desacralization of the nation and citizenship voiced in the early eighties. See, for example, the colloquium organized by CIEMI in 1982 (Cahiers de la Pastorale des Migrants 1982) on the political rights of immigrants, where part of the discussion centered around the need for a "diminution of the force of the concept of nation" (e.g., pp. 14–15).

26. Left communitarianism was in part the implicit articulation for the human need of community. The ambiguous language of left communitarianism recalls Michael Ignatieff's eloquent argument that, "of all the needs I have mentioned the one which raises this problem of the adequacy of language in its acutest form is the need for fraternity, social solidarity, for civic belonging . . . our task is to find a language for our need for belonging which is not just a way of expressing nostalgia, fear, and estrangement from modernity" (1986:138–139).

27. Pluralist themes also were voiced by those with ties to France's overseas Departments and Territories (DOM-TOM), including the moderate Right presidential aspirant, R. Barre (see Perotti 1985).

28. By stressing these arguments' embeddedness in French ideologies, this analysis does not explore another direction for comparison, namely, their relation to other patterns of defining and defending citizenship in different polities and time periods. For an analysis of American conceptions of citizenship that recalls the types of arguments displayed here, see R. Smith (1997), where he distinguishes "liberal," "republican," and "Americanist" arguments; Brubaker (1992) for a comparison of French and German conceptions and patterns of talking about citizenship; Breton (1988) for Canadian understandings of national membership, and its relations to a changing nationalism in Canada; Favell (1997)

for a British and French comparison; also see Hammar (1989), Brubaker (1989), and Layton-Henry (1990) for broader comparative perspectives.

29. Several scholars point out the exclusionary logic or aspects of Sieyes's conception of the citizenry. Manin argues that Sieyes's text implicated as well an exclusionary stance, see Manin (1984). Also see Bruschi's analysis of Sieyes's texts and his position vis a vis foreigners (1987).

30. Guibert-Sledziewski (1988) identified two contradictions with the revolutionary ideal of nation. The first was within itself, the tensions between the "national-universalism" aspects of the ideal; the term referred to both practical and theoretical contradictions. The second was the way its "heritage was passed and received," including the usage of republicanism in Left nationalism, whereby "national sovereignty define(d) itself by excluding" (1988:175).

31. For example, the revolutionary movements of 1848 have been characterized as "patriotic" or nationalist movements of the Left.

32. There have been numerous books, articles and dissertations that question the construction and veracity of this "national myth," particularly in the past decade or two. For a sampling, see Weber (1976); Braudel (1990); Noiriel (1988); Citron (1988); and Krulic (1988b).

33. Though some scholars wish to distinguish between a "cultural idiom of nationhood" and "ideologies" of nationhood, claiming that idioms are "longer-term, more anonymous, and less partisan," and that *unlike* ideologies, they are "not neutral vehicles for the expression of pre-existing 'interests': they *constitute* interests (underline in the original) as much as they express them" (Skocpol cited in Brubaker 1992). This study, however, follows more closely Geertz's definition of ideologies (1973) that understands ideologies as constitutive of interests as well. Furthermore, this study diverges from the former interpretation in so far as it links ideologies of nations with nationalist ideologies, a link that interpretation strenuously resists.

34. Michelet's work exemplifies this celebration of an open, universalizing French nationalism. See *Légendes Démocratiques du Nord*, *La France devant l'Europe*, and his 1869 preface to *L'Histoire de France*; see also, Viallaneix, *La Voie Royale, Essai sur l'Idée de peuple dans l'oeuvre de Michelet* (1959), all cited in Jennings (1990).

35. It was not until the nineteenth century, however, that the term nationalism appears explicitly in the texts and in politics (cf. Gallisot 1986).

36. For example, "patriotism of the left" is expressed in French colonialism, especially in the movement in the ninteenth century to universalize French education, to bring its civilizing mission and to construct the "national myth" (Gallisot 1989:31).

37. These counternationalisms have also been traced to the French revolution.

38. It should be noted that these may be considered the major strands of French nationalism, but this portrayal is certainly not exhaustive. See, for example, Sternhall (1983); Winnock (1990); Taguieff (1984, 1988).

39. See the special issue of *Intervention* (1984) on "Republicanism"; Bergouinioux and Manin (1980); and Birnbaum (1979).

40. In a translation of his work, Nora suggested that the phrase, "lieux de mémoire" has no English equivalent, and so, the French version should be retained even in translation (Nora 1989).

41. Renan's scholarship on the Orient, which were in many respects anti-Semitic and anti-Orient, makes it especially ironic when immigrant activists refer to Renan's plebiscite as part of their definition of the French national community.

42. Sternhall, it should be noted has been strongly critiqued by other French scholars; see Taguieff (1988).

43. During the conflict over the Nationality Code in the 1920's, which led to the 1927 revision of the code, two warring conceptions of the nation informed the debates: a "voluntarist" and "open" understanding of the nation versus the "exclusive and apprehensive (frileuse)" one advocated by the "nationalist right" (Lochak 1985:182). Though the expansive revision of the Code was enacted with the 1927 reform, pushed in part by the additional pressure of France's demographic needs, the reform required candidates for naturalization to pledge loyalty in an oath of allegiance, affirming their assimilation into French cultural community. Interestingly, an oath of allegiance was finally dropped from the current revision attempt, because, in the words of one conservative, it did not conform to French traditions of nationhood.

44. The controversies over terminology, of whether to use "insertion" or "integration" as replacements for the tainted "assimilation" during the eighties reveals the tension in circles on the Left, in particular, between the underlying priority of assimilationism in republicanist ideology, and the Left's unwillingness to use the term, "assimilation" (Costa-Lascoux 1989a).

45. By differentialist politics, I am referring to the far Right's racial sounding "national preference" logic that was denounced by the majority of the political class, and to the proposed "new citizenship," calling for the disassociation of citizenship and nationality, a theme rejected by the majority as well.

46. The nativist arguments were more confined to the far Right, and segments of the Right, and did not really constitute a point of overlap between the Right and the Socialists.

5. The Reform, the State, and the Political Process

1. The victory of the Right RPR-UDF coalition in the 1986 parliamentary elections ushered in a period of "cohabitation" for the first time in France. Cohabitation describes a split partisan executive, the coexistence of a president from one party and a prime minister from another party or bloc. Chirac called for President Mitterrand's resignation in 1986, but Mitterrand refused. Mitterrand

and Chirac more or less carved out distinctive areas of jurisdiction, with Chirac holding responsibility over most domestic policy domains. On the phenomenon of divided governance in France, see Feldblum (1996).

2. The analysis presented here of the internal reform process within the state is based on several sources of information: (1) internal documentation, memoranda, summaries of meetings, and reform drafts (including most of the dozen "motures" or drafts that the Bureau of Nationality formulated in the summer of 1986), which were furnished to the author by an informant at the Bureau of Nationality; (2) archival research at the Ministry of Foreign Relations; (3) interviews with officials at the Bureau of Nationality (Ministry of Justice), Ministries of Foreign Relations, and Interior, Directorate of Migrant Populations, and Council of State; (4) documentation found in the archives of the Nationality Commission; and (5) newspaper reports of the reform's progress.

3. The total number of people affected by the various proposed revisions fluctuates depending on which articles would be abrogated. For example, Mazeaud's proposal mentions neither Article 84 nor Articles 153 and 156 of the CNF. Furthermore, it should be underlined that statistics for those attributed or acquiring French citizenship under Articles 23 and 44 of the CNF, and 23 of the Law of 1973 are only estimates.

4. "Article 23 du Code de la Nationalité Française," N.D., 10 pp. Officials in the Bureau of Nationality wrote this internal document in April 1986 in response to the Right's proposals, and in anticipation of their being asked to draw up a "proposition" to revise the CNF (Interview, Bureau of Nationality).

5. Bureau of Nationality's documentation included "Note à l'Elysée du 25 Octobre 1985," pp. 8–11; "Modification des Conditions D'Acquisition de la Nationalité Française à raison de la Naissance et de la Résidence en France" N.D.; "Article 23 Code de la Nationalité Française" N.D.; "Réforme de l'Article 23 du Code de la Nationalité Française ou Réouverture de Négociations avec l'Algérie" N.D.

6. "Reforme de l'Article 23 du Code de la Nationalité Française ou Réouverture de Négociations avec l'Algérie," pp. 1–2.

7. "Article 23 du Code de la Nationalité Française," pp. 2–10. For example, one formulation proposed was: "This rule is not applicable to the children born in France of parents born in Algeria and became of Algerian nationality since January 1, 1963."

8. Article 44 states, "all individuals born in France of foreign parents acquires the French nationality at the age of majority, if at that date, he has in France his residence, and if he had 'during five years' which preceded his habitual residence in France or in the territories or countries for which there is the attribution or acquisition of French nationality, or was during his residence, governed by special dispositions." See *La Nationalité Française* (1985:25). In addition, the government may refuse the acquisition of citizenship for "indignity or for lack of assimilation," as per Article 46 of the code. But, such refusals are rare.

There was much furor in the press over the exigencies of Article 79. Immigrant supporters accused the Chirac government of requiring those of immigrant origin to be even better than the French. For its part, the Bureau of Nationality was "astounded" at the "counter-truths" in the press, given that Article 79 already existed in the code. All the Bureau was doing was "clarifying" and "extending" the provision (Interview, Bureau of Nationality). But see Lochak's argument in (LDH 1987) for a rebuttal of this view.

9. According to the Bureau of Nationality, they had the most difficulties with the "little Portuguese" because Portuguese youth often left school early, remained unemployed. The result being that these youth could not furnish proof of their residence in France for the five years prior to the age of majority (Interview, Bureau of Nationality).

10. On its part, the state also has a right to refuse these requests to decline French citizenship.

11. Bureau of Nationality, "Article 23 Code de la Nationalité Française" N.D.

12. Indeed, officials at the Ministries of Foreign Affairs and Justice underscored the point that, in terms of problems associated with dual nationality, the state experienced more problems and cases of fraud with the "Franco-Camerouns," than with the Franco-Maghrebis (Interviews).

13. The principle concerns of French officials were (1) the status and interests of the French abroad, and (2) the inequitable and arbitrary application and interpretation of the convention by different countries. The officials' tolerance for dual nationality did not preclude them from expressing frustration and intolerance about the dual nationality held by Franco-Algerians, and by others originating from North African and Africa. First, these officials argued that it was unfair that the convention of Strasbourg affects most of all French nationals of European origin. They cited cases of Franco-Algerians, who can have both nationalities to demonstrate the frustration felt both by themselves and French who complain about the convention. Second, they specified how Algerians and Africans can acquire French nationality and maintain their original nationality while the French, who acquire a nationality of a neighboring country, which is "so close in culture," lose theirs.

14. The number of these children attributed French citizenship increased from the 1970s to the 1980s, but still remains small in comparison to the Algerian population. In 1975, the figure was estimated at 2,294, in 1982 at 6,091, and in 1985 at 8,033.

15. Bureau of Nationality. "Suppression de l'Article 23 de la Loi du 9 Janvier 1973." N.D. p. 2.

16. These acquisitions averaged between 4,000 and 4,500 yearly. Though in 1985, with 4,972, and 1986, with 6,182, the number of acquisitions increased.

17. Since the 1973 reform, the number of "declarations" through Article 37-1 increased significantly. While before 1973, the annual number was below

500, from 1974 to the mid-eighties around 147,000 persons acquired French citizenship through Article 37-1. In 1985, 15,190 persons acquired French citizenship through marriage.

18. Bureau of Nationality, "Fiche no. 3: Projets Paraissant Neccessaire ou Utile Mais Politiquement Plus Teintes." N.D., p. 1.

19. Birnbaum writes, "In socialist France . . . the state, of its own accord, shows itself willing to sacrifice a part of the state differentiation habitual within the Jacobin tradition." He also notes that this process is longer term: "The French state is . . . threatened with the loss of certain aspects of its differentiation, for a number of private interests are already an integral part of its structures" (1988:187).

20. Haut Conseil de la Population et de la Famille, "Déclaration du Haut Conseil de la Population et de la Famille sur la Politique d'Immigration. Adoptée à l'unanimité lors de la séance du 14 Janvier 1986"; also see Haut Conseil de la Population et de la Famille, "Mesures Proposées à Favoriser L'Insertion des Jeunes d'Origine Etrangère dans la Société Française," 6/10/86, p. 14

21. Secrétariat Général du Government. "Compte-Rendu de la réunion interministerielle tenue le lundi 15 septembre 1986 sous la présidence de M. Benmakhlouf, Conseiller technique au cabinet du Premier Ministre et de M. Valroff, Conseiller technique au cabinet du Premier Ministre." 9/17/86, 5 pp.

22. Elsewhere, officials at the Directorate of Migrant Populations remarked on how they were not consulted on the legislative drafts by the department of justice until the September and October readings of the draft proposal (Interview, Directorate of Migrant Populations).

23. The issue of dual nationality was particularly salient for the Ministry of Foreign Affairs. According to its figures, the number of French dual nationals accounted for approximately 30 percent of the French living abroad. In 1985, it conducted a survey of the consuls dealing with French dual nationals abroad. The report's conclusions contained a section on how to reduce the incidence of dual nationality as well as a section on how to facilitate and maintain links with dual nationals (Ministere des Affaires Etrangères, "Les Doubles Nationaux à l'Etranger," 6/19/86, 3 pp).

24. The Council of State is not a judicial body as much as it is "the supreme jurisdictional and consultative body for the French administration" (*Larousse*). The state is obliged to seek the consultation of the Council of State on propositions of law. But it is not always obliged to follow the Council's advice. See Massot and Marimbert (1988:14–19).

25. Nationality Commission Archives. Conseil d'Etat, Section de l'Interieur et Section Sociale Réunies, No. 341-106, "Projet de Section," Assemblée Générale, seance du 30 Octobre 1986, 6 pp.

26. It also slightly modified the strict revision of Article 79, that enumerated the type of convictions that candidates for Article 44 must not have on their records.

27. The analysis of the interaction of immigrant associations, human right groups, and parties during the protest against the code is based on several sources

of research: (1) interviews with immigrant activists (e.g., CAIF, France-Plus, SOS-Racisme, Portuguese groups), party officials (PS, PCF), and social support associations (GISTI, LDH, CIMADE); (2) comprehensive press analysis for this time period; and (3) unpublished, internal party and association memoranda, as well as their published documentation.

28. Parti Socialiste, Secretariat National aux relations exterieures (N.D.) "France-Plus." 2 pp.

29. Immigrant activists saw their linkage with the churches as an important asset for the organization of the protest. A CAIF activist claimed "It was the CAIF that led the churches" into the protesters' organizing process (Interview, chief CAIF activist, 1988). Also see Costes (1988).

30. Most centrists, like Mayoud, did not aim to overturn the territorial principle. It was not the gist of Article 23—of attributing to third-generation immigrants citizenship—that was upsetting to many on the Right, rather it was its particular application to Algerian, second-generation immigrants. See Brubaker (1992).

31. The events of 1986 recalled for many the events of 1968. In 1968, the peaks in strike activity corresponded with periods of intense political contestation; and the strikes further contributed to the environment of political instability.

32. For example, SOS-Racisme, formerly an insistently nonpartisan organization (though it certainly was linked to the Socialist party), forged visible and explicit alliances with the Socialists during this period, including SOS leaders running for party posts.

33. It is to be noted, however, that the government's project was *not* "directed against this young man," who as a Franco-Algerian via Article 23 would not have been affected by the revisions. Nonetheless, in terms of its symbolic import, the reform remained interpreted as an attack against the Maghrebis in France, while other populations actually targeted by the revisions, such as the Portuguese were ignored; and indeed, the Portuguese, themselves, largely ignored the furor over the code. See Cordeiro (1987b).

34. Brubaker (1992) convincingly shows how the government reshaped their arguments to focus on the "manner" of becoming French, and not "fact" of being French.

35. Mills writes, "motives are of no value apart from the delimited societal situations for which they are appropriate vocabularies. They must be situated" (1984:22).

6. Reconstructing Citizenship

1. See also Baudrillard (1983) and Debord (1967) for earlier discussions about the meaning and operation of spectacle. While Rogin identified political

spectacles as one of the "political peculiarities of the postmodern American empire," it resonates in European terms as well; and not only because the Commission saw itself, and its hearings as "inspired by Irangate."

2. C. W. Mills defines a "vocabulary of motives" as the "ultimate of discourse," the kinds of justifications and rationalizations for action that are legitimized in a society in a given time. These discourses are part of institutional patterns, and Mills notes, following Weber, that constellations of motives may change along stratified and occupational lines. Mills argues that we need to locate "vocabularies of motives in historic epochs and specific situations. Motives are of no value apart from the delimited social situations for which they are the appropriate vocabularies" (1984:22). The Commission's crystallization of a vocabulary of motives can be situated along national lines, and located in the national terrain, at a point in time where tensions are growing between a nationalist and ethnic politics of citizenship, not only in France, but elsewhere in Western Europe as well. In other ways, however, my analysis situates the Commission in much less purposive terms than Mill's term would imply. The power of the commission may be understood not as "a possession of agents who exercise it to define the options of others, but a set of pressures lodged in institutional mechanisms which produce and maintain" norms (Connolly, 1984:156). Whereas Mills's "vocabulary of motives" could be identified with an "Anglo-American" view of an agent "in which the self is an agent, 'capable of forming intentions, of deliberately shaping . . . conduct to rules,' other dimensions of the Commission bring forth a "Foucaultian view of the subject as an artefact of power" (Shapiro, 1984:10).

3. The research on the Commission is based on several sources: (1) interviews conducted in 1988 with thirteen of the sixteen members of the Nationality Commission (Long, Kaltenbach, Bresson, Goldman, Varaut, Rivaro, Catala, Loussouarn, Chaunu, Touraine, Schnapper, Boutbien, and Kacet), and with the main "reporter" for the Commission (J. C. Mallet); (2) comprehensive analysis of the documentation contained in the Commission's archives, to which I had free access; (3) extensive press analysis of the entire period of the reform process; and (4) commentary and analyses on the Commission (e.g., Verbunt 1988b; Krulic 1988a; Weil 1988c) and special journal issues (e.g., *Plein Droit* 1988; *Lignes* 1988).

4. These were S. Kacet, who was of Algerian origin and became French through marriage to a French national, and H. Carrère d'Encausse, who became French through Article 44, and Goldman and Verneuil who were naturalized French.

5. The central figures within the Commission, who helped shaped its deliberations were Long, Touraine, and Catala; Carrère d'Encausse, Chaunu, and Schnapper played important roles; others, such as Kacet, Goldman, Rivaro and Verneuil were active in certain areas of discussion as well.

6. Nationality Commission Archives. J. Chirac, "Installation de la Commission du Code de la Nationalité" 6/22/87.

7. Nationality Commission Archives. "Compte Rendu Analytique," meeting of the commission, 7/8/87. Others at the meeting placed concurrent emphases on acting as a "catharsis" and "setting the rules" for the public debate.

8. From the first of their meetings, the majority of the Commission members expressed their preoccupations with defending the "nation" (Interview, J. C. Mallet).

9. Nationality Commission Archives. A. Touraine, "Notes Pour la Commission" (dated 10/24/87 10 pp.), p. 1.

10. For analyses and commentary of the Commission's understanding of the nation, see Verbunt (1988c); Renaut, "Quelle Idée de Nation" (*La Croix* 2/28–29/88); *Plein Droit* (1988); Krulic (1988a).

11. These definitions of national identity elaborated by the commission members come from a variety of sources, some contradictory. For example, while Goldman was effusive in his elaboration of a national identity in interviews, in his internal memoranda to the Commission he was explicitly more reticent than most of the other Commission members about questions of national identity and nation.

12. On a discussion of essentialist nationalist views, see Handler (1988:33–49).

13. Nationality Commission Archives. P. Catala, "Notes Sur le Droit de la Nationalité" (11/2/87 6 pp.), p. 6.

14. Nationality Commission Archives. Mme. Schnapper, "Quelques Points de Réflexion Provisoires." (10/22/87, 6 pp.), p. 2.

15. Nationality Commission Archives. "Compte Rendu Analytique," meeting of the commission, 7/8/87.

· 16. Nationality Commission Archives. "Installation de la Commission," p. 4.

17. Nationality Commission Archives. P. Catala, "Notes Sur le Droit de la Nationalité," p. 6.

18. Bruno Etienne was replying to a question of Touraine's, "How do you see the role of the nation?" Etienne later elaborates on this remark in a subsequent book of his (1989a), where he argued that the Unique European Act leads to a "transnational citizenship." In the same study, he claimed that the Muslim population in France is also a challenge to the social and historical practices of the French Republic, including concepts of secularity, nationality, and citizenship.

19. Long's concern about the European context and defense of the nation can be understood, in part, as reflecting growing preoccupations of the French state, particularly the Council of State. In an examination of the French state's position toward European integration, Rambaud has argued that the Council of State, in particular, has asserted that special attention must be given to penetration of European Community law into French law, and that the Council of State

must be "vigilant" against those laws that may be "against the French nation" (Rambaud 1989:62).

20. More generally, some scholars have pointed out that European integration was leading to a resurgence of "the ideology of the nation" in French politics, forcing "debates between national integration and [European] community subversion, between community integration and national subversion" (Rambaud 1989:61).

21. Nationality Commission Archives. A. Touraine, "Notes Pour la Commission." The Commission reporter, J. C. Mallet distributed a long questionnaire to all the members, of which several questions focused on the extent to which the Commission needed to elaborate its own definition of the nation and national identity. The majority opinion thought that it was necessary.

22. The Commission did not use the term, "national integration" in its definition of integration in its reports, but its members distinguished their approach to integration as a "national integration." See below. The report's initial definition of integration subscribes to the approach that the "the passage from one national membership to another must be organized in a *conscious manner*, it being understood . . . the integration to the French nation does not signify cultural assimilation." While disclaiming the imperative of assimilation, the commission argues for a notion of a strong integration (Long 1988, vol. 2:86).

23. For studies on the historical process of national integration or the ethnicization of the polity in France, see Gordon (1978); Lafont (1968); and Weber (1976).

24. Nationality Commission Archives. "Présentation du Rapport de la Commission de la Nationalité par Marceau Long, Président de la Commission" (4/11/88, 14 pp.), p. 4.

25. Nationality Commission Archives. A. Touraine. "Notes Pour la Commission," pp. 2, 6.

26. Nationality Commission Archives, "Présentation du Rapport de la Commission de la Nationalité par M. Marceau Long, Président de la Commission," p. 8.

27. The report notes that the process of integration has been called a "policy of assimilation. The expression is regrettable." The regret the report expresses appears for the negative connotations associated with the term, in particular, that it has assumed a complete erasure of the previous culture, than with the term itself. The report notes that when it uses "assimilation . . . it refers to the phenomena of acculturation of the people concerned" (Long 1988, vol. 1:24).

28. Nationality Commission Archives. P. Catala, "Notes sur le Droit de la Nationalité," p. 6.

29. In the Commission, as elsewhere in French politics, there were debates over the appropriateness of terms, between "assimilation" and "integration." Though some Commission members asserted that they were not requiring assimilation, the difference between terms often was more semantic than substantive.

30. Nationality Commission Archives. "Note de M. Rivaro à la Suite de la Réunion de 27 Octobre" (7 pp.), p. 7.

31. Nationality Commission Archives. A. Touraine, "Notes Pour la Commission."

32. See Leca (1985) and Noiriel (1988) for discussions about the weakening of the classic French integrationist institutions.

33. Nationality Commission Archives. A. Touraine, "Notes Pour la Commission," pp. 1–2.

34. See Perotti (1988) for an analysis of the conflict over the code as a reflection of the limited capacity of French integration, a debate "saying much more on French society than Islam," and revealing "French fears about its capacity for integration" (Bruno Etienne in Long 1988, vol. 1:130).

35. Nationality Commission Archives. A. Touraine, "Notes Pour La Commission," p. 7. See also, Schnapper (1987:363).

36. The date chosen for this march, November 29, was indicative of the subtexts to integration, notably the rejection of difference, and especially of an Arab, Muslim specificity. November 29, 1947 was the date the U.N. passed a resolution recommending the split of Palestine, a "black day in the Arab world." One of the points of conflict between SOS-Racisme and the Beur associations was the Desir's and his organization's refusal to align themselves with the Palestinian protests against Israel. The Arab-Israeli and Muslim-Jewish tensions became another text in the struggles to define integration as the Jewish "assimilation" was held up as the model for the Maghrebi populations. Thus, accepting to march on November 29 could be understood symbolically not just as a protest for antiracism and integration, but as a rejection of an Arab-affiliated identity (see *IM'media* 1987–1988:11). See also, Leveau and Schnapper (1987) on a comparison of Jewish and Muslim integration in France.

37. There were important differences in the way the Commission situated the different immigrant groups in France. The Commission clearly identified the Muslim, Maghrebi, non-European populations as the immigrants, whose process of national integration was neither complete nor successful. In contrast, the Portuguese population is not at all situated in terms of a national integration. The Commission describes how the 1981 Portuguese law permitting dual nationality lifted an important obstacle "for the pursuit by the Portuguese population of its *judicial integration* accompanying its already successful social integration" (Long 1988, vol. 2:46).

38. Nationality Commission Archives. "Présentation du Rapport de la Commission," p. 5.

39. A glimpse of this aspect is seen in a later testimony, when Chaunu and an Algerian immigrant activist comes to odds. Angered by her more differentialist discourse and commodified view of citizenship, Chaunu brings up the lives lost by the Harkis and his emotional outburst.

40. Rosaldo (1989) defines "imperialist nostalgia" where "people mourn the passing of what they themselves have transformed" and "destroyed."

41. These provisions would later provoke the disapproval of many immigrant associations and support organizations. See below.

42. Nationality Commission Archives. "Compte Rendu-Analytique," July 1987.

43. Nationality Commission Archives. J. Mallet, "Essai de Syntheses des Principeaux Themes Abordees par la Commission," (9/9/87 20 pp.), pp. 2, 5.

44. Nationality Commission Archives. "Présentation du Rapport de la Commission," p. 9. Also see Long (1988, vol. 2:89–90).

45. This was not a new observation, notably Costa-Lascoux (1987a) underlined the same pattern of reversals. On the other hand, Lochak, during the hearings, argued against that reasoning because the cases were not compatible (Long 1988, vol. 1). This study has also distinguished between the Left's support for a "negative" voluntarism in the seventies and early eighties, and the "positive" voluntarism gaining support in the eighties.

46. For example, the Commission member LeRoy Ladurie declared after Finkielkraut's testimony, "The elective conception of the nation supposes a decision, a desire for adhesion on the part of the youth issued from immigration" (*Le Matin* 10/21/87).

47. Nationality Commission Archives. A. Touraine, "Notes Pour La Commission," p. 4.

48. Pierre-Bloch's testimony caused a furor in his own organization, which opposed a code reform. See *Liberation* (10/10–11/87).

49. The human rights discourse reinforced various aspects of the Commission's propositions. It defined its refusal to allow parents to claim the nationality for their minor children, and its elimination of parental authorization for requesting and claiming French nationality between the ages of sixteen and eighteen in terms of human and individual "rights." "We have placed very high the right of the child," claimed Long (*Liberation* 2/17/88).

50. Commission members reacted passionately and strongly to suggestions that citizenship acquisition in France should be automatic. Interestingly, they did so in terms evoking colonialist/colonized imagery. When the JALB representative asserted her views of an automatic citizenship, P. Chaunu protested in the "name of those who spilled blood for France"; when H. Desir called for a similar citizenship, P. Boutbien protested that he felt "attacked" by Desir.

51. Nationality Commission Archives. B. Goldman, "Note de B. Goldman Sur la Situation de la Personne Née en France de Parents-Etrangers dont Accun n'y est Né" (10/26/87, 9 pp.); "Note de B. Goldman Sur l'Acquisition de la Nationalité par Marriage" (10/26/87, 2 pp.); and "Reponse de B. Goldman au Questionnaire remis le 27 Octobre 1987" (5 pp.).

52. Though it was also true that the Department of Interior advocated some devolution of authority for the cases in which no negative recommendations were given by the local offices because of the heavy load of cases (Interview, Ministry of Interior).

53. These officials noted that the CSFE, the organization representing French abroad, was particularly enraged by the Commission's statements on dual nationality. See Conseil Superieur de l'Etranger (1987).

54. This point is debated among the commentary and analyses of the Commission's proposals. For example, officials at the Bureau of Nationality claimed that the commission's propositions were in many respects more restrictive than the actual code (Interview, Bureau of Nationality). See Brubaker (1992) and Costa-Lascoux (1989a, c) for analyses that argue the Commission proposed a significantly more liberalizing version. See *Plein Droit* (1988) and Verbunt (1988b) for alternative interpretations.

55. "Any modification of the nationality code supposes a large national consensus. . . . I will delay (the reform project) till after the presidential elections in order for it to be done in serenity and not in polemics" (Chirac in *Le Figaro* 9/9/87).

56. Again, it was Jospin who rejected more bluntly the need for a positive voluntarism. Commenting on the proposal to institute a step requiring the youth to request French nationality, Jospin asserts, "This is stupid. They are (French). They do not need to ask to be it" (*Libération* 1/12/88).

57. Parti Socialiste. "Cohesion Sociale," undated, 1 p.

58. For a sampling of the critiques issued by social organizations, see Commission Diocésaine et al. (1988), and La Ligue des Droits de l'Homme (1988).

7. Who's Wearing the Veil?

1. The Anglo-Saxon model of ethnic politics refers to a general mode of integration by way of ethnic groups, ethnicity as a focus for group mobilization for political ends, and conflicts defined in terms of group interests and not issues. See Glazer and Moynihan (1975).

2. In 1989, the percentage of foreigners in the school population in France was estimated to be 8.9 percent (Perotti et al. 1989). At least 6 percent of all students were Muslim, and the estimate covered only the foreign Muslim resident population, and not French nationals (*Le Monde* 12/1/89).

3. The Jacobin model and republicanist traditions are themselves ambiguous and contradictory. For example, scholars have begun to question "if there is a Jacobin model?" (Gallisot 1989).

4. Scholarship on immigration in France has shown that, in part, this "French" model is myth, and it has been contested by previous waves of immigrants. For example, see Noiriel (1988).

5. By substantive differences, I refer to differences deriving from membership in a group which is subjectively or objectively viewed as a minority within the national collectivity. See Lochak (1989b).

6. See, for example, the article in *Le Nouvel Observateur*, "Élections: Les Beurs au Charbon" (2/23–3/1/89).

7. This portrayal of Islam is not French-specific, as seen in the Rushdie affair. The Rushdie affair was recalled during the foulard drama as an example of the rising Islamic fundamentalism (Leveau 1990). It is interesting to note that the difficulties in situating and legitimating Islam-based conflicts within categories of ethnic politics has not been confined to France or to countries with no history of ethnic politics.

8. The extent to which the school system has actually fulfilled this function is disputed. Since the early 1980s, the "failure" of the French integration institutions has been a topic of discussion. See, for example, Leca (1985) and Noiriel (1988).

9. It is telling that Franco-Maghrebis are often categorized as foreigners and not French in polls, as evidenced by the IFOP poll cited earlier. In an analysis of voting by Franco-Maghrebi youth, Muxel (1988) states, "The French are the French of French society; the "immigres," who could also have French nationality are designated here by their "immigrant identity characteristics."

10. See Haut Conseil à l'Intégration (1991, 1992, and 1993).

11. For example, in my interviews with the Commission members and in their interviews with others, many of the Commission members defined their perspective as "patriotic," and not "nationalist," even as they relied on the ambiguities between the two. Thus, Goldman, in an interview, asserted, "The reinforcement of the identity could also be conveyed by a greater civic-mindedness, and a greater patriotism . . . I do not say nationalism, which would be dangerous, I speak only about starting a national conscience . . . and why not patriotism . . . You know, I am very chauvinistic" (*Plein Droit* 1988). For a sampling of the debates over the separation of patriotism and nationalism, see Anderson (1983:129–140), Gilroy (1987:52–59), Ignatieff (1986:133–142), MacIntyre (1984), and Balibar and Wallerstein (1988). For a sampling of the debates between "cosmopolitans" and "nationalists," see the collection of articles in Brown and Shue (1981), Beitz (1983), Walzer (1983), Zolberg (1987), and *Ethics* (1988).

8. Nationality Reforms in the 1990s

1. See "La nouvelle Léglislation sur les étrangers comporte des 'atteintes excessives' aux droits fondamentaux," 8/16/93:1. For a critical analysis of both laws, see the special issue of *Plein Droit*.

2. See Géraud de la Pradelle, "Sang et Nationalité," *Plein Droit*, (1994:31).

3. See Nathaniel Herzberg, "En 1995, L'acquisition de la nationalité française a baissé de près de 27%," *Le Monde* 1/26–27/97:22.

4. See P. Bernard, "Immigration nationalité intégration," *Le Monde* 11/14/97; P. Bernard, "En droit du sol à geométrie variable," *Le Monde* 11/29/97.

5. Weil cites in his report the cases of the region of Basse-Normandie, where the rejection rate was 7 percent, Bretagne where it was 6 percent, and the Lorraine, 5.3 percent. Within regions, seven Departments posted rejection rates higher than 10 percent, including one Department (Morbihan) with a 41.2 percent rejection rate. Also see Fulchiron (1996).

6. Weil was commissioned by the Socialist Prime Minister Lionel Jospin to produce two reports, one on nationality reform and the other on immigration reform. Weil submitted his reports on July 31, 1997, and the documents were quickly reprinted in the press.

7. Completing the formal request process at sixteen may reflect strategic thinking on the part of immigrant youth given that as they got older, the difficulties in meeting the conditions of the request processes could increase. Under the pre-1993 regime, for example, establishing residency proved difficult for those youth who dropped out of school.

8. Bernard cites figures showing that around 15,000 children a year became French through this manner before 1993.

9. See P. Bernard, "Ce qui reste de la manifestation de volonté," *Le Monde* 11/27/97; J. B. de Montvalon, "Les PC et les Vert ne s'opposeront pas au projet de loi sur la nationalité," *Le Monde* 11/27/97.

10. See P. Bernard, "Lionel Joseph impose un compromis sur le code de la nationalité," *Le Monde* 11/14/97; also see *Le Monde* 11/6/97.

11. Cited in P. Bernard, "Simone Veil, Présidente du Haut Conseil à l'intégration. Une démarche pragmatique et un projet de loi cohérent," *Le Monde* 10/16/97.

12. See P. Bernard and J. B. de Montvalon, "Le Front National est à l'arrière-plan du débat sur la nationalité," *Le Monde* 11/30/97:6.

13. For example, in one city, the National Front sought to implement a "municipal allocation" for the birth of a child that would be based on "the national preference," according to which the *allocation* would be given to all families in which at least one of the parents were "French or a national of the European Union" (*Agence France-Presse*, "L' 'allocation naissance'vitrollaise: le préfet saisit la justice," 2/4/98).

14. Weil argues that the logic that the child born in France of immigrant parents remains foreign until the acquisition of citizenship "was equally the logic of the law of 1889" (1997, chapter 3). However, the 1889 law stressed that the vocation of the child was to become French. With both the 1993 and 1997 reforms, that vocation is qualified.

15. The legislation left it at the discretion of the family to decide if mention of the nationality at birth was to placed on birth certificates and in the official "livret de famille" (Philippe Bernard, "Les dispositions adoptées en première lecture," *Le Monde* 11/30/97).

16. P. Bernard, "Dominique Schnapper, Revenir sur la loi Méhaignerie me paraît inutile et plutôt dangereux," *Le Monde* 8/1/97.

17. See the reports by C. Chambraud, "François Léotard ne souhaite pas un référendum sur la nationalité," *Le Monde* 12/2/97:7; and C. Fabre, "La Droite sénatoriale demande à M. Chirac d'organiser un référendum sur la nationalité," *Le Monde* 12/19/97.

18. See "Loi no. 98-170 du 16 Mars 1998 relative à la nationalité," *Journal Officiel de la République Française* 3/17/98:3935–3138.

19. Mazeaud was cited in Thierry Bréhier, "La loi de 1973 avait été votée dans un climat d'unanimité," *Le Monde* 11/26/97.

20. See Patrick Weil (1991) on the legislative history and processes leading to the 1984 immigrant entry and residency legislation.

21. Jospin's letter of July 1, 1997, to Patrick Weil is reprinted in Weil's report (Weil 1997).

22. A renewed attention to domestic political factors can be seen in some work on comparative immigration policy. The political scientist Gary Freeman has argued that "political factors should be at the centre of the explanation of comparative immigration policy" (1998:102).

23. See Schönwälder (1996) and Alan Cowell, "Like It or Not, Germany Becomes a Melting Pot," *New York Times* 11/30/97.

Bibiliography

Aissou, A. 1987. *Les Beurs, L'École et la France*. Paris: CIEMI, L'Harmattan.

Alouane, Y. 1979. *L' Émigration Maghrebine en France*. Tunis: Ed. CERES Production.

Assouline D., and S. Zappi. 1987. *Notre Printemps en Hiver: Le Mouvement Étudiant de Décembre 1986*. Paris: Ed. La Découverte.

Anderson, B. 1983. *Imagined Communities: Reflections on the Origins and Spread of Nationalism*. London: Verso.

Après-Demain. 1986. Devenir Français. Dossier, vol. 286, Juillet–Septembre.

Autrement. 1977. Culture Immigrée. Intégration ou Résistance. (11).

Apter, D. 1964. "Ideology and Discontent." In *Ideology and Discontent*. New York: The Free Press.

Badie, B., and P. Birnbaum. 1983. *The Sociology of the State*. Chicago: University of Chicago Press.

Baechler, J. 1988. "Dépérissement de la Nation?" *Commentaire* 41:104–113.

Baldwin-Edwards, M., and M. A. Schain, eds. 1994. *The Politics of Immigration in Western Europe*. Essex: Frank Cass.

Balibar, E. 1984. "Sujet ou Citoyens." In *Les Temps Modernes*. 452–454:1726–1753.

———. 1988a. "L'Avenir du Racisme." *Lignes* 2:7–12.

———. 1988b. "Propositions on Citizenship." *Ethics* (98) 4:723–730.

Balibar, E., and I. Wallerstein. 1988. *Race, Nation, Class. Les Identités Ambiguës*. Paris: La Découverte.

Bariani, D. 1985. *Les Immigrés, Pour ou contre la France*. Paris: France Empire.

Bauböck, R., and D. Cinar. 1994. "Briefing Paper: Naturalization Policies in Western Europe." In M. Baldwin-Edwards and M. Schain, eds., *The Politics of Immigration in Western Europe*.

Baudrillard, J. 1983. *Simulations*. New York.

Beer, W. 1980. *The Unexpected Rebellion: Ethnic Activism in Contemporary France*. New York: New York University Press.

Beitz, C. 1983. "Cosmopolitan Ideals and National Sentiments." *Journal of Philosophy* 80:591–600.

Belorgey, M., D. Lochak, and H. Leclerc. 1985. "Pour Une Participation des Etrangers à la Démocratie Locale." *Presses et Immigrés en France* 129.

Bendix, R. 1977. *Nation-Building and Citizenship*, 2nd ed. Berkeley: University of California Press.

Ben Jelloun, T. 1984. *Hospitalité Française. L'Histoire Immédiate*. Paris: Seuil.

Berger, J. 1968. *A Seventh Man. A Book of Images and Words about the Experiences of Migrant Workers in Europe*. London: Verso.

Berger, S. 1979. "Politics and Anti-Politics in Western Europe in the Seventies." *Daedalus* 108 (1).

———, ed. 1981. *Organizing Interests in Western Europe*. Cambridge: Cambridge University Press.

Bergouinioux, A., and G. Grunberg. 1984. "Le Socialisme et la République." *Intervention* 10:26–33.

Bergouinioux, A., and B. Manin. 1980. "L'Exclu de la Nation." *Le Débat* Octobre.

Bergquist, J. 1986. "The Concept of Nativism in Historical Study Since *Strangers in the Land*." *American Jewish History* (7) 2:125–141.

Beriss, D. 1990. "Scarves, Schools and Segregation: The *Foulard* Affair." *French Politics and Society*, vol. 8 (1) Winter.

Berlin, I. 1974. *Four Essays on Liberty*. New York: Oxford University Press.

Berque, J. 1985. *L'Immigration à l'Ecole de la République*. Rapport au Ministère de l'Education Nationale. Paris: La Documentation Française.

Birnbaum, P. 1979. *Le Peuple et les Gros*. Paris: Presses de la Fondation Nationale des Sciences Politiques.

———. 1982. *The Heights of Power*. Chicago: University of Chicago Press.

———. 1988. *States and Collective Action: The European Experience*. Cambridge: Cambridge University Press.

Body-Gendrot, S., B. D'Hellencourt, and M. Rancoule. 1989. "Entrée Interdite: La Législation sur l'Immigration en France, au Royaume-Uni, et aux Etats-Unis." *Revue Française de Sciences Politiques* 39 (1).

Bohning, W.R. 1978. "International Migration and the Western World: Past, Present, Future." *International Migration* 16:11–22.

Bourdieu, P. 1980. "L'Opinion Publique n'existe pas." In *Questions de Sociologie*. Paris: Éditions de Minuit.

Braudel, F. 1990. *The Identity of France*: vol. 1, *History and Environment*. New York: Harper & Row.

Breton, R. 1988. "From Ethnic to Civic Nationalism: English Canada and Quebec." *Ethnic and Racial Studies* 1:85–102.

Bruschi, C. 1987. "Droit de la Nationalité et Egalité des Droits de 1789 à la fin du XIXᵉ Siècle." In S. Laacher, ed., *Questions de Nationalité*.

————. 1988. "Le Droit de Cité dans l'Antiquité: un Questionnement pour la citoyenneté aujourd'hui." In C. W. de Wenden, ed., *La Citoyenneté*.

————. 1988a. "Citoyenneté et Nationalité: les Ambiguïtés de l'Histoire." *Les Cahiers de l'Orient* 11:85–102.

Brown, P. G., and H. Shue, eds. 1981. *Boundaries: National Autonomy and Its Limits*. Totowa, NJ: Rowman and Littlefield.

Brubaker, W. R., ed. 1989. *Immigration and the Politics of Citizenship in Europe and North America*. Washington, DC: German Marshall Fund of the United States and the University Press of America.

————. 1989a. "Introduction." In W. R. Brubaker, ed., *Immigration and The Politics of Citizenship in Europe and North America*.

————. 1989b. "Citizenship and Naturalization: Policies and Politics." In W. R. Brubaker, ed., *Immigration and The Politics of Citizenship in Europe and North America*.

————. 1989c. "Membership without Citizenship: The Economic and Social Rights of Noncitizens." In W. R. Brubaker, ed., *Immigration and the Politics of Citizenship in Europe and North America*.

————. 1992. *Citizenship and Nationhood in France and Germany*. Cambridge: Harvard University Press.

————. 1996. *Nationalism Reframed: Nationhood and the National Question in the New Europe*. Cambridge: Cambridge University Press.

Boulot, S., and D. Boyzon-Fradet. 1988. *Les Immigrés et l'École: Une Course d'Obstacles*. Paris: L'Harmattan, CIEMI.

Bouamama, S. 1988. "De l'Anti-racisme à la Citoyenneté." *IM'media Magazine* 8:20–21.

Cahiers de l'Orient. 1988. Dossier: Immigration—Citoyenneté—Nationalité. 11:69–162.

Cahiers de la Pastorale des Migrants. 1982. "Les Droits Politiques des Immigrés." CIEM. 10–11. 1er et 2e trimestres.

Callovi, G. 1990. "Regulating Immigration in the European Community." Paper presented at the 7th International Conference of Europeanists, Washington, D.C.

Catani, M., and Pallida, S., ed. 1987. *Le Rôle des Mouvements Associatifs dans l'Évolution des Communautés Immigrées*. Paris: FAS/DPM.

Carens, J. H. 1988. "Membership and Morality: Admission to Citizenship in Liberal Democratic States." In W. R. Brubaker, ed., *Immigration and the Politics of Citizenship in Europe and North America*.

Castles, S. 1984. *Here for Good. Western Europe's New Ethnic Minorities*. London: Pluto Press.

————. 1988. "The Bicentenary and the Failure of Australian Nationalism." *Race and Class*, vol. xxix (3).

———. 1989. *Migrant Workers and the Transformation of Western Societies*. Occasional Paper No. 22. Center for International Studies: Cornell University.

Castles, S., and G. Kosack. 1985. *Immigrant Workers and Class Structure in Western Europe*, 2nd ed. London: Oxford University Press.

Cercle Pierre Mendes France. 1988. "Un Nouveau Regard sur l'Immigration" *Projet* 210.

Césari, J. 1988. "Les Musulmans à Marseille: Enjeux d'une Reconnaissance Politique." *Pouvoirs* 47:123–132.

———. 1989–1990. "Le Comportement Politique des Immigrés Maghrebins." *Les Cahiers de l'Orient*, Nos. 16–17, 4ème trimester-1er trimestre.

Charlot, M. 1986. "L'Emergence du Front National." *Revue Française de Science Politique* 36.

Chebel, M. 1988. "Visages." *Les Cahiers de l'Orient* 11:151–162.

CIMADE Information. 1987. Dossier: Code de la Nationalité. Un Projet en Veilleuse. 2:11–25.

Cinar, D. 1994. "From Aliens to Citizens. A Comparative Analysis of Rules of Transition." In R. Baubock, ed., *From Aliens to Citizens, Redefining the Status of Immigrants in Europe*. Aldershot: Avebury.

Citron, S. 1987. *Le Mythe National. L'Histoire de France en Question*. Paris: Les Éditions Ouvrières.

———. 1988. "L'Histoire: Réflexions Sur une Carence." *Hommes et Migrations* 1112:50–57.

Club 89. 1985. *Maîtriser l'Immigration. Reconnaître Les Réalités Qui Préoccupent Les Français-Engager Une Politique Cohérente et Responsable*. Paris: L'Albatros.

Club de l'Horloge. 1985. *L'Identité de la France*. Paris: Albin Michel.

Cohen, R. 1994. *Frontiers of Identity: The British and the Others*. Harlow: Longman.

Connolly, W. 1984. "The Politics of Discourse." In M. Shapiro, ed., *Language and Politics*. New York: New York University Press.

Cordeiro, A. 1981. *Pourquoi l'Immigration en France? (Critique des Idées Reçues en Matière d'Immigration)*. Office Municipal des Migrants de Creteil.

———. 1985. "Mouvement Associatif et Communautés Issus de l'Immigration." Centre de Recherches en Sciences Sociales du Travail, Université de Paris-Sud, Sceaux.

———. 1986. *Enfermement et Ouvertures: Les Associations Portugaises en France*. Paris: CEDEP.

———. 1987a. "Pour Une Définition de la Nouvelle Citoyenneté." *CAIF*, 3ème Forum. Paris.

———. 1987b. "Voyage en 'Tosmanie': Jeunes d'Origine Portuguaise en France." *Accents Multiples* 7.

Costa-Lascoux, J. 1984. "Quelle Nationalité?" *Le Temps Modernes* Mars–Mai.

———. 1986. "La Politique Française de l'Immigration. Textes Législatifs et Réglementaires (Mai 1981–Mars 1986)." *Revue Européenne des Migrations Internationales* 2:205–240.

———. 1987a. "L'Acquisition de la Nationalité Française, une condition de l'Installation." In *Questions de Nationalité, Histoire et Enjeux d'un Code.* Paris: CIEMI, L'Harmattan.

———. 1987b. "Nationaux Seulement ou Vraiment Citoyens?" *PROJET* 204 Mars–Avril.

———. 1989a. *De L'Immigré au Citoyen.* Paris: La Documentation Française.

———. 1989b. Interview in *Libération* 11/6/89.

———. 1989c. "Une Citoyenneté au delà du Sol et du Sang." In J. F. de Raymond, ed., *Les Enjeux des Droits de l'Homme.* Paris: Larousse.

Costa-Lascoux, J., and E. Temine, eds. 1985. *Les Algériens en France. Genèse et Devenir d'une Migration.* Paris: Publisud.

Costain, A. 1992. *Inviting Women's Rebellion. A Political Process Interpretation of the Women's Movement.* Baltimore: Johns Hopkins University Press.

Costes, A. 1988. "L'Église Catholique dans le débat sur l'Immigration." *Revue Européenne des Migrations Internationales*, vol. 4, no. 1–2:29–48.

Cuches, D. 1982. "Les Bornes de la Tolérance ou la Tolérance Bornée: Notion et Usage du 'Seuil de Tolérance.' " *Pour* 86.

Darras, L. 1986. La Double Nationalité. Thèse du Doctorat d'Etat. Paris: Université de Droit, d'Économie et de Sciences Sociales.

Dazi. F., and R. Leveau. 1988. "L'Intégration par la Politique: Le Vote des Beurs." *Études* Septembre.

Debord, G. 1967. *La Société du Spectacle.* Paris: Buchet/Chestel.

———. 1990. *Comments on the Society of the Spectacle.* London: Verso.

De la Pradelle, G. 1993–1994. "Sang et Nationalité." *Plein Droit* no. 22–23:28–31.

De Rham, G. *See* Rham, G. de.

De Wenden, C. W. *See* Wihtol de Wenden, C.

Desir, H. 1987. *S.O.S. Désirs.* Paris: Calmann-Levy.

Diaz, M. 1988. "Interculturalité et Nouvelle Citoyenneté: l'Example Portugais." In C. W. de Wenden, ed., *La Citoyenneté.*

Différences. 1988. L'Immigration et le Racisme dans le Débat. Dossier (77) April.

Dray, J. 1987. *SOS Génération: l'Histoire de l'Intérieur du Mouvement des Jeunes de Novembre–Décembre 1986.* Paris: Ramsey.

Droit et Liberté. 1996. "MRAP: Documentation," No. 447, February.

Dubet, F. 1988. "SOS Racisme et la Revalorisation des Valeurs." *Hommes et Migrations* Janvier.

———. 1989. *Immigrations: Qu'en Savons-Nous? Un Bilan des Connaissances.* Paris: La Documentation Française.

Dummont, A., and A. Nicol. 1990. *Subjects, Citizens, Aliens and Others: Nationality and Immigration Law*. London: Weidenfield and Nicolson.

Echanges Méditerranéens. 1987. *Moi et l'Autre*. Marseille.

Edelman, M. 1971. *Politics as Symbolic Action. Mass Arousal and Quiescence*. Chicago: Markham.

———. 1985. *The Symbolic Uses of Politics*. Urbana: University of Illinois Press.

Etienne, B. 1987. *L'Islamisme Radical*. Paris: Hachette.

———. 1989a. *La France et l'Islam*. Paris: Hachette.

———. 1989b. "Pour un Islam Français" *L'Express*, 12 Mai.

Espace 89. 1985. *L'Identité Française* Paris: Tierce.

Esprit. 1966. Les Etrangers en France. Special.

———. 1985. Francais-Immigrés. Special. Mai–Juin.

Ethics. 1988. Symposium on Duties Beyond Borders. (98) 4.

Etudes. 1982. Les Droits Politiques des Immigrés. Janvier.

Evans, P. B., D. Rueschemeyer, and T. Skocpol, eds. 1985. *Bringing the State Back In*. Cambridge: Cambridge University Press.

Expressions. 1988. Pour Une Nouvelle Citoyenneté. Dossier. (55) Juillet.

Fassmann, H., and R. Munz. 1994. "Patterns and Trends of International Migration in Western Europe." In H. Fassmann and R. Munz, eds., *European Migration in the Late Twentieth Century*. Aldershot: Edward Elgar Publishing Co.

Favell, Adrian. 1997. *Philosophies of Integration: Immigration and the Idea of Citizenship in France and Britain*. London: Macmillan; New York: St. Martin's Press.

Feldblum, M. 1993. "Paradoxes of Ethnic Politics: the Case of Franco-Maghrebis in France." *Ethnic and Racial Studies*, vol. 16, no. 1:52–74.

———. 1996. "France." In B. E. Shafer, ed., *Postwar Politics in the G-7 Orders and Eras in Comparative Perspective*. Madison: University of Wisconsin Press, pp. 117–155.

Fenet, A., and G. Soulier, eds. 1989. *Les Minorités et Leurs Droits Depuis 1789*. Paris: L'Harmattan.

Finnemore, M. 1996. *National Interests in International Society*. Ithaca, NY: Cornell University Press.

Fitzgerald, K. 1996. *The Face of the Nation: Immigration, the State, and the National Identity*. Stanford: Stanford University Press.

Foucault, M. 1984. "The Order of Discourse." In M. Shapiro, ed., *Language and Politics*.

Freeman, G. P. 1979. *Immigrant Labor and Racial Conflict in Industrial Societies*. Princeton: Princeton University Press.

———. 1986. "Migration and the Political Economy of the Welfare State." *Annals of the American Academy of Political and Social Sciences* 485:51–63.

————. 1995. "Modes of Integration Politics in Liberal Democratic States." *International Migration Review* 29/4 Winter, 881–902.

————. 1998. "The Decline of Sovereignty? Politics and Immigration Restriction in Liberal States." In C. Joppke, ed., *Challenge to the Nation-State*. Oxford: Oxford University Press.

Fuchs, G. 1987. *Ils Resteront: Le Défi de l'Immigration*. Paris: Eitions Syros.

Fulchiron, Hugues, ed. 1996. *Être Français Aujard'hui. Premier bilan de la mise en oeuvre du nouveau droit de la nationalité*. Lyon: Presses Universitaires de Lyon.

Gallissot, R. 1985. *Misère de l'Antiracisme: Racisme et Identité Nationale*. Paris: Arcentere.

————. 1986. "Nationalité et Citoyenneté." *APRES-DEMAIN* 286:8–15.

————. 1989. "Droits de l'Homme: Citoyenneté-Nationalité. Quel est le Sens du Jacobinisme, si Jacobinisme Il y a?" In A. Fenet and G. Soulier, eds., *Les Minorités et Leurs Droits Depuis 1789*.

Gaspard, F., and C. Servan-Schreiber. 1984. *La Fin des Immigrés*. Paris: Le Seuil.

Geertz, C. 1973. "Ideology as a Cultural System." In *The Interpretation of Cultures*. New York: Basic Books.

Gellner, E. 1983. *Nations and Nationalism*. Ithaca: Cornell University Press.

George, P. 1986. *L'Immigration en France: Faits et Problèmes*. Paris: A. Colin Actualité.

Gilroy, P. 1987. *There Ain't No Black in the Union Jack. The Cultural Politics of Race and Nation*. London: Century Hutchinson.

————. 1993. *The Black Atlantic*. Cambridge: Harvard University Press

Giordan, H. 1982. *Démocratie culturelle et Droit à la Différence*. Rapport au Ministre de la culture. Paris: La Documentation Française.

Girardet, R. 1983. *Le Nationalisme Français. Anthologie 1871–1914*. Paris: Le Seuil.

Glazer, N., and D. Moynihan, eds. 1975. *Ethnicity: Theory and Experience*. Cambridge: Cambridge University Press.

Gleason, P. 1980. "American Identity and Americanization." In Stephan Thernstrom, ed., *Harvard Encyclopedia of American Ethnic Groups*. Cambridge: Harvard University Press.

Gonzalez-Quijano, Y. 1987. "Les 'Nouvelles' Générations Issues de l'Immigration Maghrebine et la Question de l'Islam." *Revue Nationale des Sciences Politiques* vol 36 (6).

————. 1988. "Les Autres Arabes." *Les Cahiers de l'Orient*, 3ème trimestre–1er trimestre.

Gordon, D. 1978. *The French Language and National Identity (1930–1975)*. The Hague: Mouton.

Greenfield, Liah. 1992. *Nationalism. Five Roads to Modernity*. Cambridge: Harvard University Press.

Grillo, R. D., ed. 1980. *'Nation' and 'State' in Europe. Anthropological Perspectives*. London: Academic Press.

Griotteray, A. 1984. *Les Immigrés: Le Choc*. Paris: Plon.

Gross, A. 1968. "Political Process." In *International Encyclopedia of the Social Sciences*, vol. 12. New York: Macmillan and The Free Press.

Guibert-Sledziewski, E. 1988. "La Nation, Idéal Contradictoire." *Projet* 213:168–177.

Guillon, M. 1988. "Etrangers et Immigrés dans la Populations de la France." In C. W. de Wenden, ed., *La Citoyenneté*.

Guillon, M., and I. Taboada-Leonetti. 1986. *Le Triangle de Choisy: un Quartier Chinois à Paris*. Paris: CIEMI, L'Harmattan.

Hall, P. 1986. *Governing the Economy. The Politics of State Intervention in Britain and France*. New York: Oxford University Press.

Hall, P. 1993. "Policy Paradigms, Social Learning and the State. The Case of Economic Policymaking in Britain." *Comparative Politics* 25:275–296.

Hall, S. 1988. *The Hard Road to Renewal*. London: Verso.

Hammar, T., ed. 1985a. *European Immigration Policy*. Cambridge: Cambridge University Press.

———. 1985b. "Dual Citizenship and Political Integration." *International Migration Review* 19:438–450.

———. 1986. "Citizenship: Membership of a Nation and of a State." *International Migration* 4:735–747.

———. 1989. "State, Nation, and Dual Citizenship." In W. R. Brubaker, ed., *Immigration and the Politics of Citizenship in Europe and North America*.

———. 1990. *International Migration, Citizenship, and Democracy*. Aldershot: Gower.

Handler, R. 1988. *Nationalism and the Politics of Culture in Quebec*. Madison: University of Wisconsin Press.

Hannoun, M. 1985. *Français et Immigrés au Quotidien*. Paris: l'Albatros.

———. 1986. *L'Autre Cohabitation: Français et Immigrés*. Paris: L'Harmattan.

———. 1987. *L'Homme est l'Espérance de l'Homme*. Rapport sur le Racisme et les Discriminations en France au Secrétaire d'Etat auprès du Premier Ministre Chargé des Droits de l'Homme. Paris: La Documentation Française.

Hansen, R. A., and P. Weil, eds. 1999. *Citizenship, Immigration and Nationality: Nationality Law in the European Union*. London: Macmillan.

Haut Conseil à l'Intégration. 1991. *Pour un Modèle français d'intégration. Premier rapport annuel*. Paris: La Documentation Française.

———. 1992. *La connaissance de l'immigration et de l'intégration. Novembre 1991*. Paris: La Documentation Française.

———. 1993. *La connaissance de l'immigration et de l'intégration. Décembre 1992*. Paris: La Documentation Française.

Hayward, J. 1978. "Dissentient France: The Counter Political Culture." *West European Studies* 3.

Heisler, M. O., and B. Schmitter Heisler, eds. 1986. From Foreign Workers to Settlers? Transnational Migration and the Emergence of New Minorities. *The Annals of the American Academy of Political and Social Sciences* 485 (May).

Heisler, B. Schmitter. 1986. "Immigrant Settlement and the Structure of Emergent Immigrant Communities in Western Europe." *The Annals of the American Academy of Political and Social Sciences* 485:76–86.

———. 1990. "Citizenship—Old, New, and Changing." In J. Fijalkowski, H. Merkens, and F. Schmidt, eds., *Dominant National Cultures and Ethnic Identities*. Berlin: Berlin Free University.

———. 1992. "The Future of Immigrant Incorporation: Which Models? Which Concepts?" *International Migration Review* (26) 2:623–645.

Higham, J. 1988. *Strangers in the Land. Patterns of American Nativism 1860–1925*, rev. ed. Rutgers, NJ: Rutgers University Press.

Higonnet, P. 1988. *Sister Republics: The Origins of French and American Republicanism*. Cambridge: Harvard University Press.

Hirschman, A. 1991. *The Rhetoric of Reaction. Perversity, Futility, Jeopardy*. Cambridge: Belknap Press of Harvard University Press.

Hobsbawm, E. 1983. "Introduction: Inventing Traditions" and "Mass-Producing Traditions: Europe, 1870–1914." In E. Hobsbawm and T. Ranger, eds., *The Invention of Tradition*. Cambridge: Cambridge University Press.

———. 1990. *Nations and Nationalism Since 1870. Programme, Myth, Reality*. Cambridge: Cambridge University Press.

Hollifield, J. 1986. "Immigration, Race and Politics." *French Politics and Society* (13) March.

———. 1989. "Migrants into Citizens. The Politics of Immigration in France and the United States." Paper presented at the Annual Meetings of the American Political Science Association, Atlanta, Georgia.

———. 1991a. "Immigration and Modernization." In J. Hollifield and G. Ross, eds., *Searching for the New France*. London: Routledge.

———. 1991b. "Still Searching for the New France." In J. Hollifield and G. Ross, eds., *Searching for the New France*. London: Routledge.

———. 1992. *Immigrants, Markets, and States: The Political Economy of Postwar Europe*. Cambridge: Harvard University Press.

———. 1994. "Immigration and Republicanism in France: The Hidden Consensus." In W. Cornelius, P. Martin, and J. Hollifield, eds., *Controlling Immigration. A Global Perspective*. Stanford: Stanford University Press.

Holmes Cooper, A. 1996. "Public Good Movements and the Dimensions of Political Process: Postwar German Peace Movements." *Comparative Political Studies* 29:3 (June).

Hommes et Libertés. 1985. Les Immigrés dans la Cité. Special Issue.

———. 1987. Code de la Nationalité. Ils y Ont Droit. (45/46) Janvier–Fevrier.

———. 1985. Convergence . . . Divergences . . . Des marcheurs de 83 aux rouleurs de 84. 1077:4–5.

———. 1986a. Identité Française et Assimilation. Dossier. 1088:37–62.

———. 1986b. Les Immigrés Maghrebins et L'Islam en France. Dossier. 1097:43–62.

———. 1987a. Nouveaux Aspects de La Politique Française d'Immigration en 1987. Dossier. 1100:15–24.

———. 1987b. Dossier: Le Code de la Nationalité. Sera-t-il Reformé? 1106:11–29.

———. 1990. Laïcité-Diversité. Dossier.

Horowitz, D. 1975. "Ethnic Identity." In N. Glazer and D. Moynihan, eds., *Ethnicity: Theory and Experience*. Cambridge: Harvard University Press.

———. 1987. *Ethnic Groups in Conflict*. Berkeley: University of California Press.

Husbands, C. T. 1988. "The Dynamics of Racial Exclusion and Expulsion: Racist Politics in Western Europe." *European Journal of Political Research* 16:701–720.

Ignatieff, M. 1986. *The Needs of Strangers*. New York: Penguin Books.

IM'media. 1987. Fabrikons Français. Film.

———. 1987–1988. L'Anti-Racisme. Nouvelle vertu Républicaine. Dossier. (7) Automne-Hiver.

———. 1988. Citoyenneté: Marianne Si Tu Savais. Dossier. (8) Printemps-Eté.

International Migration Review. 1985. Political Participation and Civil Rights of Immigrants. Special Issue 19(3).

Intervention. 1984. "La République." Décembre–Août, no. 10.

Ireland, Patrick. 1994. *The Policy Challenge of Ethnic Diversity: Immigrant Politics in France and Switzerland*. Cambridge: Harvard University Press.

IRIS. 1987. L'Imbroglio du Code de la Nationalité. 1:5–39.

Jaffre, J. 1986. "Qui Vote Le Pen?" In E. Plenal and A. Rollat, eds., *L'Effet Le Pen*. Paris: La Découverte/Le Monde.

Jazouli, A. 1986. *L'Action Collective des Jeunes Maghrebins de France*. Paris: CIEMI, L'Harmattan.

Jennings, J. 1990. "Liberalism, Nationalism, and the Excluded." Paper presented at the 2nd Conference of the International Society for the Study of European Ideas, Leuven, Belgium, September 3–8.

Jepperson, R. L., and J. W. Meyer. 1990. "The Public Order and the Construction of Formal Organizations." In W. W. Powell and P. J. DiMaggio, eds., *The New Institutionalism in Organizational Analysis*. Chicago: University of Chicago Press.

Kamenka, E., ed. 1973a. *Nationalism: The Nature and Evolution of an Idea*. Canberra: Australian National University Press.

————. 1973b. "Political Nationalism. The Evolution of an Idea." In E. Kamenka, ed., *Nationalism: The Nature and Evolution of an Idea.*

Karl, T. L. 1991. "Dilemmas of Democratization in Latin America." In D. Rustow and K. P. Erickson, eds., *Comparative Political Dynamics*. Stanford: Stanford University Press.

Kastoryano, R. 1989a. "L'Etat et Les Immigrés: France, Allemagne, Grande-Bretagne, et Etats-Unis." *Revue Européenne des Migrations Internationales* 5 (1) 2ème trimestre.

————. 1989b. "Les Deux Stratégies des Associations 'Beurs.' " *Le Journal des Elections.*

————. 1996. *La France, l'Allemagne & leurs immigrés: Négocier l'identité*. Paris: Armand Colin.

Kates, G. 1986. "Jews into Frenchmen: Nationality and Representation in Revolutionary France." *Social Research* 56 (1).

Kato, J. 1996. "Path Dependency as a Logic of Comparative Studies: Theorization and Application." Paper presented at the American Political Science Association Meetings, San Francisco, August 29–September 1.

Kaufman, L. A. 1990. "The Anti-Politics of Identity." *Socialist Review*, vol. 20 (1):January–March.

Kepel, G. 1987. *Les Banlieues de l'Islam. Naissance d'une Religion en France.* Paris: Seuil.

Kitschelt, H. 1986. "Political Opportunity Structures and Political Protest: Anti-Nuclear Movements in Four Democracies. *British Journal of Political Science* 16:58–95.

Kritz, M., C. Keely, and S. Tomasi. 1981. *Global Trends in Migration: Theory and Research in International Population Movements*. New York: Center for Migration Studies.

Krulic, J. 1988a. "L'Immigration et l'Identité de la France. Mythes et Realités." *Pouvoirs* (47).

————. 1988b. "Nos Mythes Fondateurs Sous Une Autre Lumière." *Projet* 210:67–73.

Kubat, D. 1979. *The Politics of Migration Policies: The First World in the 1970s.* New York: Center for Migration Studies.

Laacher, S. ed. 1987. *Questions de Nationalité Histoire et Enjeux d'un Code.* Paris: CIEMI, L'Harmattan.

Lafont, R. 1968. *Sur La France*. Paris: Gallimard.

Lavau, G. 1987. "Nationalism and the Rise of the Extreme Right in France." *French Politics and Society* 5(1–2).

Layton-Henry, Z. 1988. "The Political Challenge of Migration for Western European States." *European Journal of Political Research* 16:587–596.

————, ed. 1990. *The Political Rights of Migrant Workers in Western Europe.* London: Sage.

———. 1990a. "The Challenge of Political Rights." In Z. Layton-Henry, ed., *The Political Rights of Migrant Workers in Western Europe*.

———. 1990b. "Citizenship or Denizenship for Migrant Workers." In Z. Layton-Henry, ed., *The Political Rights of Migrant Workers in Western Europe*.

———. 1993. *The Politics of Immigration*. Oxford: Blackwell.

Lebon, A. 1987. "Attribution et Perte de la Nationalité Française: Un Bilan 1973–1986." *Revue Européenne des Migrations Internationales* 3 (1 and 2).

———. 1988. *1986–1987 Le Point sur L'Immigration et la Présence Etrangère en France*. Paris: La Documentation Française.

Leca, J. 1983. "Questions sur La Citoyenneté." *Projet* Janvier.

———. 1985. "Entretien: Une Capacité d'Intégration Défaillante." *Esprit* Juin.

———. 1988. "Entretien." In C. W. de Wenden, ed., *La Citoyenneté*.

Le Gallou, J. Y. et le Club De l'Horloge. 1985. *La Préférence Nationale: Réponse à l'Immigration*. Paris: Albin Michel.

Le Gallou, J. Y., and J. F. Jalkh. 1987. *Être Français, Ça Se Mérite*. Paris: Albatros.

Le Huu Khoa. 1985. *Les Vietnamiens en France: Insertion et Identité*. Paris: CIEMI, L'Harmattan.

Le Pen, J. M. 1984. *Les Français D'Abord*. Paris: Carrère-Michel-Lafont.

Leveau, R. 1988. "Islam, Nationalité et Citoyenneté, le Vécu quotidien pour les Musulmans." In C. W. de Wenden, ed., *La Citoyenneté*.

———. 1988–1989. "Crise de Voile ou Crise de Société." *Les Cahiers de l'Orient* (11) 3ème trimestre.

———. 1989. "Les Partis et l'Intégration des 'Beurs.'" In Y. Meny, ed., *Ideologies, Partis Politiques et Groupes Sociaux* (Etudes Réunies par Y. Meny pour George Lavau). Paris: Presses Fondation Nationale de Sciences Politiques.

———. 1990. "Islamic Veil and National Flag." *The European Journal of International Affairs* 4:41–53.

Leveau, R., and C. W. de Wenden. 1985. "L'Évolution des Attitudes Politiques des Immigrés Maghrebins." *Vingtieme Siecle* Juillet–Septembre.

———. 1988a. "Les 'Beurs' Nouveaux Citoyens." *Les Cahiers de l'Orient* 11:103–114.

———. 1988b. "La Deuxième Génération." *Pouvoirs* 47.

Leveau, R., C. W. de Wenden, and G. Kepel. 1987. "Les Musulmans En France." *Revue Française de Science Politique*, vol. 37 (6).

Leveau, R., and D. Schnapper. 1987. "Religion et Politique: Juifs et Musulmans Maghrebins en France." *Revue Française de Science Politique* 37 (6).

Leveau, R., and A. Zghal. 1989. "Islam et Laïcité en France." *Etudes*, Mai.

Lignes. 1988a. Code de la Nationalité. 2:7–28.

———. 1988b. Les Extrême-Droites en France et en Europe."

Llaumett, M. 1983. "L'Immigration en Novembre '83. et La Marche Pour l'Egalité et Contre le Racisme." *Presse et Immigrés en France* 112.

———. 1985. "Immigrés, sondages et Opinion Publique." *Presse et Immigrés en France* 129.

Lochak, D. 1985. *Etrangers: de Quel Droit?* Paris: PUF.

———. 1986. "Comment Peut-On Etre Francais?" *Après-Demain* 286:15–29.

———. 1987. "Code de la Nationalité. La Logique de l'Exclusion." *Les Temps Modernes* 490, Mai.

———. 1988. "Etrangers et Citoyens au Regard du Droit." In C. W. Wenden, ed., *La Citoyenneté.*

———. 1989a. "Les Etrangers et L'Alternance." *Projet* (216), Mars–Avril.

———. 1989b. "Les Minorités et le Droit Public Français: Du Refus des Différences à la Gestion des Différences." In A. Fenet and G. Soulier, eds., *Les Minorités et Leurs Droits Depuis 1789.*

Lochak, D., and J.-M. Belorgey. 1985. "Le Droit de Vote aux Elections Locales." *Hommes et Libertés* 37:17–19.

Long, M. 1988. *Etre Français Aujourd'hui et Demain. Rapport de la Commission de la Nationalité presenté par M. Marceau Long au Premier Ministre,* vols. 1 and 2. Paris: La Documentation Française.

Lorcerie, Françoise. 1994. "Les Sciences Sociales au Service de l'Identité Nationale." In D. C. Martin, ed., *Carte d'identité. Comment dit-on "Nous" en politique 2.* Paris: Presses de la Fondation Nationale des Sciences Politiques, pp. 245–281.

MacIntyre, A. 1984. "Is Patriotism a Virtue?" Laurence: University of Kansas. Department of Philosophy.

Manin, B. 1984. "Pourquoi la République?" *Intervention* 10:7–25.

Marangé, J., and A. Lebon. 1982. *L'Insertion des Jeunes d'Origine Etrangère dans La Société Française.* Paris: La Documentation Française.

March, J., and J. Olsen. 1989. *Rediscovering Institutions. The Organization Basis of Politics.* New York: The Free Press.

Marie, C. V. 1984. *L'Immigration Etrangère.* Paris: ADRI.

———. 1988. "Entre Économie et Politique: Le 'Clandestin,' une Figure Sociale à Géométrie Variable." *Pouvoirs* 47:75–92.

Marks, G. 1996. "An Actor Centered Approach to Multilevel Governance." Paper presented at the American Political Science Association Meeting, San Francisco, August 29–September 1.

Marks, G., and D. McAdam. 1996. "Social Movements and the Changing Structure of Political Opportunity in the European Community." *West European Politics,* vol. 18.

Marrus, M., and R. Paxton. 1981. *Vichy France and the Jews.* New York: Basic Books.

Marshall, T. H. 1965. *Class, Citizenship, and Social Development.* New York: Doubleday.

Massot, J. 1985. "Français par le Sang, Français par la Loi, Français par Choix." *Revue Européenne des Migrations Internationales*, vol. 1 (2).

Massot, J., and J. Marimbert. 1988. *Le Conseil d'Etat*. Paris: La Documentation Française.

Mayer, N., and P. Perrineau, eds. 1989. *Le Front National à Découvert*. Paris: FNSP.

McAdam, D. 1982. *Political Process and the Development of Black Insurgency 1930–1970*. Chicago: University of Chicago Press.

McAdam, D., J. McCarthy, and N. Zald, eds. 1996. *Comparative Perspectives on Social Movements: Political Opportunities, Mobilizing Structures, and Cultural Framings*. Cambridge: Cambridge University Press.

McAdam, D., S. Tarrow, and C. Tilly. 1996. "A Comparative Synthesis on Social Movements and Revolution: Towards an Integrated Perspective." Paper presented at the Annual Meeting of the American Political Science Association, August 29–September 1.

Miles, R. 1987. "State, Racism, and Migration: The Recent European Experience." Occasional Papers. Amsterdam: Center for Economic and Political Studies.

———. 1993. Racism after "Race Relations." London: Routledge.

Miller, M. J. 1981. *Foreign Workers in Western Europe. An Emerging Political Force*. New York: Praeger.

———. 1989. "Political Participation and Representation of Noncitizens." In W. R. Brubaker, ed., *Immigration and the Politics of Citizenship in Europe and North America*.

Mills, Wright C. 1984. "Situated Actions and Vocabularies of Motive." In M. Shapiro, ed., *Language and Politics*.

Milza, P. 1985. "Un Siècle d'Immigration Etrangère en France." *Vingtième Siècle* 7:3–18.

Mitterrand, F. 1988. "Lettre à Tous les Français." pp. 1–54. Paris.

Le Monde Aujourd'hui. "Les Immigrés, enjeux électoraux." Supplement to no. 12697. 11/24–25/85.

MRAP. 1986. "Contribution à un débat sur les droits civiques des Immigrés en France" *Droit et Liberte*, no. 447.

Muxel, A. 1988. "Les Jeunes Migrants de la Deuxième Génération et Leur Inscription dans le Systeme Politique Actuel." Paper presented at the Journée d'Etude de CEVIPOF, January 29.

Nettl, J. P. 1968. "The State as a Conceptual Variable." *Comparative Politics* 20.

Noiriel, G. 1984. "L'Histoire de l'Immigration. Note sur un enjeu." *Actes de la Recherche en Sciences Sociales* September.

———. 1985. "Immigration: Le Fin Mot de l'Histoire." *Vingtième Siècle* 7:141–150.

———. 1988. *Le Creuset Français. Histoire de l'Immigration, XIXe–XXe Siècles.* Paris: Seuil.

———. 1992. *Population, immigration et identité nationale en France, XIXe–XIXe siècles.* Paris: Hachette.

Nora, P. 1984. "Les Métamorphoses de la Mémoire Républicaine." *Intervention* 10:59–65.

———. 1989. "Between Memory and History: 'Les Lieux de Mémoire'." *Representations* 26:7–25.

Nordlinger, E. A. 1981. *On the Autonomy of the Democratic State.* Cambridge: Harvard University Press.

North, D. C. 1990. *Institutions, Institutional Change and Economic Performance.* Cambridge: Cambridge Univeristy Press.

Parti Socialiste. 1981. *100 Propositions Pour La France. La Liberté des Femmes et des Hommes Responsables.*

Perotti, A. 1983. " 'Marcheurs Sans Importance' Interpellent La France." *Presse et Immigrés en France* 111.

———. 1985. "La 'Préférence Nationale': Réponse à L'Immigration ou Organization de l'Egalité et Division de la Classe Ouvrière?" *Presse et Immigrés en France* 132.

———. 1986. "A propos de la Révision du Code de la Nationalité. Plaidoyer pour le Droit du Sol." *Presse et Immigrés en France* 139–140.

———. 1987. "Recentrer Le Débat Sur le Code de la Nationalité." *Presse et Immigrés en France* 150–150.

———. 1988. "L'Immigration en France: Son Histoire, Ses Nouvelles Réalités et Ses Nouveaux Enjeux." In C. W. de Wenden, ed., *La Citoyenneté.*

Perotti, A., A. Costes, and M. Llaumett. 1989. "L'Europe et L'Immigration. 1ère Partie: Les Constats." *Migrations Société* 1:23–46, CIEMI.

Philippe, B. 1981. *Etre Juif dans la Société Française* Paris: Collection Pluriel.

Pinto, D. 1984. "Vive la République." *Intervention* 10:89–90.

———. 1988. "Immigration. L'Ambiguïté de la Référence Américaine." *Pouvoirs* 47:93–102.

Piore, M. 1979. *Birds of Passage: Migrant Labor and Industrial Societies.* Cambridge: Cambridge University Press.

Plamenatz, J. 1973. "Two Types of Nationalism." In E. Kamenka, ed., *Nationalism: The Nature and Evolution of an Idea.*

Plein Droit. 1988. Dossier: Quel Discours Sur l'Immigration? (3) Avril.

———. 1993–1994. De Legibus Xenophobis. No. 22–23.

Plenel, E., and A. Rollat. 1984. *L'Effet Le Pen.* Paris: La Decouverte.

Polin, R. 1987. "Identité Nationale et Immigration." *Revue des Deux Mondes* (9) 9:623–639.

Powell, W., and P. DiMaggio. 1991. *The New Institutionalism in Organizational Analysis.* Chicago: University of Chicago Press.

Projet. 1983. Les Français qui sont aussi La France. vol. 171–172.

———. 1986. La France avec les Immigrés. vol.199.

Rambaud, P. 1989. "L'Utopie Communitaire et l'Idéologie de la Nation." *Projet* (217) Mai–Juin.

Rassemblement Pour La République. Union Pour la Démocratie Française. 1986. *Plateforme Pour Gouverner Ensemble.*

Rosaldo, R. 1989. "Imperialist Nostolgia." *Representations* 26:107–122.

Rath, J. 1990. "Voting Rights." In Z. Layton-Henry, ed., *The Political Rights of Migrant Workers in Western Europe.*

Regowski, R., ed. 1985. *New Nationalisms in the Developed West.* Boston: Allen & Unwin.

Renan, E. 1882. *Qu'est-ce qu'une Nation.* Talk presented at the Sorbonne, Paris, March 11. Reprinted in *Qu'est-ce qu'une Nation?* (et autres textes choisis et présentés par Joël Roman.) Paris: Presses Pocket, 1992.

Rendel, M. 1970. *The Administrative Functions of the French Conseil d'Etat.* London: London School of Economics and Political Science.

Revue Française de Science Politique. 1987. Les Musulmans Dans La Société Française. 37 (6) Décembre.

Rex, J., D. Joly, and C. Wilpert. 1987. *Immigrant Associations in Europe.* Aldershot: Grower.

de Rham, G. de. 1990. "Naturalization: The Politics of Citizenship Acquisition." In Z. Layton-Henry, ed., *The Political Rights of Migrant Workers in Western Europe.*

Rist, R. 1979. "Migration and Marginality: Guestworkers in Germany and France." *Daedalus* 108:95–108.

Rogers, R. 1985. *Guests Come to Stay: The Effects of European Labor Migration on Sending and Receiving Countries.* Boulder, CO: Westview Press.

Rogin, M. 1990. " 'Make My Day': Spectacle as Amnesia in Imperial Politics." *Representations* 29:99–123.

Rule, J., and C. Tilly. 1975. "Political Process in Revolutionary France, 1830–1832." In J. Merriman, ed., *1830 In France.* New York: New Viewpoints.

Safran, W. 1984. "The French Left and Ethnic Pluralism." *Ethnic and Racial Studies* vol. 7:497–61.

———. 1985. "The Mitterand Regime and Its Policies of Ethnocultural Accommodation." *Comparative Politics* 18 (1).

———. 1990. "The French and Their National Identity: The Quest for an Elusive Substance." *French Politics and Society* 8 (1) Winter.

Said, E. 1979. *Orientalism.* New York: Vintage Books.

Sayad, A. 1977. "Les Trois Âges de l'Immigration Algérienne en France." *Actes de la Recherche Sociale,* no. 15, Juin.

———. 1981–1982. "La Naturalisation, Ses Conditions Sociales et Sa Signification Chez les Immigrés Algériens." *GRECO* 13 (3–5).

————. 1984. "Etat, Nation, et Immigration: l'Ordre National à l'Epreuve de l'Immigration." *Peuples Méditerranéens* (27–28) Avril–Septembre.

————. 1987. "Les Immigrés Algériens et la Nationalité Française." In S. Laacher, ed., *Questions de la Nationalité. Histoire et Enjeux d'un Code.*

————. 1988. "Immigration et Naturalisation." In C. W. de Wenden, ed., *La Citoyenneté.*

Schain, M. 1985a. "Immigrants and Politics in France." In J. Amber, ed., *The Socialist Experiment.* Philadelphia: Institute for the Study of Human Issues.

————. 1985b. *French Communism and Local Power.* London and New York: Francis Pinter and St. Martin's.

————. 1987. "The National Front in France and the Construction of Political Legitimacy." *West European Politics* 10:229–252.

————. 1988. "Immigration and Changes in the French Party System." *European Journal of Political Research* 16:597–622.

————. 1990. "Immigration and Politics." In P. Hall, J. Hayward, and H. Machin, eds., *Developments in French Politics.* New York: St. Martin's Press.

Schields, J. 1987. "Politics and Populism: The French Far Right in the Ascendant." *Contemporary French Civilization* 11 (1) Winter.

Schmidt, V. A. 1991. *Democratizing France: The Political and Administrative History of Decentralization.* Cambridge: Cambridge University Press.

Schnapper, D. 1987. "Unité Nationale et Particularismes Culturels." *Commentaire* (38) Summer.

————. 1988. "La Commission de la Nationalité, Une Instance Singulière." *Revue Européenne des Migrations Internationales* 4:9–28.

————. 1991. *La France de l'intégration.* Paris: Gallimard.

Schönwalder, Karen. 1996. "Migration, Refugees, and Ethnic Plurality as Issues of Public and Political Debates in (West) Germany." In D. Cesarani and M. Fulbrook, eds., *Citizenship, Nationality and Migration in Europe.* London: Routledge, pp. 159–178.

Schor, R. 1985. *L'Opinion Française et les Etrangers en France, 1919–1939.* Paris: Publication de la Sorbonne.

Schreiber, T. 1966. "De La Résidence à la Naturalisation. Les Etrangers dans la Vie Civique." *Esprit* 348:808–825.

Scott, N. R., and J. Meyer, 1994. *Institutional Environments and Organizations: Structural Complexity and Individualism.* New York: Sage Publications.

Shapiro, M., ed. 1984. *Language and Politics.* New York: New York University Press.

Shklar, J. 1991. *American Citizenship. The Quest for Inclusion.* Cambridge: Harvard University Press.

Sieyes, E. 1982. *Qu'est-ce que le Tiers-Etat.* Paris: PUF.

Silverman, M., ed. 1991. *Race, Discourse, and Power in France.* Averbury: Grover.

———. 1992. *Deconstructing the Nation: Immigration, Racism, and Citizenship in Modern France*. London: Routledge.

Simon, G. 1986. "Les Portugais et la Double Nationalité." *Actualités Migrations* April 28:126:2–5.

Skocpol, T. 1979. *States and Social Revolutions*. Cambridge: Cambridge University Press.

———. 1985. "Bringing the State Back In: Strategies of Analysis in Current Research." In P. Evans, D. Rueschemeyer, and T. Skocpol, eds., *Bringing the State Back In*.

———. 1992. *Protecting Soldiers and Mothers: The Politics of Social Provision in the United States, 1870s–1920s*. Cambridge: Harvard University Press.

Smith, A. 1979. *Nationalism in the Twentieth Century*. Oxford: Martin Robertson.

———. 1991. *National Identity*. London: Penguin Books.

Smith, R. 1988. "The 'American Creed' and American Identity: The Limits of Liberal Citizenship in the United States." *The Western Political Quarterly* (41) 2:225–251.

———. 1997. *Civic Ideals: Conflicting Visions of Citizenship in U.S. History*. New Haven: Yale University Press.

SOFRES. 1983. *l'Opinion Publique 1983*. Paris: Gallimard.

———. 1985. *l'Opinion Publique 1985*. Paris: Gallimard.

———. 1988. *L'Etat de l'Opinion. Clés Pour 1988*. Paris: Seuil.

Soysal, Y. 1994. *Limits of Citizenship: Migrants and Postnational Membership in Europe*. Chicago: University of Chicago Press.

———. 1996. "Changing Citizenship in Europe: Remarks on Postnational Membership and the National State." In D. Cesarani and M. Fulbrook, eds., *Citizenship, Nationality and Migration in Europe*. London and New York: Routledge.

Stasi, B. 1984. *L'Immigration: Une Chance pour La France*. Paris: Laffont.

Steinmo, S., K. Thelen, and F. Longstreth, eds. 1992. *Structuring Politics: Historical Institutionalism in Comparative Perspective*. Cambridge: Cambridge University Press.

Sternhall, Z. 1983. *Ni Droite ni Gauche. L'Idéologie Fasciste en France*. Paris: Le Seuil.

Suleiman, E. N. 1974. *Politics, Power, and Bureaucracy in France: The Administrative Elite*. Princeton: Princeton University Press.

Taguieff, P. A. 1984. "La Rhétorique du National-Populisme." *MOTS* 12 Mars.

———. 1985. "L'Identité Française et ses ennemis. Le Traitement de l'Immigration dans le National-Racisme Français Contemporain." *L'Homme et La Société* (77–78).

———. 1986. "L'Identité Nationale Saisie Par La Logique de Racisation." *MOTS* 12 Mars.

———. 1987. *La Force du Préjugé. Essai sur le Racisme et ses Doubles*. Paris: La Découverte.

———. 1988. "L'Identité Nationaliste." *LIGNES* 4:14–60.

———. 1991. *Face Au Racisme*. Paris: La Découverte.

Taguieff, P. A., and P. Weil. 1990. "Immigration, fait National et Citoyenneté." *Esprit* 161:87–102.

Tapinos, G. 1975. *L'Immigration Etrangère en France, 1946–1973*. Paris: INED/PUF.

———. 1988. "L'Immigration en France." *Commentaire* 43 Autumne.

Les Temps Modernes. 1984. L'Immigration Maghrebine en France. Les Faits et les Mythes. 452–454 mars–mai.

Tibon-Cornillot, M. 1983. "Le Défi de l'Immigration Maghrebine." *Le Monde* 8/23–24.

Tilly, C., L. Tilly, and R. Tilly. 1979. *The Rebellious Century, 1830–1930*. Cambridge: Harvard University Press.

Tilly, C. 1978. *From Mobilization to Revolution*. Reading, MA: Addison-Wesley.

———, ed. 1996. *Citizenship, Identity and Social History*. London: Cambridge University Press.

Tribalat, M. 1986. "La Population Etrangère en France." *Regards Sur l'Actualité* 118:33–44.

———. 1995. *Faire France, Une enquête sur les immigrés et leurs enfants*. Paris: La Découverte.

Turner, B.S. 1986. "Personhood and Citizenship." *Theory, Culture, and Society* 3:1–16.

———. 1990. "Outline of a Theory of Citizenship." *Sociology* 24:189–217.

Verbunt, G. 1977. "Une Culture pour le Folklore ou pour la Lutte." *Autrement* 11:6–11.

———, ed. 1985. *Etat National, Diversité Culturelle, Société Industrielle*. Paris: CIEMI.

———. 1988a. "Citoyenneté, Nationalité, et Identité." In C. W. de Wenden, ed., *La Citoyenneté*.

———. 1988b. "Peut-On Etre Français Sans l'Etre." *Les Cahiers de l'Orient* 11 3ème trimestre.

Verbunt, G., F. Bovenkerk, and R. Miles. 1988. "Le Racisme et les Réactions de l'Etat à La Migration: Les Sujets d'une Etude pour Definir un Champ de Recherche." Paper presented at the Colloque International, "Les Mutations Economiques et les Travailleurs Immigrés Dans les Pays Industriels." Vaucresson, January 28–30.

Vernon, R. 1986. *Citizenship and Order in French Political Thought*. Toronto: University of Toronto Press.

Vichniac, J. 1990. "French Socialists and 'Droit à la Différence.'" Paper prepared for the 7th International Conference of Europeanists, March 23–25, Washington, D.C.

———. 1991. "French Socialists and 'Droit à la Différence': A Changing Dynamic." *French Politics and Society* (9) 1:40–56.

Vingtième Siècle. 1985. Etrangers, Immigrés, Français. Juillet–Septembre.

Voisard, J., and C. Ducastelle. 1988. *La Question Immigrée Dans La France Aujourd'hui*. Paris: Calmann-Levy.

Wahl, N. 1980. "Foreword." In W. Beer, *The Unexpected Rebellion. Ethnic Activism in Contemporary France*. New York: New York University Press.

Walzer, M. 1981. "The Distribution of Membership." In P. Brown and H. Shue, eds., *Boundaries: National Autonomy and Its Limits*. Totowa, NJ: Rowman and Littlefield.

———. 1983. *Spheres of Justice: A Defense of Pluralism and Equality*. New York: Basic Book.

Weber, E. 1959. *The Nationalist Revival in France, 1905–1914*. University of California Publications in History, vol. 60. Berkeley: University of California Press.

———. 1976. *Peasants into Frenchmen* Stanford: Stanford University Press.

Weil, P. 1988a. L'Analyse D'une Politique Publique. La Politique Française d'Immigration. Thèse du doctorat, Paris, Institut d'Etudes Politiques.

———. 1988b. "La Politique d'Immigration." *Pouvoirs* 47:45–60.

———. 1988c. "La Politique Française d'immigration et la Citoyenneté." In C. W. de Wenden, ed., *La Citoyenneté*. Paris: La Nouvelle Encyclopédie, Foundation Diderot, Fayard.

———. 1991. *La France et ses étrangers. L'aventure d'une politique de l'immigration 1938–1991*. Paris: Calmann-Levy.

———. 1997. *Mission d'étude des législations de la nationalité et de l'immigration*. Paris: La Documentation Française.

Wihtol de Wenden, C. 1982. "Les Immigrés et Le Discours Politique Municipal." *GRECO 13. Recherches Sur les Migrations Internationales* 4–5:68–79.

———. 1985a. "Du Bon Usage Politique des Immigrés." *Projet* 191:45–57.

———. 1985b. "Etat des Etudes en Matière de Citoyenneté et de Nationalité." *Dossier-Migration-CIEM* 24, Janvier–Fevrier, 4 pp.

———. 1987. *Citoyenneté, Nationalité, Immigration*. Paris: Arcentere.

———. 1988a. *La Citoyenneté et les Transformations de la Structure Sociale et Nationale de la Population Française*. Paris: La Nouvelle Encyclopédie, Foundation Diderot, Fayard.

———. 1988b. *Les Immigrés et la Politique*. Paris: Presses de la Fondation Nationale des Sciences Politiques.

Winnock, M. 1990. *Nationalisme, Anti-Sémitisme, et Fascism en France*. Paris: le Seuil.

Young, I. 1989. "Polity and Group Difference: A Critique of the Ideal of Universal Citizenship." *Ethics* (99) 2:250–274.

———. 1990. *Justice and the Politics of Difference*. Princeton: Princeton University Press.

Ysmal, C. 1984. "Le RPR et UDF au Front National: Concurrences et Connivences." *Revue Publique et Parlementaire* (913).

Zald, M. 1996. "Culture, Ideology and Strategic Framing." In D. McAdam, J. McCarthy, and M. Zald, eds., *Comparative Perspectives on Social Movements*. Cambridge: Cambridge University Press.

Zolberg, A. R. 1981. "International Migrations in Political Perspective." In M. Kritz, C. Keely, and S. Tomasi, eds., *Global Trends in Migration. Theory and Research on International Population Movements*.

———. 1987. "Wanted but Not Welcome: Alien Labor in Western Development." In W. Alonzo, ed., *Population in an Interacting World*. Cambridge: Cambridge University Press.

Official Publications and Documentation

Assemblée Nationale. 1986. Bulletin des Commissions. No. 31, 2–4 Décembre. Paris: Service des Commissions de l'Assemblée Nationale.

Assemblée Nationale. 1986. Bulletin des Commission. No. 32, 9–12 Décembre. Paris: Service des Commissions de l'Assemblée Nationale.

Chirac, J. 1986. "Déclaration de Politique Générale du Gouvernement." Assemblée Nationale. No. 627. April 7. Paris.

Conseil National des Populations Immigrées. 1985. La Nationalité Française. October 17. Paris.

Conseil Superieur des Français de l'Etranger. 1987. Dossier Pour la Commission de la Nationalité. 9 pp. Paris.

FAS (Fonds d'Action Sociale). 1989. "Cheminements de l'Intégration: 1985–1988." *Hommes & Migrations*, no. 1119.

INSEE (Institut National de la Statistique et des Études Economiques). 1992. Recensement General de la Population de 1990. Paris: INSEE.

Journal Officiel. Paris.

La Nationalité Française: Textes et Documentation. 1985. Paris: La Documentation Française.

OMI (Office des Migrations Internationales). 1989. "La Naturalisation. L'Aboutissement d'une Intégration Réussie." *Actualités Migrations* no. 267–268.

Ministère des Affaires Sociales et de la Solidarité Nationale (Direction de la Population et des Migrations). 1986. *1981–1986. Une Nouvelle Politique de l'Immigration*. Documents Affaires Sociales. Paris: La Documentation Française.

Ministère des Affaires Sociales et de la Solidarité Nationale (Direction de la Population et des Migrations). 1988. *1986–1987 Le Point sur l'Immigration et la Présence Etrangère en France.* Documents Affaires Sociales. Paris: La Documentation Française.

Solidarity and Immigrant Association Documentation

CAIF (Conseil des Associations Immigrées en France). 1986. Assemblée Générale. 20 pp. Octobre 5 and 6. Ecoublay.

CEDEP (Collectif Pour l'Etude et la Dynamisation de l'Emigration Portugaise). 1988. "Les Portugais de France et la Question de la Nationalité." Brochure no. 10. June. Paris.

CEDEP. 1988. "Les Portugais de France et le Débat sur le code de la Nationalité." *Actualité Migration.*

Commission Diocésaine. "Justice à Paris," Service Interdiocésain des Travailleurs Immigrés. 1986. "Nationalité. Un Nouveau code?" 8 pp. Paris.

Commission Diocésaine, "Justice à Paris," Service Interdiocesain des Travailleurs Immigrés. 1988."Nationalité . . . Le Rapport des 'Sages.' " April. Paris.

FASTI (Fédération des Associations de Solidarité Avec des Travailleurs Immigrés). 1987. "Motion d'Orientation. Vers Une Nouvelle Citoyenneté. La Faim des Immigrés: La Citoyenneté." 11ème Congrès. June 6–8, Nantes.

FASTI. 1985. "Argumentaire: Pour le Droit de Vote des Immigrés." Paris.

GISTI (Groupe d'Information et de Soutien des Travailleurs Immigrés). 1983. "Note sur les Jeunes Algériens en France." Paris.

GISTI. 1988. "Quel Discours sur l'Immigration." *Plein Droit* 3.

LDH (La Ligue des Droits de l'Homme). 1987. "Nationalité: La Réforme en Question." 32 pp. Paris.

LDH (La Ligue des Droits de l'Homme). 1988. "Commentaire des Propositions de la Commission de la Nationalité." Paris.

MEMOIRE Fertile. 1988. "Citoyenneté 'Horizon 2000': Agir Pour Une Nouvelle Citoyenneté." Etats Généraux de L'Immigration. May 27–29, St. Denis, France.

MRAP (Mouvement Contre le Racisme et Pour l'Amitié entre les Peuples). 1985. "Contribution à un Débat sur les Droit Civiques des Immigrés en France." Paris.

MRAP. 1986. "Code de la Nationalité Française: Pour le Retrait du Projet de Réforme." 12 pp. Paris.

MRAP. 1987. "Identité, Egalité, Citoyenneté dans la France et l'Europe en Mutation." Congrès de Paris, November 14–15.

MRAP. 1988. "Des Supports Pour Faire Avancer la Réflexion sur la Citoyenneté." Paris.

SOS-Racisme. 1988. "Réflexions sur le Rapport de la Commission de la Nationalité. April.

Newspapers, Journals, and Newsletters

Agence Républicaine d'Information
Aspects de la France
Cahiers de la Pastorale des Migrants
CAIF Informations
Démocratie Moderne
Eurobaromètre
L'Evénement du Jeudi
L'Express
L'Humanité
La Croix
La Lettre de la Nation
Le Figaro
Le Matin
Le Monde
Le Monde Hebdomaire
Le Nouvel Observateur
Le Quotidien de Paris
Le Rivarol
Le Spectacle du Monde
Le Témoignage Chrétien
Libération
Lutte Ouvrier
New York Times
Paris-Match
Réforme
Reuters
Rouge
Sans Frontière

Index